GoFailMe

GoFailMe

The Unfulfilled Promise of Digital Crowdfunding

Erik Schneiderhan

and

Martin Lukk

STANFORD UNIVERSITY PRESS
Stanford, California

Stanford University Press
Stanford, California

Printed in the United States of America on acid-free, archival-quality paper

ISBN 9781503609044 (cloth)
ISBN 9781503636927 (paperback)
ISBN 9781503636934 (electronic)

Library of Congress Control Number: 2022058401

Library of Congress Cataloging-in-Publication Data available upon request.

Cover design: Jason Anscomb
Cover photograph: iStock
Typeset by Newgen in Vollkorn Regular 10/14.5

With Gratitude and Love to Our Parents:
Cathryn and Paul Baird
and
Piret and Toomas Lukk

Contents

Acknowledgments

We would like to start by acknowledging what has been a productive and fulfilling partnership as coauthors of this book. It has been a long and, at times, grueling ride. Our partnership made the trip easier.

Books like this one are not simply the product of author labor. They involve significant teamwork. This research project had at least nine research assistants working on it at one time or another. Without their efforts, this book would not exist. Cinthya Guzman and Hammad Khan provided invaluable work during early research on crowds and crowd-funding, helping to launch the project. Joanne Soares, our coauthor on our first publication related to this project, brought energy and intelligence to our data collection, analysis, and writing. Patrick Leduc helped us get the crowdfunding data we needed. Patrick's quantitative data skills and computer acumen were invaluable and critical to our data collection. Jasmine Anthony, Rose Davis, and Sienna Woodhall worked tirelessly from beginning to end, helping us collect the data, make sense of it, and get it on the page. Without them, this project would never have made it off the ground. Rena Friesen also worked on several drafts and provided significant support fact-checking and editing. Carmen Lamothe kept everything moving forward. She worked alongside us, kept the project organized, interviewed some of our study participants, oversaw data analysis, and made sure we kept on schedule. Carmen's research skill and expertise were a driving force behind the project.

Money helped as well. We would like to thank the Canadian government—specifically the Social Science and Humanities Research Council (SSHRC)—for funding this project with an Insight Development Grant. Without this financial support, it would have been difficult to cover the costs of gathering our data.

A number of people offered us support at various stages over the past five years. Erik's friends at Harbord House—particularly Joe Adelaars, Sue Anderson, Judy Carroll, Donna Chabot, Neil Chesworth, Cristina and Dave Getson, George McGowan, and John Oakes—offered encouragement during the entire journey. Martin thanks Ella and Daniel Becker, Cinthya Guzman and Sébastien Parker, Mart-Matteus Kampus, Kenzie O'Keefe and Abbie Engelstad, Daisy and R. M. Pellant, Loore and Oskar Viires, and Markus Lukk for good humor and thoughtful conversations throughout this time; Friida Prisk has provided support and encouragement from the very beginning. We would like to thank audience members at the 2017 Canadian Sociological Association Annual Conference, the 2018 American Sociological Association Annual Meeting, and the 2019 Social Science History Association Conference. We received valuable feedback at all of these presentations, and our work is better as a result. In particular, we would like to thank Lis Clemens, who attended several of these presentations and provided invaluable input. Fergus Heywood was a supporter from beginning to end, read several drafts, and provided insightful and useful comments and suggestions. The anonymous reviewers at Stanford University Press who read our draft manuscript (during the pandemic!) and provided substantive and thoughtful feedback made this book better. We are very grateful to them. Letta Page worked her editorial magic for us at several points, and the book is cleaner, smarter, and more effective as a result. Marcela Maxfield at Stanford University Press oversaw the entire publishing process and gave us encouragement and advice all along the way. We want to thank Marcela and the team at Stanford for believing in this project and guiding it to publication. We also want to thank everyone who agreed to tell us about their experiences using crowdfunding for this book through interviews and surveys. We are grateful for their time, thoughtfulness, and generosity in sharing their stories with us.

Erik would like to offer particularly heartfelt thanks to the members of his writing accountability group: Ginger Ferguson, Meredith Martin, and Glenda Musoba. These three amazing academics and friends were there for all the ups and downs of the writing and production process. Their encouragement and understanding made all the difference.

Finally, we would like to thank our partners, M. P. Stevens and Angela Hick, for being there during years of trial and tribulation related to producing this book. Your support was invaluable and uplifting, and kept us going until we reached the finish line. Thank you.

We dedicate this book to our parents.

GoFailMe

Introduction

Robert and his partner Lisa saw their lives change in an instant when they learned Lisa had terminal brain cancer. At most, the doctor said, she had two years. In the time since her first consultation, Lisa's brain had swelled and pushed through the opening where the spinal cord enters the skull. The pressure on her vertebrae had paralyzed her from the neck down. Robert, a substitute teacher in the local school system and a part-time professional hockey referee, was already feeling the financial pressure of staying home during her illness. How would they make ends meet if he continued to stay by Lisa's side until the end? Hospital parking alone was $14 per day, not to mention the cost of rent, groceries, and keeping the lights on at home. He decided to stop working anyway.[1]

Some friends suggested that Robert and Lisa ask for help. Robert was reluctant at first. The idea of asking friends and family for money, let alone strangers, was humiliating. But after a second round of surgery, Lisa told him: "Hey, if this thing goes sideways, take the help this time." Confronting what was sure to be a long ordeal, Robert relented and gave his friends the green light to set up a page on the website GoFundMe. The dollars poured in, and after five months they had raised over $70,000, roughly Robert's annual pay.[2] With all the bills, they weren't out of the woods financially, but they could stop worrying about short-term expenses. They were also able to make Lisa more comfortable by purchasing a communication device—not covered by insurance—since she could no longer speak because of her blocked airway.

When a loved one becomes very ill, practically overnight the choices are excruciating: work to pay the bills and keep a roof over your partner's head but miss what little time you might have left together, or take time off but risk financial ruin. It's a helpless and frustrating dilemma. Often the government can't or won't help. In that case, unless you have a rich benefactor, the only way out is to ask others for money. It can get the job done, though the money isn't free. It can come with obligations to those who helped you out. It may feel like an admission of defeat—not to mention the humiliation of putting yourself at the mercy of others. Robert got the money he needed but at what personal cost? Does it work out for everyone who tries raising funds this way? More important, where did this practice come from and why did Robert end up using it?

Mark woke up ready to start a new and exciting chapter in his life. He had been offered his dream job in New York City. All that was left were a few errands and he was off to the airport to board his flight, then settle in at his new apartment. He had been feeling a bit stiff from all the stress of the move, so he decided he would see his chiropractor before the flight. Several minutes into the visit, the chiropractor's adjustment of Mark's neck went wrong and the trauma caused a stroke. Mark lay on the floor for several hours before the chiropractor called an ambulance to take him to the ER, where he was misdiagnosed. He survived but with massive neurological damage that kept him from taking his job in New York and forced him to move in with his family. Weak state malpractice laws prohibited him from seeking compensation, and his insurance wasn't adequate to cover his health-care needs. Because of fear that it would lead the chiropractor to file a lawsuit against him, Mark was unable to publicly raise money for his needs. Seventeen years after the trauma occurred, Mark's lawyer told him that the threat of defamation suits had passed, in large part because the chiropractor had lost their practice and the ER had been sanctioned for other malpractice events. Full of anger at the system and full of hope that people would support his cause, Mark finally decided to try GoFundMe. In his words, "I had just seen a couple families . . . who posted hard luck stories about people who'd had an injury. The one family . . . their campaign caught fire, and they raised, like, a quarter of a million dollars in two days. So I thought, 'We have to give this a try.'" Mark tried. He asked for funds to help pay for his ongoing medical care and to make ends meet because he couldn't work full-time. He didn't receive a single donation. The humiliation of this defeat took years to shake off. He likened the whole experience to "shouting into that well of sadness, hoping people will see and hear you."

At first, Tonika thought it was a mistake. She checked to see if it was really her name on the email and then broke into tears. In 2015, at age thirty-two, Tonika had already faced significant challenges. She had dropped out of high school at nineteen and experienced homelessness. She worked and saved as she went back to school, earning a bachelor's degree and landing a job helping others navigate the education system. She wanted the tools that would help her make more of an impact in the world of education, so she applied to Harvard's Master's in Education program. And she was accepted. Yes, Tonika could probably have gone to a similar and equally high-quality program at home in Canada, where some (but not all) of the costs would have been covered. But this was *Harvard*. The problem was the $71,000 in tuition, fees, and expenses. She needed to show that she would have it within weeks or she couldn't get a visa. She shared her triumph and challenge with a few friends, who suggested she set up a crowdfunding page on GoFundMe. In a story reported across Canada and the US, the money came in a torrent and she quickly blew through her initial goal. She raised more than $75,000 in total.[3]

When faced with a tragedy like a house fire, a sick loved one, or a crushing tuition bill, people feel suddenly and completely overwhelmed. *How do I handle this?* Usually, they do what people have always done in the face of hardship: ask others for help. Although the risks and challenges facing people today are distinct from those in previous eras—seen in the high incidence of diseases like cancer and increasingly severe weather events caused by climate change—individuals and families still turn to familiar and long-standing sources of aid. Many look to family members and good friends. Others seek help from local community organizations and from churches, mosques, synagogues, and temples. Many organize bake sales, yard sales, and 5K runs. No less important are professional charities like United Way and The Salvation Army, which emerged in the nineteenth century and continue to be significant sources of aid. People and organizations like these have formed a reliable, informal safety net in both the US and Canada and in countries around the world. There's also aid from local, regional, and federal governments, which, as seen during the COVID-19 pandemic, can make a real difference.

But until relatively recently, cries for help were reliant on older technologies like mail, telephone, television, and face-to-face appeals. This changed with the rise of the internet. Increasingly, people in need are turning to a previously unrecognized source—the digital crowd.

Although some of the names have been changed, the stories here are all true; they motivated the writing of this book. In the twenty-first century, people like Robert and Lisa, Mark, and Tonika are finding help among strangers through *crowdfunding*, a novel form of internet-based charitable fundraising that has received substantial attention since the early 2010s. Crowdfunding involves individuals and groups using dedicated websites to post requests for help with covering costs for any of a variety of reasons. Once a request is posted to one of several public crowdfunding sites, it's used to solicit donations from other internet users—the "crowd"—whether friends and family or complete strangers.

There are countless examples of successful and highly publicized crowdfunding. A campaign to support victims of a mass shooting in Las Vegas in 2017 raised more than $11 million. A tragic bus crash that killed fifteen members of the Humboldt Broncos junior hockey team in Saskatchewan in 2018 led to $11.5 million in donations. Jennie and Gary Landsman, parents from Brooklyn, New York, raised more than $1.25 million to help their sons, who have a rare brain disorder known as Canavan disease. A COVID-19 first responders fund started in 2020 raised $8.2 million to provide supplies to those at the forefront of the pandemic response. These cases are a testament to how innovative internet technologies can help individuals come together and make a real difference for those going through incredibly tough situations.[4]

Crowdfunding donations can be sought for almost any cause, from replacing a stolen bicycle to building shelters after a hurricane. In practice, however, most requests on crowdfunding sites—and some of the largest campaigns recorded—are associated with costs for health care and personal medical emergencies, as well as children's educational opportunities after the death of a parent. The online crowd has quickly become a key welfare provider for people affected by life's tragedies who have nowhere else to turn. Our social safety net has gone digital.[5]

GoFundMe and For-Profit Fundraising

Although there are dozens of crowdfunding websites out there, GoFundMe is by far the most popular. In 2021, GoFundMe announced that, since its creation in 2010, more than 150 million people had used it to donate over $15 billion, making it the world's largest crowdfunding site for personal causes. This is a staggering amount of money raised from a massive number of donors through a process that barely existed a decade ago. By comparison, The Salvation Army, among the largest and best-known American charities, raised roughly $2.4 billion via private donations through its US operations in 2020, the same year that United Way Worldwide (America's largest traditional charity in terms of donation dollars and an organization comprising hundreds of local charities in more than forty countries and territories) reported raising $3.4 billion. GoFundMe doesn't disclose how the total donations it receives break down across the different countries where it operates. But given how established GoFundMe is in the United States, it makes sense that much of the platform's yearly fundraising comes from Americans helping Americans. Comparing the scale of donations collected by GoFundMe with those of America's traditional charities shows that, in a matter of only a few years, it has come to rival—if not surpass—the efforts of some of the country's longest-standing philanthropic institutions, becoming a leader among charitable giving organizations.[6]

Unlike America's time-honored charities, though, GoFundMe is a for-profit business. In many countries, including the US and Canada, the activities of charitable entities and other nonprofit organizations are closely monitored and highly regulated. In the US, nonprofits receive generous tax exemptions under Section 501(c)(3) of the tax code, and being certified as a 501(c)(3) organization is taken as a sign of legitimacy.

To obtain this status, organizations must demonstrate that they exist solely for one or more charitable purposes (e.g., promoting literacy) and that their governance structure and activities are designed exclusively to achieve these charitable ends.[7] Their operation is subject to strict rules to ensure that their activities and earnings don't benefit private interests. They must also file wide-ranging annual reports on their finances and activities. This is how we know, for example, how many fundraising dollars America's largest charities raised in 2020—and how they spent those dollars. It's also why we don't see much beyond broad brushstrokes when it comes to the fundraising activities of GoFundMe and platforms like it.

As a private company, GoFundMe is subject to very few reporting requirements. Thus we know very little about what goes on inside this massive charitable entity—only the snippets of information that have made it into the business press and interviews. In 2015, for instance, GoFundMe's founders sold their majority stake in the company to an investor group in a deal that valued the company at around $600 million. Other fragments of information about the company's performance and revenue have trickled out through journalists' accounts over the years—for example, it projected earning $100 million in revenue in 2016 on a more than 20 percent operating profit margin.[8]

The only information available about the donations GoFundMe collects are from its annual "reports," stylized and highly selective disclosures of its fundraising efforts in the previous year. The company is to be commended for releasing any information at all, since it isn't required to, but these disclosures are meager in comparison to those required by the 501(c)(3) charities that likely compete with GoFundMe for fundraising dollars. Notably, when GoFundMe's 2021 annual report announced that it had raised over $15 billion since 2010, it didn't say what share of the total went directly to campaigns, what went to operational costs, what went to profits, and so on. As of 2017, the site no longer charges a mandatory 5 percent fee on funds raised for personal campaigns in the US and Canada, yet much of the link between the donations it facilitates and the profits it generates for shareholders remains opaque. What's clear is that crowdfunding is a widely used means of charity in the twenty-first century whose commercial nature sets it drastically apart from the traditional charity organizations that predate it. Led by companies like GoFundMe, crowdfunding also appears to be highly profitable and growing.[9]

Why We Wrote This Book

Our interest in crowdfunding as a way of helping others came in part from previous research and writing on nineteenth-century charity. In North America, as in much of the industrialized world, private charities and voluntary organizations were the primary providers of relief for the poor until well into the twentieth century. Throughout this period, making a living and getting by was by all accounts extremely difficult: rapid industrialization and urbanization were accompanied by dangerous, exploitative working conditions in factories and unsanitary living conditions in the working-class neighborhoods of expanding cities. Life was particularly hard for the millions of immigrants, often with limited English, who had arrived on the continent seeking work and better wages, as well as for Black Americans in the wake of the Civil War and Abolition. Though various aid societies, churches, and other community organizations came together at the local level to help specific groups, there was no national system of social support as we know it—no safety net. Instead, whatever help was to be had in nineteenth-century North America came from a patchwork of limited local government assistance programs and the relief efforts of private, often religious charities and voluntary associations. Typically, the help provided to the needy by these groups came with significant conditions, and so it was also extremely common for individuals to instead ask for help directly, in person, from neighbors as well as strangers.[10]

But how was one to know who was "worthy" of help and who was simply taking advantage of the kindness of others? These concerns, combined with the rise of a philosophy of pulling yourself up by your bootstraps grounded in Social Darwinism and Malthusianism, led to the emergence of Charity Organization Societies, which tracked relief recipients through a central registry and diagnosed whether or not people were truly in need. Individual donors could then give to their local charity organization, where staff ensured that funds were used to help those thought to have genuine need. Though this shift began to organize the distribution of aid, it still largely amounted to a free-for-all approach to society's well-being. There was little oversight, and disbursements were based on local, personal evaluations of worth and need.[11]

Americans and Canadians had moved away from this system by the middle of the twentieth century. In response to the haphazard, inequitable, and mostly private assistance that came before, industrialized countries began to establish what scholars call welfare states. In these political arrangements, national governments actively played a role in bolstering the social and economic well-being of their citizens by ensuring access to resources like health care, education, and protections against the fallout from illness and unemployment. The origins of the US welfare state are usually traced to the 1930s and a series of policies enacted under President Franklin D. Roosevelt's New Deal—most notably the Social Security Act of 1935—which authorized federal assistance programs to combat the economic devastation of the Great Depression. In Canada, a similar expansion took place after World War II and went far beyond US efforts by including features such as universal health care. These systems, different and imperfect in their own ways, ensured a basic level of well-being and security for most citizens and eliminated much of the need for individuals to ask others for help.[12]

This historical background bubbled to the surface when we first heard about Tonika Morgan's case on CBC Radio in Canada in 2015. What happened to Tonika had distinct echoes of nineteenth-century charity. It was an inspiring story, to be sure—a woman of color who was once homeless is now going to Harvard. But as sociologists we're trained to take individual stories and relate them to the broader social world. Anecdotal success tells us next to nothing about the big picture. Tonika got the money she needed, but what about other people? And how is this any different from nineteenth-century stories of people begging strangers for help? Our societies had made conscious choices to move away from this form of getting and providing help in decades past, so why was it back?[13]

These questions aligned with the ones we saw raised by a small but growing group of researchers thinking critically about crowdfunding. Some asked important ethical questions: What responsibility did websites bear for preventing fraud? Were campaigners being asked to give up too much privacy? Was the process fair? Other scholars, including ourselves, were asking how the rise of crowdfunding was connected to shortcomings in government help and whether everyone who needed help could get it this way. Further, what were the long-term consequences of crowdfunding for how we thought about who deserves help?[14]

Concerns about crowdfunding resonated with red flags cropping up across academia, industry, and the media as commentators worried about the increasingly invasive and potentially destructive role of the internet in our lives. Social media companies like Twitter and Meta (formerly Facebook) allowed the spread of misinformation and political radicalism; after the 2016 US presidential election, many wondered about the tension between democracy and the business models these platforms relied on. Soon there were prominent calls for greater regulation of "Big Tech" and the algorithms, or automated decision-making tools, that shaped what we could and would see while browsing. Critics saw algorithms as the pernicious keys to ongoing efforts to track online behavior and predict desires to make us spend more time on websites, thus driving profits at the expense of our privacy and well-being. Algorithms, researchers showed, were equally problematic in that they encoded the biases of their creators, meaning that they perpetuated race and gender-based inequities. In another part of the Web, different platforms were building the "gig" and "sharing" economies characterized by their critics as a new model of work featuring precarity and hardship for workers under the guise of freedom and flexibility. And what about people unable to use digital services because they had trouble with access, equipment, or know-how? The more we thought about it, the more we understood that GoFundMe, as a dominant, for-profit internet platform driven by automated decision-making, illustrated many of the issues animating debate in so many domains.[15]

Though questions about crowdfunding abounded, there were few answers, especially ones based on systematic and rigorous empirical investigation. Early evidence was concerning. Crowdfunding campaigns for health care appeared to be more common in places where fewer people were insured. Platforms also often featured campaigns raising money for dubious, unproven, and potentially dangerous medical treatments that wouldn't normally be covered even for the insured. In our early research on crowdfunding in Canada, we found that campaigns often asked for help with costs in areas known to be underfunded in the public health-care system, like cancer care, suggesting that crowdfunding was connected to broader social and political issues. Crucially, older people and racial and ethnic minorities tended to be less successful at raising money in crowdfunding, pointing to inequities and perhaps discrimination. As a process, it seemed that crowdfunding encouraged highly individual, emotional stories of need but drew public attention away from the systemic issues surrounding the hardships of crowdfunding's hopefuls.[16]

Findings from early studies seemed to corroborate critics' concerns and challenge the neat and largely positive stories cited in the media and promoted by crowdfunding companies themselves. The same studies raised many new questions and made clear how little we knew about this new and massively popular fundraising model. Suggestive data from analyses of small samples of online campaigns was not enough to draw conclusions, and studies at this stage featured little commentary from those at the center of crowdfunding, namely the people creating and benefiting from its campaigns. Analyzing what people wrote on their campaign pages didn't tell us about the bigger picture, including how people came to use crowdfunding, what the process was, and how it fit with other, more traditional ways of getting help. Importantly, reading online crowdfunding pages also fell short in telling us how campaigns ended up or what thoughts and feelings people took away from them. Given our interest in social policy and the history of social welfare, we saw an opportunity to expand the scope of existing analyses to consider how different places compared in terms of crowdfunding uptake and examine how crowdfunding was used to address social welfare needs beyond medical care.

This book builds on a small but compelling body of research to shed more light on this novel and poorly understood form of digital fundraising. Representing years of research and based on a unique, expansive set of evidence, we believe the pages that follow provide the most comprehensive sociological overview of crowdfunding to date.

How We Gathered Our Data

As there was no current, comprehensive, and publicly available dataset on crowdfunding in either the US or Canada, we drew on approaches from computational social science to create our own. First, we gathered data on almost 2 million crowdfunding campaigns created on GoFundMe in the US and Canada between 2018 and 2021. We focused on GoFundMe because it had become the dominant crowdfunding platform and its name was becoming synonymous with the practice, akin to Polaroid or Kleenex or Google. The dataset we constructed contains information on how much money campaigns asked for and how much they raised, among other things, and it allows us to tackle some of the big questions surrounding crowdfunding. With our dataset in place, we asked over 600 people across the US and Canada to complete a survey about their experiences using crowdfunding to raise money for healthcare and education costs. The survey allowed us to understand the people participating in crowdfunding in even greater detail, how they felt about it, and more generally what they thought about how people get help in the US and Canada today. Finally, we conducted in-depth interviews with 50 people across the US and Canada who had used crowdfunding to get help. Their stories, at times heartbreaking and at times exhilarating, helped us see beyond the numbers and construct a vivid picture of what was involved in this new way of getting help.

We've chosen to consider crowdfunding in the US and Canada simultaneously because doing so allows comparative study across a pair of countries that are in some ways remarkably similar and in others strikingly different. Canada, in sharp contrast to the US, is regularly pictured as a friendly, progressive haven, where higher taxes help ensure that everyone's needs are met. America's liberal politicians, Bernie Sanders most notably, have pointed to Canada as an example of what national health care ought to look like and have suggested the Canadian system as a blueprint for US health-care reform, so it's reasonable to expect lower crowdfunding need in Canada. Nonetheless, while it deserves credit for its relatively generous approach to citizens' well-being, the Canadian system has shortcomings too. There are critical gaps that leave many Canadians vulnerable in ways that are similar to gaps in the American system. These often-overlooked flaws in Canada's acclaimed social in-surance system mean that Americans and Canadians facing many of life's misfortunes have much more in common than they might realize.[17]

This is why, when we speak of "we" or "us" we're generally referring to Americans and Canadians together. But we also compare the use of crowdfunding between Americans and Canadians to get a better sense of how similar or different people in these countries really are in terms of getting the help they need for basic costs. Are Canadians turning to sites like GoFundMe for help with medical costs? If yes, why is this when Canada has universal health care but the US doesn't? Looking at the two side by side, as well as at the different regions in each, allows us to draw conclusions about the different political arrangements that contribute to the prevalence of crowdfunding, something we couldn't do with just a single case. In Chapter 2, we expand this analysis further by comparing US and Canadian crowdfunding with crowdfunding around the world. Taking crowdfunding use as an indicator of the strength of a country's social services and by comparing crowdfunding in the US and Canada, we reveal the strengths and unexpected weaknesses of different forms of social support globally.

To sum up, we spent years gathering online data, conducting sur-veys, interviewing crowdfunding users, and then analyzing it all. All of these different types of data form the backbone of this book, allowing us to make strong, evidence-based claims about crowdfunding. For those looking for more details on our data and methods, we provide a method-ological appendix that has all relevant information.

A Revolution in Welfare Crowdfunding

GoFundMe and others like it are part of a new and revolutionary system, an overall digital transformation in how we help each other. *Crowdfund-ing*, as a general term, is quite broad. We use *welfare crowdfunding* to focus solely on the crowdfunding that attempts to fund people's social wel-fare needs, notably in health care and education. Welfare crowdfunding has enormous potential, evidenced by the more than $15 billion in do-nations that GoFundMe has facilitated for all its campaigns combined. Nearly 20 percent of American adults gave to a medical crowdfunding campaign in 2020. The genie is out of the bottle, and welfare crowdfunding has now become a familiar and routine way of interacting with our communities (and well beyond) in times of need.[18]

We begin to shed light on welfare crowdfunding by drilling down on the way GoFundMe works, who gets funded, and how all of this relates to larger questions of helping. We understand that, as a private, for-profit entity, GoFundMe shouldn't be expected to solve the problems of inequality that plague the United States, Canada, and the rest of the world. But we do want to make the process of welfare crowdfunding more transparent so we can decide whether or not this mechanism is what we want to rely on to close the gaps in our social safety net.

We found a lot to like about GoFundMe. It's immediately apparent that it provides hope. When you crowdfund, there's a sense of possibility at the start—that you might get help, that things might get better. This is powerful. Hope is valuable, and any process that can provide more of it in difficult times is worth our attention.

Welfare crowdfunding can also be a stage for showing the good in us. People helping others is heartwarming. The incredible potential of family, friends, and community to lean in and reach out is there for all the world to see. And when it works, it's amazing at putting money in the pockets of people who truly need it. While we're not necessarily equipped to assess the needs of others, it was clear from the start of our research that our respondents needed every penny they asked for through crowdfunding—not to fund cushy lifestyles but to pay for cancer treatments, cover lost wages, support education goals and dreams, and get life back on track after a tragedy. And sometimes they got what they asked for. Robert and Lisa were armed with financial support in her final days. Why? Because people stepped up when they didn't have to. Whether a celebrity like Taylor Swift, a frequent donor on GoFundMe who gives thousands of dollars, or a neighbor who gives five, the act is one of caring and goodness. These gestures are inspiring. Witnessing and maybe even joining an outpouring of support is uplifting. In our view, we don't spend enough time showcasing the good things that happen in society. It's our sense that these caring behaviors might be infectious.[19]

Welfare crowdfunding streamlines and simplifies the process of getting help. As respondent Xavier told us, "it's something that was not there before, and if that platform [weren't] there, I mean, it [would] be much harder . . . asking for help or anything like that." Adam, another respondent, agreed, explaining: "It's easier to have something you can click on if you want to donate money and it can get transferred and go over right then, instead of calling somebody that's 200, 300 miles away and having to explain over the phone and *then* asking." The process highlights the best the internet has to offer—instant communication with millions of potential donors, with pictures, videos, and text providing information in a transparent fashion. Crowdfunding is a far cry from the days of knocking on doors, hat in hand, asking for money.

We can see the democratic promise of the internet here. In theory, GoFundMe and other sites provide a space where anyone can ask for help. This isn't entirely true in practice, as we show, yet it's possible that overall GoFundMe is performing a service to society. It can be seen as a diagnostic tool, showing us the scale of our social problems and taking away some of the shame of asking for and accepting help from others. Government support for the unemployed or those with low incomes is, for good reason, given discreetly, to people whose life circumstances are hidden from the public but who are nonetheless often stigmatized for receiving it, as seen in the racist stereotype of the "welfare queen," repeated during Ronald Reagan's campaign against US social programs in the 1970s and 1980s. GoFundMe has given us a window on what these struggles actually look like and who needs help. Perhaps this can spur greater understanding for what others are going through and destigmatize asking for help.[20]

Despite its potential positive contributions, our findings show that welfare crowdfunding has a fundamental problem. It doesn't work. Most people who use it don't get the help they need. Ultimately, we argue, current welfare crowdfunding brings significant profits to GoFundMe without managing to support most of those it's designed to help. Why? It will take the rest of the book to lay out our argument, but we'll give you a preview.

To start, a large segment of the population in the US and Canada can't use crowdfunding. Either they aren't allowed to or they don't have the capacity. We know, for instance, that undocumented immigrants are among our societies' most needy. They don't have accumulated wealth, they don't have access to good health care, and they struggle to find a foothold in their new home. And GoFundMe won't permit them to raise funds. There are obvious legalities involved—for example, without legal documentation it becomes tricky to facilitate bank transfers. But does anyone really believe there's no way around this issue? Churches and immigrant aid groups provide undocumented workers with financial and material help regardless of legal status. Another large swath of society can't use welfare crowdfunding because of the digital divide. There are those who don't have access to a computer, smartphone, or tablet. And there are those who don't have access to the internet. We show that those on the far side of the digital divide have less education, are older, and are more likely to be people of color. That raises alarms because we know that Whites with higher levels of education, those who likely have a digital toolkit at their disposal, tend to already have better access to the resources needed to face unexpected hardships.[21]

For those who can get in the door, the welfare crowdfunding system is unequal and unfair. In other words, the digital divide doesn't end at internet access. It continues with people's differing abilities to use the internet effectively. We found that race, age, social capital, and technological and marketing skills are among the determinants of successful crowdfunding. Older people, people of color, and those lacking necessary skills and connections just don't do as well. This points to inequalities in both social network access and technical skills, and it may point to intersecting forms of discrimination in this online marketplace. What becomes apparent is a disconnect between the assurances given by crowdfunding platforms like GoFundMe, that anyone can raise money through these services, and the reality that only a small fraction of funding campaigns ultimately meet their goals.[22]

As part of the emotional rollercoaster of crowdfunding, individuals give crowdfunding platforms a lot of personal data and cede some measure of privacy. This is worrisome. All of a person's struggles are there for all the world to see. It can be embarrassing and humiliating. Who feels good about publicly declaring that they have testicular pain? Who wants to publicize that they're in an abusive relationship? Who wants salt rubbed in the raw wounds that come with losing a child to cancer? All this data regarding our struggles becomes the property of crowdfunding platforms like GoFundMe. And they use it to make their services better, meaning "make more money," in a pattern of behavior that the scholar Shoshana Zuboff has termed "surveillance capitalism"—economic activity led by large technology companies that involves collecting and analyzing data about user behavior at massive scales and using it to personalize advertisements and online services in increasingly profitable ways.[23]

Why is it a problem that GoFundMe is single-mindedly pursuing profits? After all, this is the purpose of a corporation. More generally, why are the inequities and personal costs tied to welfare crowdfunding worth understanding? Because a growing reliance on digital technologies, which many people are unable to use effectively to do important tasks, risks making inequalities in income, well-being, and opportunity even worse than they already are—and even harder to undo. We should care about these inequalities, for one because they threaten the principles of meritocracy and equal opportunity that our liberal democratic societies are built on. More important, exclusion from digitally mediated activities can mean deprivation and exclusion from achieving basic standards of living and full, dignified membership in society, not to mention maximizing human potential.[24]

It would be one thing if the internet and the services it makes possible were simply nice to have. But in the twenty-first century many essential activities, like applying for a job and accessing government services, largely happen online, especially in geographically remote areas where access to resources, both public and private, is already challenging. Like the telephone and automobile before it, the internet has gone from a luxury good to a necessity for meaningful participation in society. If the internet is key to doing the many things that improve our life circumstances, then those who can't use it—either effectively or at all—are left out of important opportunities and so are disadvantaged compared with skilled internet users.[25]

In an era characterized by drastic inequality and in which governments have over decades pulled back support of their citizens, GoFundMe has become a major way to make up the difference. If people who desperately need help in the wake of a tragedy or are trying to afford college can't make use of this valuable resource because they lack internet access, then the money this site brings in is distributed un-equally, creating cause for concern.

But the problems with GoFundMe go much deeper. Proponents of welfare crowdfunding, and most notably GoFundMe itself, describe it as an empowering practice from which anyone can benefit. As we've found, however, crowdfunding users rarely make their goals, so it hardly works even for those who can use it. And the experience comes with significant emotional costs. Our respondents spoke of humiliation, wounded pride, embarrassment, helplessness, and frustration when they shared their stories in order to get help for themselves or those they love. But we don't hear these stories in the news. Failure doesn't sell. Companies like Go-FundMe are profiteering from crowdfunding while touting it as a cure-all for those in dire financial straits. Meanwhile, the promises of crowd-funding are distracting us from the broad, systemic issues behind our social problems and from more effective ways of responding to them, including solutions that don't require people's well-being to depend on donation dollars.[26]

Broadly, we find that welfare crowdfunding promotes a myth of online meritocracy. The original idea behind crowdfunding was to de-mocratize fundraising and remove biases in determining who gets funding and who doesn't. Those who succeeded would say it's because they deserved it more (or at least argued their case better). At the 2012 Web Summit, an influential technology industry conference, Danae Ringelman, one of the cofounders of the early crowdfunding platform Indiegogo, declared: "In a world where everybody is funding everything, the role of the gatekeeper will be obsolete." She went on to ask: "Who's to say who should be able to raise money and who should not?" Ringelman talked about how her platform helped the "cream rise to the top" using what for us is a pretty uncomfortable metaphor given the racialized di-mensions of crowdfunding.[27]

Today, we know that you can tick all the "right" social boxes and do all the right things to set up and manage your page but still fail to make your goal. For what it's worth, Indiegogo is a platform primarily for profitable ventures—like manufacturing and selling a new gadget you invented—where entrepreneurs take risks to hopefully attract cus-tomers and turn a profit in the future. While inequalities in access and success are still an important concern in this kind of crowdfunding, we find it less problematic. In welfare crowdfunding, the stakes are on a different scale entirely: people are asked to become entrepreneurs to meet their basic needs. And if their cause doesn't "rise to the top," the consequences can be skipping medical treatments and rent payments, not just failing to start a company.

Though crowdfunding was meant to remove gatekeepers, it seems to have merely replaced old gatekeepers with new ones, namely crowdfunding platforms themselves and in particular GoFundMe, which dominates the market. Sure, this situation might change with more government oversight in the future or as new companies enter the market, but for now GoFundMe exerts tremendous influence over who does and doesn't raise money. This happens through algorithms. Big Tech services, like Google and Facebook, love to say that they're neutral, mere conduits for the public will. But they aren't. In pursuit of clicks, user engagement, and revenue, they make choices about what we see on their sites, and they build algorithms for maximum impact. In the case of crowdfunding platforms, algorithmic decision-making funnels visitors and their dollars toward some fundraising campaigns over others in ways that maximize "engagement," thereby stimulating profits at the expense of the individual livelihoods tied to the campaigns hanging in the balance.[28]

Even when it does work, crowdfunding isn't free. You give up quite a bit in return. GoFundMe's terms of use tell us that it might sell your data, which it terms a "business asset," at some point. The truth is, we have no idea what GoFundMe is doing. The welfare crowdfunding machine, in particular the mechanism of GoFundMe, isn't transparent. This is a major problem. We can't see how algorithms shape our crowdfunding experience. We don't know what sites are doing with our personal data. GoFundMe and other for-profit crowdfunding platforms can largely do as they wish because there's so little oversight. And for most crowdfunding users, it's a case of giving something for nothing. You give data but get no donations to your cause.

Once again, we've been through this before. Problems stemming from a lack of oversight caused the US and Canada to make major changes in how we helped others in the nineteenth century. Charity organizations, settlement houses, and eventually social work and the welfare programs of the New Deal became part of a process of systematizing and regulating such efforts. We think that GoFundMe should be considered alongside Google, Apple, Meta, and Amazon, the other Big Tech companies creating unregulated platforms and economies that play by rules of their own making beyond the government's reach. Like other large platforms, GoFundMe has bought up many of its competitors, gained a virtual monopoly on donation-based crowdfunding, and created a single go-to platform, where its own rules and user biases are the law. In a growing "techlash," internet users, advocacy groups, and governments themselves are challenging the practices of major technology platforms, including through antitrust lawsuits, but it's a slow process. In the meantime, companies are raking in the profits. GoFundMe has so far avoided being lumped in with the worst of Big Tech's offenders, and we think that should change.[29]

In the world of business, winners and losers are part of the game—features, not bugs, as the saying goes. Competition makes failure an intrinsic characteristic of any capitalist society. Not every idea is a good one, and the marketplace provides a way of sorting the good and the bad. But business models and business thinking don't always travel well. Efficiency, competition, and marketing are critical to the success or failure of business ventures. But should they matter for our personal health? Our educational prospects? Paying rent? Trying to become our best selves? The crowdfunding format, originally intended for entrepreneurial use, has been transposed to the realm of individual humanitarian aid with precious few changes. This makes sociologists like us nervous. In welfare crowdfunding, those seeking help are required to present their cases in terms of entrepreneurial pitches in a competitive marketplace. Here, fundraisers must do their best to attract donor dollars while competing with others experiencing similar hardships. To have a chance, fundraisers must strive to present their campaign in a way that appeals as much as possible to internet users who have an array of campaigns they might support. Our fear, and a major impetus for writing this book, is that the crowd, its choices already constrained by platform algorithms, haphazardly picks those it feels are "worthy" and leaves the rest behind.

GoFundMe and other platforms have created a powerful system with the potential to significantly impact the global fight against poverty and inequality. The innovative technology supporting them, however, is being held back by profit motives. As such, this solution to our social problems is just not working for most people. As our title shows, we think "GoFailMe" might be a better name.

Roadmap for the Book

The motivations for and powerful potential of welfare crowdfunding are clear. But how does it all work? Why don't most people get the help they need? Taking a step back, do most people who need help ask for it through crowdfunding in the first place? Put another way, who doesn't crowdfund their welfare and why? These are a few of the questions that guided our work. Understanding welfare crowdfunding, in all its subtleties, is critical if we're going to continue to rely on it so heavily. That's why we hope readers will return, over and over across the next five chapters, to these inward questions: *Is this the way we want to fill the gaps in our health-care and education systems?* Or, more personally: *Is this the way I want to ask for help for myself or someone I love?* We follow a simple line of presentation. We start by showing how and why crowdfunding emerged in the digital age. We then look at who uses it, how the process unfolds, and what happens for those who seek help. Finally, we try to make sense of it all and tie it to future action.

In Chapter 1, we provide recent historical context and some theoretical tools to help readers understand welfare crowdfunding. We look at the origins of crowdfunding in the twentieth-first century and show how it transformed from a business tool to a tool for helping, and discuss when and how welfare crowdfunding emerged on the internet. We consider GoFundMe and the COVID-19 pandemic, showing how welfare crowdfunding exploded in popularity as people struggled to make ends meet and stay healthy during a global pandemic that, as of this writing, has claimed at least 6 million lives worldwide. As crowdfunding moved into the realm of social welfare, we argue, it brought with it principles and logics that are antithetical to social citizenship and the basic tenets of social welfare that inspired major advances in social support systems in the twentieth century.[30] Although our technologies have advanced in leaps and bounds since the early days of the welfare state in North America, our capacity to meet everyone's needs hasn't kept up and actually seems to have taken several steps back. Across this review, we offer some theoretical tools that help us make sense of the "how and why" of welfare crowdfunding in this and subsequent chapters.

Having set the stage, we turn to welfare crowdfunding users in Chapter 2. As sociologists, we mean something specific when we ask "Who?" Though this project is about real people, we aren't looking for just names and stories but demographic characteristics as well. We're really asking, "What *kinds* of people" in terms of age, gender, geographic location, race, income, education, and so on. What we argue based on our data is that online fundraising is primarily a tool of those who are already relatively privileged in age, class, race, and social capital (for instance, White people disproportionately use health-care crowdfunding). We also look at why people ask for help. Among the complex motivations, we find cancer and the creation of education trust funds to be the most prevalent, with insurance, job loss, and general financial troubles underpinning most situations.

In Chapter 3, we unpack the process of welfare crowdfunding. How does it work? Following the logic of setting up a GoFundMe page, we take the reader through the process from the initial idea to launch of the appeal. Along the way, we show how crowdfunding users attempt to market themselves, their struggles, and their stories (or those of a friend or family member). This involves the careful selection of emotive, high-quality pictures and engaging text; putting a dollar value on their struggles; and activating social networks (supposing they have any). And then, no matter how strong the network ties, no matter how much enthusiasm and energy they have for promoting their cause, there comes a moment when welfare crowdfunders have to wait and hope.

In Chapter 4, we show what happens from the moment of launch onward. Our data offers a pretty clear, simple answer: disappointment. Few people meet their crowdfunding goals. Few get the help they need. We draw on our data to show what this looks like in big-picture terms across the United States and Canada. We also get down on the ground, focusing on what this disappointment (and the loss of privacy) feels like for individuals who needed help and didn't get it.

In Chapter 5, our final chapter, we consider the big question that faces all scholars when the data and analysis are laid out: *So what?* It's our position that a system in which we publicly beg strangers, friends, and family for money isn't the best society has to offer. We offer ideas for changing welfare crowdfunding for the better so that it addresses rather than amplifies inequalities and alleviates the suffering that drives so many people to lay bare their hardest struggles in the hope that friends and strangers will help.

One

A Brief History of the Rise
of Digital Crowdfunding

If you want to understand a social phenomenon, it's often a good idea to start with its history. Origins matter, and they can help us understand the how and why of the present day. In this chapter, we consider the origins of digital crowdfunding. We try to answer the following questions: Where did crowdfunding come from? How did it become so prevalent as a way of helping others? Crowdfunding as we know it today emerged in the twenty-first century, following key developments in the internet. Though it first appeared as a tool for business and entrepreneurship, crowdfunding has only recently found use in social welfare, to cover costs associated with needs like health care and education. Our main argument is that crowdfunding didn't travel well on this journey. It smuggled along a logic and principles that are antithetical to those that inspired the creation of twentieth-century state welfare programs, namely social citizenship and the idea that governments have some responsibility for meeting the basic needs of their citizens. For-profit business and philanthropy make poor bedfellows, we argue, so welfare crowdfunding's origins should be read as damning for its current practice.

If you only read about crowdfunding in the news now and then, you might think that appealing to crowds for financial help was made possible only by the magic of the internet. This isn't the case. The crowd, whether made up of familiar people or strangers, has been a source of money for centuries. There are many prominent examples, including what is often cited as the first example of crowdfunding: In the early 1700s, author Jonathan Swift set aside £500 of his personal wealth and lent it out, interest-free, to help poor people in Ireland provided they could show they were trying to work and had ties to their community. Others soon adopted Swift's system, which amounted to a loose network of loan associations based on funds provided voluntarily by community members. Around the same time, the English poet Alexander Pope raised funds from the public to support a new English translation of Homer's *Iliad* and placed the names of donors on a list of acknowledgments in the printed work. This was an early form of crowdfunding for artistic endeavors. Donations from the public have similarly funded causes ranging from Mozart's piano concertos to the construction of the Statue of Liberty's pedestal in New York.[1]

Often-overlooked precursors to crowdfunding are different kinds of community and mutual aid groups that have been organized at various times and places, especially by members of marginalized groups. In North America, for example, the eighteenth century saw the creation of Black voluntary associations and mutual aid societies, where both free and enslaved people pooled money and other resources to care for each other in an otherwise hostile environment. The African Union Society, established in Newport, Rhode Island, in 1780, was among the first of these and involved various kinds of economic cooperation, including insurance against illness, accident, and death in addition to nonmonetary resources like educational discussions and moral guidance. Such organizations proliferated after the American Revolution, particularly in Northern urban areas, and served as pillars of Black communities. These cases show that it's possible for motivated individuals to come together and, by pooling their resources, accomplish great things in challenging circumstances. Crowdfunding proponents point to cases like these as part of a long tradition inherited by today's internet-based crowdfunding solutions.[2]

Web 2.0

In this book, we're primarily interested in the most recent phase of crowdfunding—how asking the crowd for help went digital. We begin this story in the early twenty-first century. By then, the "World Wide Web" had evolved into much more than a collection of static, text-based, informative web pages. Instead, internet users were increasingly participating as what we now call "content creators." It was the start of Web 2.0. This term, which came out of tech circles, referred not to any specific technical change in the way the internet worked but to a shift in the way it was *used*. As Brian McCullough writes in a history of this period, "if Web 1.0 was about browsing stuff created by others, Web 2.0 was about creating stuff yourself."[3] Leading this change were a spate of innovative new websites, like the online encyclopedia Wikipedia, launched in 2001, which embodied these shifts by letting anyone create or edit its entries. Web 2.0 captured the idea of an internet where content would be created by its users rather than its owners or administrators, and it was taking shape through new types of user-generated content like blogs, wikis, and (hash)tags.

Among the most significant inventions to emerge from this period of transformation were social media services, some of which we still use today. Led by companies like Friendster and Myspace, respectively launched in 2002 and 2003, these platforms innovated simple ways for everyday people to post and circulate material largely of their own making such as short messages, announcements, and photos and videos. These and other Web 2.0 networking sites found massive success on the basis of user participation, sharing, and collaborating, principles that profoundly changed the trajectory of the internet. Together, they paved the way for Facebook (now part of Meta), which came online in 2004 and surpassed all other social media sites in only a few years.[4]

Excitement about the increasingly participatory internet reached far beyond experts and tech industry insiders by the mid-2000s. A telling example is *Time* magazine's choice to award the 2006 Person of the Year to "You." Breaking with their tradition of naming specific change-makers and cultural icons, the editors chose that year to bring attention to the ever-broadening group of individuals who made up, created, shared, and shaped the digital world. YouTube, a video-sharing website, was only a year old and the novel messaging service then called "Twittr" just a few months older, but both were already finding success based on serving up user content no matter how eccentric or odd. These sites produced some of the first "viral" internet sensations, setting the stage for the meme-filled internet to come. The siloed sharing and socializing of AOL chat rooms and the text-only "bulletin boards" that came before had burst wide open. Tech journalists led the way, but now the general-audience media was paying attention too.[5]

Time's choice acknowledged that ordinary people—including you, the reader of this book, if you were on the internet in the mid-2000s—were transforming the web and media consumption in general. As websites gobbled up our writing, snapshots, and clips to serve up to our peers as "content," the digital and "real" worlds seemed more and more like the same thing. And what happened online became more and more important for "real" life. In 2007, Barack Obama announced his presidential candidacy via YouTube, undertook the first significant internet-based US political campaign, and won the first presidential election that most people followed online. Meanwhile, countries like Estonia and Switzerland were already letting their citizens cast votes via the internet, while users around the world rapidly shifted myriad everyday activities, like shopping and dating online. Nearly two decades later, large swaths of people's everyday lives take place online, and our experiences there shape important aspects of our offline lives, such as how we understand politics and whether we choose to get vaccinated. Platforms like Facebook aim to blur the boundaries between online and offline even further by moving more and more of our social lives into virtual reality worlds known as metaverses.[6]

Mass online participation in the 2000s also led to the perception that the internet was associated with freedom and democracy. If the Web was a major driver of world events, and if the Web was "you," it stands to reason that, as a newly empowered, internet-enabled individual, you could change the world, whoever and wherever you were. Those who scoffed at the idea that ordinary people might wrest control over information from traditional media companies, news organizations, and the government paused as content creators and citizen journalists entertained, inflamed, and informed across a proliferation of internet platforms.[7]

Within years, *Time*'s prediction that the Web "revolution" would "not only change the world but also change the way the world changes," seemed to have been borne out in numerous examples. Although researchers caution against overstating the internet's role in emerging movements, we would see in events like the 2011 Egyptian Revolution and the "Twitter revolutions" of Iran, Tunisia, and Ukraine that social media platforms could help citizens speak out and challenge oppressive regimes in new ways. Prominent instances of "hashtag activism"— including the spread of #BlackLivesMatter and #MeToo—further made the case that the internet could be a force for democracy as it raised awareness of social issues and urged collective responses.[8]

Silicon Valley embraced the public's surging optimism about the internet, where it resonated with long-standing ideas about the role of technology in society. The dominant economic and political beliefs animating the US technology industry have been called the Californian Ideology. This mix of ideas, which began circulating among technology entrepreneurs in the San Francisco Bay Area during the 1990s, drew together aspects of 1960s counterculture with signature features of American capitalism. It combined "the free-wheeling spirit of the hippies and the entrepreneurial zeal of the yuppies," as media scholars Richard Barbrook and Andy Cameron described it in an influential 1995 essay.[9]

From there, sociologist Elisabetta Ferrari argues, the latest iteration of the Californian Ideology adopted three interrelated tenets: (1) digital technology is inherently democratic and conducive to individual freedom; (2) social problems, like racism and sexism, should be solved through innovative digital technologies rather than laws and policy interventions; and (3) the market, not the government, should be responsible for improving people's lives.[10] These tenets represent a blending of ideologies from the political left and right, including technological determinism, libertarianism, and neoliberalism, with a belief in meritocracy and self-empowerment. Together, they have promulgated an optimistic narrative of digital technology's place in society and smoothed over the seams between its revolutionary rhetoric and its firm entrenchment in the established capitalist system. In the 2000s, the Californian Ideology helped create public perceptions of the Web as a beacon of freedom; in turn, the Web's popularity and success lent credibility to the Californian Ideology.

Of course, the many people who make up Silicon Valley's tech industry—not to mention the US tech industry more broadly—don't uniformly endorse this way of thinking. Nonetheless, the narrative captured in the Californian Ideology appears so consistently in the statements of insiders, including leaders of the largest and most influential technology companies, that we can talk about it as a dominant paradigm. When Google filed its application to become a publicly traded company in 2004, founders Larry Page and Sergey Brin wrote to potential investors that the company's goal was "to develop services that improve the lives of as many people as possible—to do things that matter." Nearly a decade later, Facebook founder Mark Zuckerberg used similar words when he took his company public, writing: "Facebook was not originally created to be a company. It was built to accomplish a social mission—to make the world more open and connected." Unusually for an executive courting investors, Zuckerberg went on to say, "We don't build services to make money; we make money to build better services."[11]

Scholars have systematically traced the use of such "solutionist" ideas, which position commercial digital technologies as the best tools for solving society's problems, in the interviews and speeches of today's tech leaders and the writings of the technology press, demonstrating that the Californian Ideology remains a guiding spirit of contemporary digital capitalism.[12] These dominant ideas are important to understand, regardless of whether technology leaders truly believe they're changing the world, because they're used to justify tech companies' activities to lawmakers and the public, not to mention their employees. They're also important to understand because they form the backdrop to many of the influential technologies and services that came out of the first decade of the new millennium—including crowdfunding. It would be another decade before this techno-optimism was seriously shaken by repeated charges that tech companies were putting profits before principles through their complicity in spreading misinformation, harming children's self-esteem, and the like, spurring fierce debates about industry regulation.

Crowdsourcing

Before there was crowdfunding, technology commentators were talking about *crowdsourcing*. This was part of contemporary digital capitalism's second wave of social change. Journalist Jeff Howe, writing in the technology magazine *Wired* in 2006, coined the term to identify a common feature of a novel breed of website appearing in the Web 2.0 era and making new online activities possible. Crowdsourcing can be understood as a way of using the internet's networking capabilities to connect people with diverse skills and aptitudes to accomplish goals that would be challenging or impossible for a single person or small team. It means turning to the vast "crowd" of internet users, wherever and whoever they might be, to complete tasks typically accomplished by individuals. Rather than outsourcing tasks to experts, new services made it possible to crowdsource tasks with the help of the digital public.[13]

Crowdsourcing takes many forms. In its most optimistic incarnation, it's about improving the circulation of expertise and ideas in the service of creative problem-solving. This happens through dedicated websites that connect both amateurs and professionals with highly specialized scientific and engineering problems that have in many cases stumped the research and development teams of major companies and organizations. Among these websites is InnoCentive, a still-running service highlighted as an early example of crowdsourcing. InnoCentive allows organizations to post "challenges" to its network of "solvers," who attempt to solve the challenges to earn money (as many as tens of thousands of dollars for successful ones). Examples of challenges posted to the website, by major pharma and chemical companies, nonprofits, and government agencies, include developing an environmentally sustainable, nonplastic mini butter dish for a large dairy producer and designing a system to automatically identify agricultural fields in satellite imagery for the National Geospatial-Intelligence Agency.[14]

What makes crowdsourcing work is that it leverages the "wisdom of crowds." This is the idea that a large group of people—a crowd—is better at making decisions and finding creative and innovative solutions than a few elite specialists, regardless of how well trained and educated those specialists are. What is thought to make crowds "wise" is that, unlike small groups of specialists, they're made up of loose interpersonal connections. Network scholars refer to these as "weak ties" (in contrast to "strong ties," which we share with the people we're closest to and spend time with, like friends and intimate partners). Strong social connections are important for our well-being; however, they're much less useful when it comes to finding a job or a new apartment. This is because our closest friends tend to move in the same social circles that we do and share many of the same contacts. On the other hand, people we barely know—former coworkers, schoolmates, and friends of friends—are the ones most likely to know about opportunities we wouldn't otherwise hear about. Social scientists have shown that these social connections do indeed facilitate career advancement—and may even be sources of intimacy and emotional support.[15]

Weak ties are also useful for coming up with new ideas. They make crowds wise. In the same way that loose social connections help us find practical opportunities by linking us to information from people we don't personally know, they expose us to new insights and knowledge. Our circle of friends is limited because everyone in it tends to have access to the same information that we do. What's more, our friend groups tend to be homogenous: they're often made up of people very similar to us in a variety of characteristics, including race and ethnicity, gender, age, education, occupation, and political views. This pattern is found across many societies, and scholars attribute it to *homophily*, or the human tendency to associate and form bonds with people who are "like us"— "birds of a feather flock together."[16]

A key implication of homophily is that it limits the kinds of people we come to know, the kinds of experiences we're likely to have, and the ideas we come up with. All this means that in the same way that our close friends are less helpful than we might think when looking for a new job or place to live, they're also less helpful for coming up with a brilliant idea or a solution to a vexing creative problem. When struggling with these matters, we're often better off turning to people we don't know. This is where the "strength of weak ties" lies.[17] Crowdsourcing takes this principle and applies it at an industrial scale: by using the internet's unique capacity to connect strangers across vast distances, it brings together large numbers of weak ties and focuses their efforts on specific goals.

By matching people with the problems they're best suited to solve, InnoCentive and similar platforms show how crowdsourcing and Web 2.0 principles can be used to spur innovation and solve pressing intellectual problems. As such, they might be seen as part of a celebrated tradition of scientific challenges and prizes used throughout history to encourage technological innovation. Famous examples include the 1714 prize established by the British Parliament for anyone developing a way to measure longitude at sea (a life-or-death issue for eighteenth-century mariners), which led to significant advances in clockmaking; and the 1919 Orteig Prize, won by Charles Lindbergh for making the first non-stop flight from New York to Paris, a boon for aviation's advancement.[18] Crowdsourcing platforms effectively launch new scientific prizes every week and in this way can be seen as playing a part in solving our era's defining challenges, such as global poverty, climate change, and infectious disease. The examples just given also show how crowdsourcing companies strive to solve the world's problems as well as generate healthy profits, embodying the techno-solutionist ethos. Of course, the fact that they're for-profit entities doesn't necessarily mean they can't provide valuable services that help the world. But they do produce unique conflicts and challenges.

When crowdsourcing is used for less lofty goals, not to solve the world's problems but to source cheap labor, its profit motives become thornier. In this incarnation, which looks more like outsourcing, the internet is used to access the productivity of the networked public for relatively simple, repetitive, and often tedious tasks that can be completed online. As Howe explains in writing about crowdsourcing in 2006, "for the last decade or so, companies have been looking overseas, to India or China, for cheap labor. But now it doesn't matter where the laborers are—they might be down the block, they might be in Indonesia—as long as they're connected to the network."[19] His account of the then-novel practice quotes executives in various industries describing how much money they're saving by offloading tasks to online workers, a sign of the highly optimistic coverage of new internet services by the mainstream technology press in the 2000s as much as a sign of the vast cost-cutting potential of crowdsourcing.

Amazon Mechanical Turk is a prime example of this iteration of crowdsourcing. Launched in 2005 by the Web services subsidiary of the e-commerce giant, MTurk, as it's also known, is a platform where companies and organizations can post small, repetitive tasks and hire members of the crowd to complete them for very low, per-task wages. Typical MTurk jobs involve labeling images, transcribing audio, and filling out surveys. The service is named after a famous eighteenth-century chess-playing machine that, rather than exhibiting artificial intelligence, was eventually revealed to contain a hidden human chess player. In the same vein, MTurk has been described as "artificial artificial intelligence"—a computer-based solution to tedious work that, beneath the surface of its online interface, is actually powered by human labor. While attractive to employers, the service has been described as a "digital sweatshop" defined by menial work and—because its workers are independent contractors rather than Amazon employees—few labor protections. This makes the work insecure and extremely low-paying, to the tune of about $2/hour for the average MTurk worker as estimated in a 2018 study.[20] MTurk and others like it thus illustrate the gloomy side of crowdsourcing, in which influential Web 2.0 technologies touted as helping save the world are simultaneously used to reinvent problematic forms of work in cutting-edge ways.

The term *crowdsourcing* was an attempt to put a name to a fast-rising evolution of the internet, ushered in by a slew of novel services, which quickly became a pillar of the increasingly participatory and collaborative Web 2.0. As we have shown, crowdsourcing uses the internet's networking capabilities to bring together the online "crowd" and leverage individual users' various talents, ideas, and insights to solve challenging technical and intellectual problems. Most accounts of crowdsourcing have focused on its potential for scientific advancement and human betterment. Yet its second form, treating the crowd as a pool of cheap reserve labor, is arguably far more influential. It has paved the way for the "gig economy" and "crowdwork" companies like Uber and Taskrabbit. Indeed, crowdsourcing and the early services that facilitated it are crucial because they established a certain way of using the internet to connect people to accomplish things.[21] Other services snapped up this blueprint and replicated it across domains, applying the logic of crowdsourcing to achieve all kinds of outcomes.

From Crowdsourcing to Crowdfunding

Instead of tapping the crowd for ideas or to accomplish tasks, as in crowdsourcing, *crowdfunding* is about using the internet to ask people for money. What makes it compelling is that it provides a way of financing projects and ventures in a variety of areas—from the arts to consumer electronics—that doesn't rely on traditional financial intermediaries such as banks, venture capital funds, or wealthy benefactors. With crowdfunding, entrepreneurs of different stripes can use the internet's connectivity to raise money directly from the online public. In addition to opening up a large new pool of potential investors, in crowdfunding it isn't necessary to strike it big with any single donor. Instead, entrepreneurs can raise the funds they need by collecting small amounts from many individuals—whether or not they have deep pockets or fit the image of a traditional investor. The exciting idea behind crowdfunding at its inception was that it could make worthwhile commercial ideas a reality through the power of people's spare change.

Among the first to adopt this way of financing projects were musicians, whom we don't usually think of as entrepreneurs but nonetheless often fit the mold. They seek capital to create commercially viable products. Given the inherent uncertainty surrounding the profitability of any creative venture, musicians and other artists—especially those working in less popular genres—have traditionally faced high barriers to financing their visions.

The website ArtistShare, launched in 2003 and often cited as the first crowdfunding website, proposed a solution it called "fan-funding." Through its online platform, independent musicians could post proposals for new projects, like albums, and their fans could donate money to support them. In return for their support, fans would receive rewards determined by the artist, such as a physical copy of the recording, a thank-you card, or an album credit. Similar websites soon launched, making mainstream what amounts to an accessible and Web-based form of arts patronage. Recently, platforms like Patreon and Substack implemented the patronage principle through a subscription model, in which users sign up to make regular payments to support creative producers (e.g., writers, musicians, digital artists) in exchange for exclusive access to their work.[22]

As we approached 2010, this new way of giving and getting money had been termed *crowdfunding* and was spreading across hundreds of websites. Indiegogo and Kickstarter, launched respectively in 2008 and 2009, became the most prominent and successful. They allowed users to raise money for creative endeavors like music and films as well as more conventional commercial products like apparel, board games, and kitchen gadgets. Contributions could even help build physical businesses like bakeries and breweries. Project supporters received rewards, usually based on the size of their donation, that included early access to the products they sponsored. The platforms facilitating these exchanges earned revenue by charging fees: Indiegogo and Kickstarter, for example, both collect 5 percent of the money raised by a campaign in addition to approximately 3 percent for processing each donation. Having grown to suit diverse purposes, crowdfunding has also grown to encompass diverse funding models: along with reward-based crowdfunding, crowdfunding today can be donation-based (donors don't expect anything in return), lending-based (donors lend money and are repaid with interest), and equity-based (donors receive shares of future profits).[23]

Befitting its techno-optimistic era, crowdfunding was positioned by the tech press and by platforms as a force for good that democratized entrepreneurship, making it possible for ordinary, everyday people to bring good ideas to life. It was touted for bringing investment opportunities to the masses. Jeff Howe, the *Wired* journalist, described crowdfunding as "flattening hierarchies" in investing and entrepreneurship and as "radically shifting" the fundraising landscape. "Who's to say who should be able to raise money and who should not?" mused Danae Ringelman, cofounder of the platform Indiegogo. "We don't believe it's anybody's right to make that decision . . . you want a system where the cream rises to the top based on meritocratic reasons, not someone's biased opinions. . . . We're in the business of truly democratizing funding." Today's biggest crowdfunding platforms channel the Web 2.0 zeitgeist, insisting they fulfill the internet's democratic promise. They embody the attitude that ordinary people can change the world, in business and the arts, and they aim to channel "you" and "your" collective power toward active participation in, not passive consumption of, the digital world.[24]

Crowdfunding was pitched as liberating because it purported to reduce the influence of gatekeepers in entrepreneurial and creative pursuits. When Ringelman, the Indiegogo founder just quoted, scorned "someone's biased opinions," she was suggesting that by delegating funding decisions to the crowd, we end up with more objective assessments of deservingness. Cutting out the usual gatekeepers—banks, investors, record labels, and the like—whose judgments are clouded by shallow concerns about profitability and mainstream appeal—and leaving decisions to the crowd is thought to allocate funds more equitably and in ways that better align with projects' inherent quality. Once a project is funded by the crowd, the absence of traditional intermediaries should also give its creators greater control over its execution (think of the proverbial record executive telling a band to go back to the studio until they come up with a hit).

This rosy view was widely shared among crowdfunding's biggest authorities. Yancey Strickler, one of the cofounders of Kickstarter, explained the idea behind the platform with references to the early struggles of The Beatles and George Lucas and the lesson that "good ideas go unrecognized, experts get it wrong, perseverance prevails." The problem was that fundraising, "for everyone who doesn't have a rich, benevolent uncle . . . sees only profit or predictability. Not art or passion or talent or an incredible story of inspiration." Kickstarter, he said, was a way to give everyone a chance to fund their ideas and "discover that we can offer each other value through creation without a middleman dictating the product and terms." Slava Rubin, another crowdfunding founder, similarly decried the influences of "the venture capitalist, the banker, the grant maker at an institution . . . the right person at the government," and described crowdfunding as "a marketplace for access to capital" and a way to "eliminate the gatekeeper and give everybody the opportunity."[25] The emphasis of such narratives on democracy, freedom, equality, opportunity, and improving people's lives through the market and innovative commercial technologies placed these companies securely within the tradition of the Californian Ideology and the techno-solutionist thinking characteristic of Silicon Valley entrepreneurship.

Crowdfunding was an almost instant success. By forging an innovative union of new internet technology and entrepreneurship, it created business opportunities and made many new creative ventures possible. Among its major "wins" were the commercial successes of the popular game Cards Against Humanity and the Oculus Rift virtual reality headset—whose makers later sold their company to Facebook.

But as research emerged, it became clear that crowdfunding wasn't a magic bullet. Scholars began to warn that crowdfunding might not be as fair and equitable as it seemed—and as its founders aspired for it to be. Studies showed that entrepreneurs' success in crowdfunding depended on factors other than just the merits of their projects. The kind of project, the social and geographic location of the person behind it, and the characteristics of that person all play their part in determining which campaigns are funded. For one, investors are attracted to certain types of projects over others. They tend to prefer campaigns supporting tangible products like books or digital devices, which they can acquire after investing. Campaigns with less tangible deliverables, like those seeking support for environmental projects, are thus at a disadvantage in crowdfunding. Investors also like projects that involve smaller, more incremental innovations rather than radical ones, putting campaigns that think "too big" at a disadvantage. Campaign success is likewise influenced by how the campaign is presented. Pitches with proper spelling, a relatable style, and a particular narrative and phrasing tend to do better, as do campaigns with videos introducing the project and providing frequent updates to investors.[26]

Beyond campaign characteristics, who you know and where you live affect your chances of attracting crowdfunding dollars. Studies repeatedly find that the size of someone's personal social network matters greatly for crowdfunding success; contacts developed from previous entrepreneurial ventures are especially helpful. Crowdfunding also exhibits "home bias"—investors are more likely to support projects whose creators live near them.[27] This is for numerous reasons, including the fact that personal networks tend to be made up of people who are nearby, and that the benefits of many crowdfunding ventures primarily accrue to those physically near it (e.g., a campaign to support a local café). Investors in smaller, less densely populated areas who don't have a large community to call upon may be disadvantaged by this bias.

Finally, the crowd makes investment decisions based on who you are. For example, it prefers campaigns with people who list advanced degrees like MBAs and other credentials, which might reasonably be taken as signs of experience and trustworthiness by investors. However, other signals affecting its decisions are more problematic. Notably, studies of crowdfunding platforms have found that campaigns by Black American entrepreneurs are significantly less likely to receive funding compared with similar projects by White entrepreneurs. Moreover, experimental research shows that campaigns featuring Black entrepreneurs tend to do worse compared with White entrepreneurs even when they're raising funds for the *exact same* project. Potential investors also tend to rate identical projects as being of inferior quality when the creator is Black. There is less evidence of gender-based disadvantage, although the majority of crowdfunding is done by men. As you may recall from the Introduction, long-standing research on the "digital divide" has documented significant gaps in internet access—and differences in its use—based on age, income, education, and race. There is no reason to expect that internet-based crowdfunding would be spared these tendencies, and findings from crowdfunding research confirm that who you are matters not only for crowdfunding success but for whether you use crowdfunding at all.[28]

Crowdfunding was meant to democratize finance, bringing it to everyone and especially to those traditionally overlooked by banks and venture capital funds. It was also meant to be meritocratic, based solely on the quality of an entrepreneurial vision, rather than "someone's biased opinions." But it turns out that the crowd holds its own biases and stereotypes, which figure into its decision-making in ways that feel less than "wise" and advantage some campaigns and entrepreneurs over others.

What has become clear is that, as is true for business in general, you need many specific skills and characteristics (which not everyone has) to be successful in crowdfunding. Although crowdfunding has the potential to connect investors with projects across great distances, its success is still based on old-school factors like physical proximity and personal networks. And because real-world patterns of discrimination, based on characteristics like race and ethnicity, are reproduced in the behavior of online crowds, it has never worked the same for everyone who wants to raise money regardless of how deserving the cause; some people lose out. It thus behaves much like traditional markets so that, while it does bring opportunities for business and investment to some people who didn't have it before, there will always be "losers." Despite its innovations, crowdfunding has fallen well short of radically upending the existing system, flattening oppressive hierarchies, and sweeping away traditional barriers to inclusion.

In other words, crowdfunding platforms appear to have merely replaced old gatekeepers with new ones that bring their own problems. While record and movie company executives and venture capitalists no longer have as much say in which ideas are funded, this authority has been passed on to a biased crowd. Crowdfunding has thus not liberated artists from the influence of industry gatekeepers, but has simply led to an exchange of one master for another. What's more, many of the same traditional organizations whose influence crowdfunding should have eliminated have slipped back in and joined the crowd themselves, including investment funds and other financial institutions eager for profit-making opportunities.[29]

Crowdfunding platforms themselves have taken up the role of gatekeeper. This happens through the many ways platform companies shape the visibility of campaigns. Thousands of individual campaigns are live and accepting investments on any major crowdfunding site at any given moment, yet the platforms' home pages feature only a tiny fraction of them. When we visited Indiegogo, for example, its front page highlighted "Cool & Clever Finds" and projects deemed "Team Favorites." Kickstarter underscored "Featured Projects" and "Fresh Favorites," and campaigns that have been awarded badges for being "Projects We Love" get major boosts in visibility. According to Kickstarter, these badges are doled out by a "team that works to surface extra-bright projects," about which the team is "extra excited." They say that chosen projects tend to have "well-crafted videos, striking images, a clear plan, an excited community, and a lot of creativity." Kickstarter offers a few tips on becoming a "Project We Love," but the process is otherwise opaque.[30]

To the extent that the featured campaigns are simply the ones already getting attention and investments, these interventions entrench the crowd's existing decision-making patterns. But since relatively unpopular campaigns are also featured, we know there are other considerations involved. The platforms' business models are based on collecting fees for facilitating successful campaigns, so there are good reasons to think that profitability plays a role in choosing campaigns to highlight.[31] Private companies are well within their rights to manipulate their platforms, but doing so belies crowdfunding's promise to eliminate gatekeepers entirely. The fact that crowdfunding is dominated by a handful of major players amplifies the effect of a platform's decisions for shaping crowdfunding as a whole.

As we mentioned in the Introduction, algorithms are another major way platforms shape outcomes of crowdfunding campaigns. These automated processes determine (among other things) what content websites display to which users, choosing what rises to the top as we browse the Web. Google's algorithms make decisions about which websites show up at the top of our search results, Facebook and Twitter determine which announcements and posts we see, Netflix picks movies for us to watch, food delivery apps guess what's for dinner, and dating apps set us up with potential mates. All algorithms receive some input and direction from their programmers—and websites might leave room for featured content handpicked by humans—but the rules governing algorithmic decision-making are rarely known to users.[32]

And algorithms don't necessarily make the right call. Scholars have demonstrated that they make biased decisions all across the internet. They bring bias into the services we use to learn, communicate, and entertain ourselves online—as well as the institutions we interact with "in the real world." Google search results discriminate against people of color and promote problematic racial stereotypes. Government offices like housing authorities and unemployment offices determine who to investigate based on the decisions of novel computer systems that end up punishing the poor. Police departments use big data and algorithms to decide who to surveil and investigate in ways that endanger privacy and liberties. The uses of algorithms and data analytics in various sectors also have knock-on effects, contributing to wide-ranging public issues like clickbait journalism, misinformation, labor exploitation, and political repression.[33]

Because algorithms are trained based on patterns in human decision-making, they inherit the biases and prejudices of the past—"garbage in, garbage out" as the saying goes. The massive extent to which these technologies—what author Cathy O'Neil calls "weapons of math destruction"—have been deployed across different sectors of the economy and society, and the power they're given, makes them highly concerning.[34] In crowdfunding, they further erode the idea that platforms are neutral, open marketplaces where success is determined by objective merit alone (something we take up more in Chapter 2). To the extent that algorithms mimic the decision-making patterns of the broader population—who are also members of the crowd—they magnify the biases and prejudices the crowd exhibits.

Crowdfunding's Migration from Business to Welfare

Internet-based fundraising quickly found uses in areas beyond entrepreneurship. It morphed from a platform seeking business investments into one seeking donations for a variety of causes, including scientific research, journalism, litigation, various charity and community projects, and political campaigns. It also became a platform to promote individual needs in the case of, for example, medical emergencies and educational opportunities (which fall into the category we call welfare crowdfunding). Stories of people raising thousands of dollars for everything from board game development to rock band tours were compelling for those who needed help. Although research produced early warning signs that crowdfunding wasn't working well for everyone, it became massively popular for covering personal costs. Before long, media articles and platforms themselves began to present crowdfunding as a "digital safety net."[35]

Although this kind of fundraising wouldn't go into full swing for another decade, following the trailblazing success of crowdfunding for entrepreneurial ventures, some had seen crowdfunding's potential for humanitarian work as early as the year 2000. It was then that Charles Best founded DonorsChoose, a website for teachers to raise funds for classroom supplies and materials. A public high school teacher in the Bronx, Best saw a need based on his own experiences cobbling together resources for his students and often spending his own money to get things done. DonorsChoose, a nonprofit, created a space for donors to support specific classroom projects and see where their money was being spent. It became a huge success and remains a significant resource for teachers across the United States. It took a few years, but eventually the mainstream humanitarian world followed. The Great Recession, which made it more difficult to raise funds for just about everything, was a major impetus because many people needed financial help and the technology was there to help make it happen.[36]

Between 2008 and 2011, four main players emerged as crowdfunding sites for humanitarian needs. In 2008, GiveForward was created primarily for medical expenses. GoFundMe, originally CreateAFund, also emerged in 2008. Its entrepreneurial founders, Brad Damphousse and Andrew Ballester, at first provided their service, for posting fundraising campaigns and sharing them through social media, for free or sold it to charities on a subscription basis. Soon, when PayPal made it possible to split payments, the company started collecting a service fee from every donation. It grew rapidly after that and a few years later was renamed GoFundMe. Another company, YouCaring, was created in 2011 by a group who were inspired to help others after returning from religious missions abroad.[37]

These dominant sites and their lesser-known counterparts all used social media to promote fundraising campaigns: you share your cause via Facebook with a few easy clicks, the word gets out, and the money comes in. And in one model, refined by YouCaring, each donor was given the option to give a little to the platform making it all possible. In a 2017 interview, Dan Saper, CEO of YouCaring, said that approximately 70 percent of users made some sort of extra donation to the company: "We treat people like adults and let them decide who to support and how much to give." GoFundMe followed a different model in its early years, charging a fee of 5 percent for each donation plus additional money for credit card processing, much like conventional crowdfunding platforms for entrepreneurship. It would take nearly a decade, but GoFundMe's approach clearly emerged as the more profitable model: in the late 2010s, it was able to swallow up most of its competitors in a series of acquisitions.[38]

The public was certainly taking notice of the highly publicized early successes of crowdfunding. By 2016, roughly one-quarter of Americans had contributed to some sort of online fundraising project. Traditional brick-and-mortar charities were noticing that things were changing too. The Salvation Army's efforts to help victims of flooding in Louisiana in 2016, for example, raised $4 million. By contrast, GoFundMe campaign creators raised over $11 million for causes related to the same disaster. Ron Busroe, head of The Salvation Army's community relations and development arm, indicated in 2017 that the organization would likely use crowdfunding going forward. It soon formed a partnership with the nonprofit fundraising software company MobileCause to allow Salvation Army "corps and units" to create crowdfunding pages at no cost. During this same time, the Red Cross began to work with CrowdRise, later acquired by GoFundMe. Going online enabled it to access a younger demographic than its typical donors. In a 2017 interview with *Time*, Jennifer Elwood, vice president of fundraising and marketing, said the Red Cross "wouldn't have been here this long if we [hadn't continued] to adapt and evolve." The twenty-first-century version of crowdfunding was here to stay.[39]

Even as charities tried to adapt, for-profit crowdfunding companies were rapidly gaining momentum. In 2014, Indiegogo moved to a "free" model of humanitarian fundraising, later creating a separate website called Generosity, part of an extension of their existing 25 percent discount for nonprofits. A company press release said, "And because human goodness shouldn't have limits, Generosity is free of the fees common to most personal and nonprofit fundraising sites, so more money goes straight to the causes you care about most." Of course, it wasn't free—the fees were simply voluntary, like a tip at a restaurant. From 2014 to 2016, YouCaring head Dan Saper estimated that 80 percent of its donors gave an average of 6 percent as a tip on a total of $300 million in donations. That likely amounted to millions of dollars in tips in two years.[40]

The year 2015 saw new CEOs Josh Chapman (formerly chairman of Cars.com) and Rob Solomon (a venture capitalist) take the helm at

GiveForward and GoFundMe, respectively. Chapman would go on to oversee GiveForward's acquisition by YouCaring in 2017, the same year Solomon would steer a merger with CrowdRise, a site cofounded by actor Edward Norton and used by the American Cancer Society and the Red Cross for online fundraising. Facebook also entered the fray around this time, launching a charitable giving tool enabling its users to raise money for their favorite nonprofits. Capping a series of head-spinning moves, GoFundMe also acquired YouCaring in April 2018 after changing its own fees to a "free" model, dropping the fixed percentage charges. According to an industry analyst at the time, "it could be that GoFundMe decided to bring in YouCaring either to help it build out its business in the tips-based space, or to work more closely with high-profile fundraisers, or (more cynically) to take out its closest independent rival in order to have less competitive pressure around how it chooses to build out fees and tips in the future." At the end of this tumultuous period, GoFundMe had emerged with a virtual monopoly. By its reckoning, it raised more than $9 billion from approximately 120 million donors by year's end 2019.[41]

The point of chronicling all this is to show that crowdfunding sites aren't first and foremost charitable enterprises. They're businesses driven by profit imperatives that pivot to new approaches and merge with other companies as the entrepreneurs who lead them try to capture market share, maximize revenue, and make serious money. For them, the gaps in American and Canadian social welfare provisions have become profit opportunities. Although their goal is to connect people to the help they need, they run businesses before anything else, accountable to their shareholders and ultimately acting as vehicles for financial gain.

Contextualizing the Rise of Welfare Crowdfunding

As scholars focused on growing inequality and the shortcomings of government support, we wondered how and why GoFundMe, a for-profit company, became dominant in meeting people's needs. Crowdfunding sites seemed to be helping thousands of people every day, at least based on news reports. The emotional cases in our newsfeeds were exciting and uplifting but contained echoes of nineteenth-century charity, with people knocking on the doors of strangers with hat in hand. How did we get here?

Directly asking strangers for money or other help had grown less common as the United States and Canada became modern welfare states in the middle of the twentieth century. Welfare states are political arrangements, commonly found among capitalist societies, where the national government plays an active role in ensuring the social well-being of its citizens by creating insurance schemes and benefit programs that protect them from common risks such as illness, unemployment, and injury. Welfare states provide support for particularly vulnerable groups, like children and the elderly, through special programs providing pensions, parental leave, social housing, and the like. They also invest in citizens' future productivity and well-being through measures like public education and job training. Welfare states are found among countries all around the world and take many different forms, differing substantially in the strictness of eligibility requirements for different programs and the generosity of program benefits.[42]

The US welfare state originated in the 1930s and the New Deal policies enacted by President Franklin D. Roosevelt during the Great Depression. Most notable among these was the Social Security Act of 1935, which established a series of government social welfare programs providing aid to the elderly, families with children, and the unemployed. These programs responded to the massive poverty, unemployment, and suffering brought about by the Depression and for the first time established a public social welfare system in the United States, which had previously relied on a patchwork of often haphazard and inequitable aid provision through churches and private charities. The Social Security Act also set the stage for the creation of Medicare and Medicaid in the 1960s.[43]

Canada's welfare state emerged slightly later, following World War II, and soon offered similar programs, including old-age pensions and benefits for the unemployed and families with children. Compared with the wealthy, industrialized countries of Western Europe and Scandinavia, the US and Canada have very limited welfare states in terms of the generosity and scope of the benefits provided, which leave individuals personally responsible for many aspects of their well-being. Comparing the two countries with each other, however, shows that the Canadian welfare state provides more generous and expansive programs, best exemplified by its publicly funded universal health-care system. Though imperfect and limited in their own ways—and leaving plenty of space for individual responsibility and private-sector solutions—the US and Canadian welfare systems enshrined a basic level of support for individual social and economic well-being as part of the legal and institutional fabric of society, and they represented a giant leap forward from the unforgiving world of nineteenth-century charity. Welfare states had their heyday in the years following World War II, as governments in capitalist countries around the world increased the scope and depth of their social expenditures during a thirty-year period of economic growth and prosperity.[44]

The 1970s marked the end of the golden age of welfare states and the beginning of a period of retrenchment or cutbacks in welfare programs and a general repudiation in many places of state-funded social support. The decade, marked by oil shocks and a recession, signified the end of the postwar economic boom. High unemployment and inflation meant that people began drawing more heavily on social supports at the same time as slowed economic growth and fewer workers devastated the tax base, making it impossible to continue providing the same benefits as before, which was already becoming more difficult with aging populations and a changing workforce. Welfare states in their previous forms had become unsustainable.[45]

At the same time, political ideals also changed. Policy-makers took up neoliberal thinking, which understands the welfare state and government intervention not as the solution but as the problem and the cause of the era's economic troubles. Epitomized by President Ronald Reagan in the United States, and Prime Ministers Brian Mulroney and Jean Chrétien in Canada, neoliberal leaders in the 1980s and 1990s advocated for less government intervention and fewer regulations curbing the freedom of businesses. Meanwhile, social problems like unemployment were seen as the result not of systemic failures but of individuals' lack of motivation to find work, due in part to the excessive generosity of welfare state benefits. In response, neoliberal politicians reduced social services, eliminated job protections, deregulated industries, and privatized state-owned enterprises. Although government social expenditures didn't plummet overnight because of neoliberal policies, social security systems increasingly failed to keep up with citizens' needs as eligibility criteria became harder to meet, program budgets stagnated, and policies stopped adjusting to new social risks.[46]

This period of political upheaval led to the growth of insecurity and inequality across industrialized countries, particularly in North America, and made it more difficult to access many kinds of services to meet people's basic needs. In the case of health care, Americans have traditionally relied on private health insurance provided through their employers. The exceptions are the elderly and those with disabilities or very low incomes, who receive coverage through Medicare and Medicaid, created in the 1960s and representing the height of health protection coverage in the US. Since the sixties, because of changes in employer and insurance industry practices, the costs of health services have ballooned at the same time that fewer employers are providing coverage for employees, leaving a growing proportion of Americans uninsured. Despite progress made in increasing insurance coverage with enactment of the Affordable Care Act (ACA) in 2010, America's public health insurance programs, for those who are eligible, are still underfunded and limited in scope, passing much of the risk of illness onto individuals' ability to pay out of pocket. Canada's celebrated national health insurance program has enjoyed relative stability through this same period, but shows growing coverage gaps—most notably when it comes to prescription drugs—as it fails to keep up with new health risks and treatment approaches.[47]

As health care has gotten more expensive and harder to acquire, Americans have had to spend more than they can afford to or have simply gone to the doctor less frequently. These circumstances have obvious negative consequences for people's health and financial well-being. Higher costs and more limited access lead people to skip necessary trips to the doctor and do without prescription medicines, making it harder to catch conditions early or manage existing ones, resulting in worse prognoses and ultimately higher medical bills when care can no longer be put off. For those who do seek health care, its high costs can lead to financial ruin or neglecting other necessary expenses. Scholars have found, for example, that the US saw a considerable decline in primary care visits, even among insured people, between 2008 and 2016, and increases in costs per visit. Among cancer survivors, another study found, 42.4 percent of the 9.5 million people diagnosed between 2000 and 2012 had depleted their life savings within two years. Although the situation doesn't appear to be as dire as in the US, research shows that Canadians too, especially those with poorer health and lower incomes, face problems with out-of-pocket medical expenses, and that they're regularly unable to afford necessary medications and forego necessities like food and heating because of drug costs.[48]

We can see in both countries that there are shortfalls and gaps in health care and other social supports, like education and housing, yet government welfare programs continue to make a major difference in the lives of tens of millions of people. In their present form, they just can't meet the basic needs of all members of society—needs many of us believe should be met. Crowdfunding wasn't a direct response to late twentieth-century welfare state retrenchment, but the rise of inequality and insecurity as we entered the twenty-first century was a key part of the context out of which welfare crowdfunding and companies like GoFundMe emerged. Most of us know that inequality remains a massive social problem. There is significant variation in wealth, income, and access to opportunities for realizing one's full potential, and those who have less of these things are turning to the internet to get help in facing their challenges.[49]

And then COVID-19 happened. The pandemic amplified and made it far harder to ignore the gaps in social welfare supports that widened so quickly as the pandemic strained already overburdened systems. Alongside this, we saw an unprecedented increase in crowdfunding activity on GoFundMe, with thousands of new pages created in the first few days of pandemic lockdowns. People turned to crowdfunding for help with everything from personal protective equipment to hospital costs, lost wages, and funeral services.[50]

In the first months of 2020, the coronavirus raced around the world. US and Canadian governments implemented measures to limit its spread. These mitigation efforts, like mandated physical distancing and the closure of offices and retail stores, amounted to a shutdown of large parts of the economy. Shutting down spurred bankruptcies, layoffs, and furloughs, particularly in the retail sector but also in white-collar industries like technology and legal services. At the same time, essential workers who remained at their jobs—including nurses, grocery store clerks, and bus drivers—faced increased risk of illness and death as they continued to work and be in contact with the public. Some, but not many, received various forms of "hazard pay," but it was hardly enough to offset the trauma and fear involved in their day-to-day work and dissipated quickly.

The economic recession spurred by the pandemic led to historic unemployment rates in both the US and Canada. In the US, the unemployment rate peaked at 14.7 percent in April 2020, the highest recorded rate since the government started collecting standardized unemployment numbers in 1948. Canada similarly broke records with a 13.7 percent unemployment rate in May 2020, not seen since the first half of the twentieth century. The average joblessness rate across all wealthy, industrialized countries approached double digits in 2020, reflecting the enormous and far-reaching economic consequences of the pandemic.[51]

The pandemic was exceptional not only because of the size and scope of its impact but also because of how quickly it devastated livelihoods. The soaring unemployment rates in both countries soon translated into soaring claims for unemployment benefits. In the US, an average 5 million new jobless claims were made each week in the first month of mandated lockdowns, a volume worse than the worst weeks of the Great Recession and far outstripping the previous record of 695,000 new claims each week set in 1982. The 22 million new unemployment claims filed in those first four weeks roughly matched the total number of jobs created in the previous ten years. By early July, almost four months into the pandemic, roughly *one out of every five American workers*—over 31 million people—was collecting an unemployment check. This was at the same time that the country was registering new record-high coronavirus cases daily and the epicenters of new infections shifted from New York to Florida, Texas, Arizona, and other states.[52]

In Canada, applications for unemployment benefits and emergency assistance soared too. In a country of 38 million people (roughly the population of California), nearly a million Canadians applied for employment insurance in the first week after physical distancing requirements forced businesses to shut down or significantly reduce activities. Twice as many jobs were lost in that single week in 2020 as were lost in the worst *month* of the Great Recession. When, in early April, Canada launched a benefit program for those who didn't otherwise qualify for unemployment insurance (similar to the Pandemic Unemployment Assistance program in the US)—including the self-employed and those on reduced hours because of the lockdowns—almost 3.5 million people applied before week's end. By July, more than one-quarter of working-age Canadians had reported receiving some kind of government unemployment benefit since the beginning of the pandemic.[53]

With literally breathtaking speed, millions of us became sick, unemployed, or both. Governments seemed just as shocked as everyday people. They were caught off guard when unemployment offices were flooded with claims but staffed to deal with the historically low jobless rates of the late 2010s. Understaffed and using systems poorly equipped for the surge in demand, all the while adapting workplaces to the pandemic, service provision faltered. In late April, laid-off or furloughed workers were met with long, frustrating wait times while applying for benefits over the phone, some only days before the rent was due. In some states, applicants made hundreds of calls but were unable to get through. Because unemployment application websites crashed under the rush of visitors, going online was no better.[54]

When benefit claims actually went through, newly unemployed people in many states still faced weeks of delays before receiving payments. In many cases, this was due to the inflexible, decades-old computer systems used to administer social security to millions of Americans. These systems needed to be adjusted to process unemployment insurance as well as the new, hastily crafted benefits programs enabled by the Coronavirus Aid, Relief, and Economic Security (CARES) Act, passed by Congress in March 2020. Again, the systems were underfunded and running on software from the 1960s that few programmers knew how to work with. Benefits processing lagged (except when it failed entirely). The size, scope, and timing of the benefits made possible by the CARES Act—whose $2 trillion price tag made it the largest economic relief package in American history—provided enormous help to individuals, families, businesses, and state and local governments despite the setbacks. Policy analysts generally praised the federal government's initial economic response and characterized it as timely, sufficiently large, and effective in reaching broad swaths of the economy, including gig workers, the self-employed, small businesses, health-care services, and state and local governments.[55]

Nonetheless, experts quickly pointed out significant gaps in the sprawling aid package. For example, benefits required having filed a federal tax return, leaving out many of the up to 30 million Americans—seniors, veterans, people with disabilities, those on very low incomes, and the like—who don't file taxes and represent some of the most vulnerable people in the country. Those living in the country without legal authorization were similarly excluded from federal aid.[56]

Further, because relief funds were linked to employment, those who had *not* lost their jobs were entitled to little or no help. Among these were frontline workers fulfilling essential roles in hospitals, on public transit, and in grocery stores, who despite keeping their jobs often lived below the poverty line and were now working through the worst of the pandemic.[57]

Outdated systems exacerbated the already leisurely pace of benefits provision. Would those who qualified for benefits and granted aid receive the money in time for rent or grocery payments? Particularly if they were receiving paper checks, the answer was no. Direct deposit was useful to some, but the obstacles already posed by delayed deliveries and lost mail were made worse for recipients who didn't have access to adequate banking services. It was unclear what these recipients would do with a paper check at a time when even predatory check-cashing services were closed. Finally, critics took issue with the limited duration of the funds. The original CARES package of benefits was set to expire by August 2020, potentially leaving millions of struggling Americans in the lurch.[58]

The Canadian government, for its part, announced a large and comprehensive aid package that was generally thought of as a successful response to the early pandemic needs of most citizens. Prime Minister Justin Trudeau announced the C$82 billion COVID-19 Emergency Response Act in March 2020. Its provisions included a variety of modifications to existing programs, such as a temporary increase in child benefits and an interest-free period for student loans, as well as new benefit programs for individuals and businesses.

Most notable among the new benefits was the Canada Emergency Response Benefit (CERB), which provided a $2,000 monthly payment to those who had lost their jobs or had seen their work hours drastically reduced due to the pandemic. As Trudeau stated, the country was in "a time where you should be focused on your health, and that of your neighbors, not whether you're going to lose your job, not whether you're going to run out of money for things like groceries and medication." The government intended to help. Benefits were also created for university students and high school graduates who had seen summer job opportunities vanish, and for businesses to continue paying for rent and payroll. Canadians already enjoyed the benefits of a single-payer national health-care system, which covered the costs of medical treatment for COVID-19.[59]

For those who qualified, obtaining benefits was in many respects easier in Canada. In the US, unemployment insurance has traditionally been the responsibility of individual states, unlike many other programs including Medicare and Social Security. This gives states broad freedoms to shape their insurance programs and requires each to run its own system for administering benefits, including the $600 weekly payment, on top of a state's unemployment benefits, provided by the federal government through the CARES Act. This meant that Americans attempting to access financial support during the pandemic faced a variety of state-specific insurance systems at different levels of preparedness, with different application procedures and with various obstacles to receiving funds when they didn't work.[60]

Canada, by contrast, features a single, federal unemployment insurance program for all residents. Getting financial help during the pandemic meant using a single application system, and many of the complications seen in the US were avoided by unemployment benefit payments being sent directly from the federal government rather than through individual provinces. What's more, Canadian officials stated that no one who applied for the job-loss benefit would be denied the money. They admitted that running a financial assistance program based largely on the honor system—where applicants only needed to *attest* to their eligibility—would invite fraud. But they insisted that the risks were justified by the need; a comprehensive audit would deal with fraudulent applications later. Canada's was thus a streamlined system that sought to pay benefits first and ask questions later. In the US meanwhile, pandemic aid was paid out by individual states whose systems were in many cases designed to make obtaining unemployment benefits as hard as possible, through onerous filing requirements and surprises such as needing a fax machine or remembering a PIN created years ago.[61]

The Canadian approach still ran into issues. Early on, some Canadians reported going weeks without income as they—and the government agencies they relied on—adjusted to new, hastily created programs. Some laid-off workers applied for benefits under the old unemployment insurance program before the pandemic-specific programs were created. But those applications didn't recognize "pandemic" as a reason for job loss, leading to incomplete applications, additional information requirements, and delayed payments. When the pandemic-specific programs did become available, however, those same workers were unable to apply because they already had pending applications for the old benefit program. They were stranded. Like Americans, many Canadians were left listening to hold music because their call centers were unable to keep up with the unprecedented demand.[62]

Policy experts pointed to gaps in government support, particularly for populations left out. Canada already had a more robust social support system than the US, with universal health-care and various programs for seniors, people with disabilities, and those on low incomes. Thus, with some exceptions, pandemic-specific programs didn't target these vulnerable groups. There were concerns that they had been forgotten—a scary situation for those who were already struggling before the pandemic and reliant on shelters, food banks, libraries with public internet, and the like, which were shut down or greatly disrupted by physical distancing mandates.[63] With the closure of many community tax clinics in the middle of tax season, there were also concerns that low-income Canadians who needed help with filing taxes would be shut out from income benefits they already relied on—and whose eligibility depended on tax returns.

Much as in the States, scholars drew attention to "essential" workers—in sectors like retail, transportation, and medical services—whose jobs continued, only with greater risks. Such jobs are often low-paying and nonunionized, have few benefits, and usually can't be done remotely. They're also disproportionately filled by women, people of color, and vulnerable groups such as those with disabilities and chronic health conditions, who in the best of times may find it difficult to juggle shift work with caregiving responsibilities, medical treatments, and other obligations. The new challenges presented by the pandemic work-place were likely to be the hardest for groups already marginalized in the labor market. Although these Canadians were fortunate to have a job, their jobs, for the most part, didn't provide economic security before the pandemic. Getting by got much harder during the pandemic and in ways that government supports didn't anticipate.[64]

With the onset of COVID-19, social welfare gaps sometimes became chasms. The government in both the US and Canada launched unprecedented economic relief packages that made a big difference for many but had difficult application procedures, payment delays, and overlooked populations. In a matter of days, the coronavirus ushered in the greatest economic and public health catastrophe in a hundred years. Millions were suddenly struggling to pay for food and rent. Those who had already been scrambling to survive a medical emergency or tuition bill were pushed to the brink. If their savings ran dry and the government's safety net failed to catch them, they did what many others had started doing in recent years. They turned to the internet for help.

From the earliest weeks of the pandemic, people were helping each other. In April, as reported by *NPR*, Nicolena, a single mother who had lost her job as a hair stylist, reported receiving only the state portion of her unemployment benefits—$340 a week in Virginia, where the amount is based on previous earnings. The federal portion—the additional $600 a week she was entitled to under the CARES Act—was delayed for her and millions of Americans whose applications were backlogged. With firm, looming deadlines on her bills, the assurances that she would eventually get the payment in full were hardly helpful. In the meantime, some of Nicolena's friends, organizing through the internet, started a fundraiser; she was able to use its proceeds to continue paying for groceries, rent, and health insurance for her and her daughter until her benefits arrived.[65]

As reported in *The New York Times*, Nadine, a 46-year-old woman in New York, lost her job on March 13, 2020, when the office of the federal agency where she worked closed indefinitely. She filed for unemployment benefits. Two months passed. Before she received the benefits to which she was entitled, she negotiated a payment extension with her phone company, made numerous unsuccessful calls to the New York Department of Labor about her claim, and tweeted at the governor. In April, six weeks into her wait, she started asking strangers on social media to send her money to help with food, mentioning her username for Cash App, a mobile money transfer service, in her request.[66]

That people were turning to the internet for help in massive numbers during the pandemic was unmistakable by October, 2020, when Go-FundMe announced a brand-new fundraising category: Food, Rent, and Monthly Bills.[67] Before then, the company was already responding to the pandemic. It was still early March 2020 when GoFundMe's nonprofit charity arm created a "general relief fund" for donations that it passed on to coronavirus-related causes. Later that month, it partnered with Yelp, the crowdsourced restaurant and business review website, to automatically generate GoFundMe campaigns for many small businesses—a practice it quickly discontinued after business owners expressed dismay at not being informed that money was being raised in their name. The fundraising category introduced in October 2020 announced a new kind of deprivation, for which seeking online donations was no longer a last-ditch effort to survive an extraordinary accident but had become a way to maintain a minimal daily existence. There had never been a better time to be in the crowdfunding business.[68]

Markets and Helping Don't Mix

This brief history of the rise of digital crowdfunding takes us up to the present day and the data we collected on welfare crowdfunding using GoFundMe. Understanding the history (and logic) of crowdfunding and the meteoric rise of GoFundMe contextualizes the data we present in the next three chapters. The history matters because it reveals the market-focused, techno-solutionist Californian Ideology that drives contemporary crowdfunding. Recall the ideology's basic tenets: digital technology by its nature is democratic and promotes individual freedom, and the market does a better job than government in improving people's lives. Yet even when it's used in the business world, because of systemic social biases, the digital divide, and biased algorithms, crowdfunding has *never* worked the same for everyone who wants to raise money. Most people lose out. As we show, the same is true when it's used in the world of social welfare. Crowdfunding didn't travel well from business to personal causes, no matter how much we cheered when it began to enter the realm of helping others just as gaps in American and Canadian social programs widened. So far, we have failed to acknowledge (and fix) the problems inherent to this way of raising money. Migrating from business to social welfare, crowdfunding carried the baggage of ideas antithetical to the principles of social citizenship and meeting basic needs that inspired twentieth-century welfare state programs and that many still believe are key to healthy and flourishing societies.

We are now ready to consider the people who need more help than ever. Who does (and who doesn't) use welfare crowdfunding to meet those acute needs and why? What does it mean to go online and, with the help of the crowd, try to sell our misery, tug at heartstrings, bring in money, and if we're really lucky, cover the bills for social goods like education and medical care?

Two

A Well of Sadness

When we began our research on welfare crowdfunding, it seemed as if everyone was doing it. But this wasn't the case. Based on our data, welfare crowdfunding is primarily a tool of those who are already relatively privileged in terms of age, class, race, and social capital. We also learned there are complex factors behind the question of *why* people ask for help. With the assistance of large amounts of data, collected and analyzed over the last few years, and research findings reported by many other scholars, this chapter goes beyond home pages to look at algorithm-driven success stories as well as stories whose asks go unfulfilled. It's time to meet some crowdfunders.

A Few Stories to Set the Stage

Let's start with Tom.

When we started this book project, neither of us had firsthand experience with crowdfunding campaigns. No one in our circles of acquaintances, friends, and family had crafted their own appeal, until Tom, an acquaintance of Erik's, experienced massive kidney failure. Needing a kidney transplant was tough news on its own, but as the sole earner for his household (which includes four children, one with special needs), Tom was almost as troubled by his sudden inability to work.

Tom's wife Mary says of this period, "The biggest issue, no matter who you are, is *How are we going to afford this?*" The couple is Canadian, so most of Tom's medical expenses would be covered, but all their other obligations, Mary told us, were urgent and immeasurably stressful. Tom agreed, remembering the sense of desperation: "Yeah, I was gonna go back [to work] even if it killed me. And it would have killed me." By his own admission, the former rock drummer had been a heavy drug user, leading a life of excess in his younger days. But with encouragement from Mary, he eventually cleaned up, got sober, and became a personal trainer. Kids came soon after, and the family was, on the whole, doing well. This was a redemption story that seemed to have a happy ending, but then Tom's body broke down. After weeks of tests, he found out his kidneys were shot. Probably it was the hard living, but who knows? What Tom did know is that without his body, he couldn't do his job, and fitness training is typically contract employment: you don't work, you don't get paid. Tom could barely get out of bed for his weekly dialysis appointment, let alone lead vigorous workouts.

The lost income was real. Tom's family wasn't eligible for provincial welfare because their past income was too high. It would take time for disability support to arrive. Theoretically, Mary could go back to work full-time, though it would mean giving up homeschooling for their four children—a last-resort option given that one of their boys is autistic and needs extra learning support.

With Tom hospitalized, drifting in and out of consciousness, Mary's thoughts turned to crowdfunding. "I had an ex-coworker who had done it a few years ago when she was diagnosed with . . . cancer—two young children; she was in her forties—and I just remembered that." She went on GoFundMe and drafted a fundraising page for Tom, but hesitated: "I actually didn't go on with it because I thought no one [would] donate. . . . And then I thought about it for a few days and I could see [Tom's] anxiety over income stuff . . . [so] I put it live." For the first few days, the fundraiser remained a secret, at least from Tom.

Tom's need and Mary's response changed our writing perspective. It felt similar to the whole COVID-19 pandemic experience: this kind of upheaval is abstract until it becomes personal. Though it felt a bit strange, since we were currently researching crowdfunding, it was hard to ignore the need of someone you *know*. Not helping felt wrong (another topic we'll talk about in a bit), so Erik donated.

As it turns out, across our interviews and the cases we found online, Tom's story is common. A family drops everything—including work, which isn't always possible—to come together and meet their loved one's challenge. Or they may choose (or be forced) to keep working, sacrificing personal support for earning power. With personal emergencies, it usually comes down to money at some point.

Recall Lisa and Robert, from the Introduction. Lisa's brain cancer diagnosis changed everything. As Robert put it, "we were scrambling, and I was trying to work, and I'm teaching math while thinking I should be at the hospital, right?" He dropped everything to support his wife during her hospitalization and treatment—to him there was no other choice. Plus he'd been doing all right financially, working as a professional hockey referee and a substitute teacher at his local high school. But the money dried up shockingly fast. With $14 per day for parking and buying cafeteria meals, going to the hospital was proving expensive. Hopeful their struggles would soon pass, however, Robert turned down his friends' initial offer to set up a GoFundMe appeal.

In fact, time and again we heard people express their initial reluctance toward welfare crowdfunding—at least for themselves. Like Mary, who drafted but stalled on posting a page for Tom, Robert regarded Go-FundMe as a last resort. He began by telling us he had hesitated because Lisa's cancer "could be . . . nothing, and they take it out and everything is all good and we just go back to a normal life after eight months." He told himself, "I can just pick up extra shifts, I can cut grass on the side in the summers, we can make ends meet after a few months, and we can get back on our feet and we can just work it off." When pressed, Robert confessed he was reluctant to ask others for help: "I don't know, I don't want to say 'proud'—I didn't want the extra attention, I didn't want the invasion of privacy or the questions or anything. I just wanted to let her deal with it and . . . once [Lisa] came to and we had a second surgery and everything, she's the one that told me: 'Hey, if this thing goes sideways, take the help this time.'" From his chair next to Lisa's hospital bed, Robert recounted how the couple's friends waited a few months before asking again to "set this thing up." This time, they got the go-ahead.

Robert figured crowdfunding might "allow me to be here rather than me worrying about work."

There are few provisions for missing work to take care of yourself or support a loved one undergoing medical care, as so many people found out during the global pandemic. Those that exist are usually for salaried employees, who make up a shrinking portion of the global economy.

It's not always about health problems or lost work, though. Crowd-funding sites also feature campaigns aimed at meeting needs usually met by governments and institutions. Public classroom fundraisers are so common now that DonorsChoose specializes in them. Delilah, an elementary school teacher in the Midwest, told us that, after a decade of teaching a traditional sixth-grade social studies class, she moved into teaching in the school's reading intervention program. She quickly realized the school couldn't provide the materials her new pupils needed, like headphones, or the supplies she needed to create a reading area. "Where [was] I going to get all this money?' You know what I mean? When I heard about [crowdfunding], I thought, 'this is really kind of cool. . . . 'I'm going to go ahead and try it.'"

Delilah wasn't entirely without reservations, feeling uncomfortable even though she was asking for funds to support her students. When her colleagues clued her into DonorsChoose, she worked to economize her ask: "Education can be very expensive, but I [tried] to make mine low-budget." She listed the basic materials her classroom needed, the cost amounting to a few hundred dollars, and posted the appeal.

> I don't like asking for money for anything, honestly. I didn't share it with my family. . . . You can share this on Facebook and all those [social networks]. I don't really want to do that, you know what I mean? I really just want to put it there and see if I get any hits anonymously because I feel like my family is going to feel guilt. . . . I don't want to guilt people into . . . giving me money.

Setting aside the fact that she wasn't asking anyone to give *her* money, just her classroom, you can still read Delilah's anxiety. She loves her community—so much so that she moved back to her hometown and into her grandparents' house in order to teach at this particular school. But there just wasn't enough money to go around: "I've been here twelve years; there's not been a good community support for the school," she commented. "The parents aren't really involved, businesses have never really been onboard," and, of course, though Delilah avoided mentioning this, public school funding has been slashed in districts throughout the United States. Welfare state retrenchment has meant cutbacks of all sorts, leaving a lot of community needs unmet. In this way, school funding campaigns are another form of welfare crowdfunding.

And then there are those who search for hope. Medical treatments aren't always covered by insurance or national health programs. Too expensive, too new, or "nontraditional," some therapies aren't approved for reimbursement by government decision-makers and insurance companies. This makes such treatments harder to find and frequently prohibitively expensive. We interviewed a woman named Jen and her Aunt Roberta, who had been diagnosed with pancreatic cancer. Her chemotherapy schedule (two weeks on and one week off for three months at a time) exhausted her and the treatment left her immunocompromised. In the midst of a global pandemic, she was in no position to keep working as a health-care practitioner. Roberta lost her income almost immediately and then learned she would have to pay for her preferred treatment regimen out of pocket. That's when her niece Jen stepped in, creating a Go-FundMe page she hoped could cover Roberta's normal expenses as well as her cancer treatment. What a feeling of powerlessness at a time when hope might be the only thing that could get you through. As Jen told us, "it makes me feel sad that the care that is out there is not available for everyone."

Illness, loss of income, government budget shortfalls, inadequate insurance—these are just a few of the reasons our interviewees turned to crowdfunding. Plus, these are stories. They capture emotional ups and downs, but they could be outliers. They might not show the big picture. Further, as researchers we understand that answers to a call for interview participants can't, on their own, tell us enough about *who* is crowdfunding across the US and Canada. We need numbers to tells us general social trends and tease out the stories that are generalizable. To get our heads around the crowdfunding phenomenon, we need both the stories and the numbers. In the next section, we provide a general, demographic picture of who crowdfunds for health and education needs.[1]

A Bird's-Eye View of Welfare Crowdfunding

To understand who uses crowdfunding in general terms, we started with GoFundMe, and analyzed how the fundraising campaigns it hosts are distributed across the countries in which it operates. As of 2022, residents of nineteen countries were eligible to create a GoFundMe campaign. These include countries with the largest English-speaking majorities: the United States, Canada, the United Kingdom, and Australia alongside Austria, Belgium, Denmark, Finland, France, Germany, Ireland, Italy, Luxembourg, the Netherlands, Norway, Portugal, Spain, Sweden, and Switzerland. The full list features some of the world's richest countries, characterized by some of the planet's highest levels of human development and well-being. Certain areas in some of these countries are notably prohibited from creating fundraisers—for instance, residents of US territories, including Puerto Rico's 3 million plus US citizens.[2]

GoFundMe campaign organizers—at least if they want to be able to withdraw the funds they raise on GoFundMe—have to meet certain eligibility requirements depending on the country and currency they select for their campaign. In most countries, organizers must provide a local phone number and mailing address, a valid bank account, and a passport or driver's license. Some countries also require a local taxpayer identification number: US residents, a Social Security number; Canadians, a Social Insurance number. If, for whatever reason, you lack the proper documents, you can't raise money on GoFundMe. That includes nearly all immigrants without legal status, a group disproportionately and often obviously in need of help.

Based on analysis of our original data, the vast majority of GoFundMe campaigns are created in the United States. Of the 2 million in our dataset created since 2018, 82 percent, or nearly 1.7 million, were located there. The United Kingdom is the second most common origin, though it accounts for just about 7 percent of GoFundMe appeals (144,000 cases). Canada is next, with 4 percent of the total (about 90,000 cases) and then

Australia, with 2 percent (49,000 cases). Though they round out the top 10, Ireland, Italy, Germany, the Netherlands, Spain, and France each boast less than 1 percent of the total. These differences are somewhat intuitive (the United States has the largest population by far), but we need to adjust for population size to get a campaign rate, or a per capita count of fundraisers.

Between 2018 and 2021, there were approximately 509 US-based GoFundMe campaigns for every 100,000 US residents. Put differently, in those three years GoFundMe hosted roughly one campaign for every 200 Americans. (For reasons we discuss more closely in the Appendix, we believe this number is a lower bound and that US-based crowdfunding is actually even more common than our data suggests.)

By population, Germany and France have the next biggest eligible populations, but their citizens don't do anywhere near as much crowdfunding as America's do. In the same three years, Germany produced 15 GoFundMe cases per 100,000 people; France, just 9. This equates to about one campaign per 7,000 residents in Germany and one per 11,000 in France. The US population is about 4 times the size of Germany's, while its GoFundMe case rate is 34 times higher. It out-peoples France by a factor of 5, but out-asks by a factor of 57.[3]

That two of the three most populous countries aren't also the top three crowdfunding countries per capita suggests that there are major cross-national differences in crowdfunding use. Yes, these numbers refer to campaigns created for *any purpose* and on a single platform (GoFundMe has competitors in all of these countries, so its fundraising activity doesn't represent the full extent of crowdfunding elsewhere). However, the magnitude of the differences we observe is consistent with the idea that large national differences underlie demand for charitable fundraising. And we believe that has to do with national political contexts. To the extent that residents have alternative sources of support, such as adequate government funding for health, job loss, and education, we imagine they have less need to raise money through crowdfunding.

Getting back to per capita rates, we see that Ireland is second to the United States in our focal period, with about 360 GoFundMe cases per 100,000 residents, and Canada takes third, boasting 240 per 100,000 (that's a bit less than half the US rate, or one campaign per 400 residents). Two other English-speaking countries, the United Kingdom and Australia, close out the top five, each with about 200 campaigns per 100,000.

Let's pause and digest. From this data, we see that crowdfunding on GoFundMe is only happening in relatively wealthy countries. Of these, whether in absolute terms or per capita, the United States is generating the most by far. In many countries, certain geographical regions and populations without the requisite country-specific documents to set up a GoFundMe campaign, are excluded. And again, it's key to remember that the excluded, like those living without legal authorization, are frequently in dire need of financial help.

Regional analysis in the United States and Canada reveals even more variation in the use of crowdfunding. A quick look at the US cases in our data shows a straightforward trend: higher numbers of GoFundMe campaigns correspond to the states with higher numbers of people. California is the largest US state and its 226,044 cases during our study period make up about 14 percent of the US total. Texas, Florida, and New York, the next three largest states, respectively account for about 9, 7, and 6 percent of crowdfunding cases, values that roughly match their population shares. States with small populations, like Wyoming, Vermont, Alaska, Delaware, and the Dakotas, likewise have the fewest crowdfunding cases, each with less than half a percent of the total.

Switching to the per capita rates helps us see how much specific states' residents engage in crowdfunding. Among the profound differences, we find that Washington DC is America's crowdfunding capital. Its 2018–2021 GoFundMe campaign rate was, in our data, about 805 cases per 100,000 residents, or 1.5 times the national average (509 cases per 100,000). Oregon, Vermont, and Colorado are regionally distant but have similar crowdfunding rates of about 700 per 100,000, or one campaign for every 150 residents. On the low end, Mississippi's 330 cases per 100,000 (about two-thirds of the national average) bring up the rear, beaten only narrowly by Iowa and Alabama, each at roughly 380 campaigns per 100,000.

When trying to make sense of this variation, it's important to remember that people use crowdfunding for a variety of reasons. Washington DC crowdfunds more than the average state, but DC is no ordinary city (and it's not a state at all). As the seat of the federal government, it's also home to the headquarters of many organizations, especially nonprofits, charities, and advocacy groups, which regularly engage in fundraising. This concentration of organizations (whose employees likely commute from surrounding states rather than live in the city) appears consequential: a look at the fundraising categories shows that Washington is home to an unusually large number of campaigns for education, community service, and volunteering (and an unusually small number of pet-related campaigns) compared with other regions.[4]

Other states' most common fundraising categories similarly appear to reflect their economies and customs. California, New York, and Tennessee are all known for their creative industries, and they're standouts when it comes to music, film, and artistic crowdfunding campaigns. Alabama, Georgia, and Virginia are among the states with high numbers of church and faith-based campaigns (to fund mission trips for example), while states recently battered by natural disasters, like hurricane-vulnerable Louisiana and wildfire-hotspot Oregon, generate lots of campaigns related to accidents and emergencies.

Just as important, there are many reasons why people in need *don't* turn to crowdfunding. Internet access, for instance, is a basic requirement for crowdfunding, and having the nation's lowest internet access rates may contribute to the low crowdfunding uptake in Mississippi, Alabama, and Louisiana.[5] That is, it's informative to compare different states in terms of the total number of campaigns they create, but it's also worth keeping in mind that these numbers obscure underlying differences between states that both promote and impede campaign creation.

Regional differences are also apparent among Canada's provinces and territories. Ontario, home to Toronto, one of North America's largest cities, is the GoFundMe hub, with a nation-leading 42 percent of 2018–2021 campaigns in our Canadian dataset (a total of approximately 35,300 cases). Three more large provinces, British Columbia, Quebec, and Alberta, follow with approximately 18, 14, and 13 percent.

Taking into account the vastly different populations of Canadian regions shows that Ontario's 241 campaigns per 100,000 puts it exactly in the middle of Canada's 13 provinces and territories—very close to the national average. The surprising outlier, when we account for population size, is the Canadian North, or The Yukon and Northwest Territories (NWT), which are distinct from the provinces and have less sovereignty in relation to the federal government. The territories are in the far north of Canada, beginning at the sixtieth parallel, east of Alaska, and extend into the Arctic Ocean. They're vast and sparsely populated, making up over a third of Canada's area but less than half a percent of its population (roughly two-thirds of Canada's population lives within sixty miles of the US border).

The Yukon, with approximately 42,000 people, has the highest number of crowdfunding campaigns per capita among Canada's major regions—roughly 500 cases per 100,000 people during the period we analyze, or almost twice the national average. Remarkably, though, this rate is still less than the US average and about the same as the rates for Hawaii and Connecticut. NWT, with a population similar to The Yukon's, has the second highest crowdfunding rate, with over 300 cases per 100,000 people, or about one-third more than the national average. If it were a US state, however, it would have the lowest per capita crowdfunding rate of any state and the District of Columbia.

A relatively large share of the population in these Canadian regions is made up of Indigenous peoples, whose ancestry dates back thousands of years to the continent's first inhabitants. Today, Indigenous peoples experience drastic inequalities compared with White Canadians—a legacy of violent displacement and forced assimilation by European colonizers—which can be seen in disparities they face in accessing resources like health care, education, housing, and clean water. And they face drastically higher unemployment, poverty, domestic violence, suicide, and substance abuse. These problems are compounded by the fact that regions in which Indigenous peoples make up large parts of the population, including The Yukon and NWT, are far removed from Canada's major population centers. With their limited infrastructure and harsh climate, services like health care can be hard to access, and even basic goods, which must be flown into many communities, can be prohibitively expensive. It makes sense, then, that medicine, emergencies, and education are their most common categories for GoFundMe appeals.

At the same time, internet access is on average slower, less reliable, and more expensive in these territories than in the rest of Canada, which likely acts as a countervailing force. People in need may not have internet service adequate for accessing help via crowdfunding. That would, in part, help explain the relatively few crowdfunding cases observed in Nunavut, home to a large Inuit population and some of the country's northernmost communities. Though Nunavut's residents surely have financial need due to the difficulties in accessing goods and services similar to those seen in The Yukon and NWT, its internet infrastructure in 2020 was the country's worst.[6]

Quebec, Canada's only predominantly French-speaking province, has the lowest per capita crowdfunding rates of the Canadian regions in our data. With just 140 crowdfunding appeals per 100,000 people between 2018 and 2021, its rate is about half the national average. Quebec's position as an outlier is noteworthy but not surprising. The Canadian federal system gives provinces considerable freedom in how they organize social services, and Quebec has a long history of doing things differently, in part because of its historic and durable ties to France, reflected in the province's approach to social welfare, which is much closer to that of France, Sweden, and Norway than the rest of Canada. These distinct politics, prioritizing relatively generous, universal social benefits and concerted investment in public education and health care, contrast with the more common North American market-based approach of fewer, more conditional benefits and more limited government involvement in citizens' well-being. Quebec's outlier status actually reinforces our sense that there's a close link between crowdfunding and the politics of social welfare (true also for crowdfunding for pet and animal needs, which is higher in Quebec than in the rest of Canada).[7]

Let's pause again to review the regional variation we've uncovered in both countries' crowdfunding activities. In the US, our data shows that Washington DC, Oregon, and Vermont have the most crowdfunding cases per capita, while Mississippi, Iowa, and Alabama have the fewest. We attribute states' differences to a variety of factors: key industries (e.g., nonprofits and charities in DC), prevalence of natural disasters (e.g., wildfires in Oregon), internet availability (e.g., low access rates in Mississippi and Alabama), and political context.

In Canada, we see that The Yukon and NWT have the highest number of crowdfunding cases per capita while Quebec has the lowest.

We attribute the high numbers in Canada's northern territories to the scarcity and cost of basic goods and services, including health care and education. We also expect barriers to internet access in the country's most remote, sparsely populated areas to keep many more people from crowdfunding even if the need for funds is there. Quebec, by contrast, has a relatively generous and comprehensive social welfare system that hews closer to that of Nordic countries. We expect there's less unmet financial need in Quebec especially when it comes to health care and education, which explains its low rate of crowdfunding appeals.

Overall, Canada's per capita crowdfunding rate is less than half that of the US. All but one Canadian region has a lower per capita rate than the lowest US state (and the Yukon, the exception, remains well below the US average). Our evidence strongly suggests that political differences across countries and regions—and specifically governments' capacity to ensure affordable access to basic services—pattern crowdfunding efforts.

Welfare Crowdfunding Demographics

Geography tells us part of the story about crowdfunding. But populations are diverse, so it's time to look at demographics and learn about the people in this story. Is everyone equally likely to participate? Who is and isn't crowdfunding? We can begin to answer these questions by looking at the breakdown of crowdfunding beneficiaries by age, gender, and race and ethnicity. We look at this demographic difference across the most widespread welfare crowdfunding—campaigns for health care— showing that some people are far more likely than others to ask for help and some people barely ask at all.[8]

Right off the bat, we see few differences between men and women crowdfunders in the US and Canada. Women have a slight edge, but make up about half of each country's population and very close to half of its combined health-care crowdfunders. Users who explicitly describe themselves as transgender or gender nonbinary in their campaign descriptions make up about 0.4 percent of US cases and 1.28 percent of Canadian cases, again fitting well with the limited statistical estimates that put the transgender and nonbinary population share in both countries at 0.4 percent (more inclusive questions in future national censuses will refine these estimates). Our data suggests that members of this group are represented in crowdfunding roughly proportionally, with perhaps greater representation in Canada. Our interviews suggest that crowd-funding is a common way of raising money for trans health-care needs, especially gender-affirming surgeries, which is in fact the reason behind most of the campaigns we observed for this group.[9]

When looking at health-care crowdfunding in terms of broad age groups, we see that adults aged 18–64 are the primary beneficiaries (accounting for about 73 percent or almost three-quarters of all US and Canadian users seeking medical or health-related help). People under age 18 account for about 20 percent, and seniors aged 65 and over account for only about 8 percent. The numbers stay steady when we separate US and Canadian user groups, and they comport well with other researchers' estimates of health-care crowdfunding among different age groups.[10]

Because people aged 18–64 make up approximately 60 percent of the combined US and Canada population, they're overrepresented in health-care crowdfunding, while children and teenagers constitute about 20 percent of the population in both countries and appear to be proportionally represented. Notably, if we look at younger users more closely, we see that infants and very young children (aged 0–2) account for about 5 percent of cases, even though all children under age 5 combined amount to roughly 5 percent of the population. This indicates that the very youngest are overrepresented in health-care crowdfunding.

The biggest gap is seen for the roughly 18 percent of US and Canadian populations that are over age 65—as mentioned, they account for 8 percent of crowdfunding beneficiaries. This is especially concerning given that older people are disproportionately heavy users of health-care services because of their increasing risk of chronic disease associated with aging and longer life spans. Medicare in the US and universal health care in Canada are relatively robust public health supports for seniors, but they don't eliminate out-of-pocket costs (which can be significant, especially for diseases like cancer). Government programs like Social Security in the US and Old Age Security in Canada have markedly reduced elderly poverty, yet many seniors, especially those with immigrant backgrounds, still experience considerable hardship in old age.

We might expect seniors to be overrepresented in health-care crowd-funding relative to their share of the population because of their greater demand for health care combined with their likelihood of having a low income. But we find the opposite. Again, we suspect that lower rates of internet use among older people account for this apparent surprise.[11]

Finally, there are important differences in terms of race and ethnicity. Health-care crowdfunding is primarily—and disproportionately—used by White people in the United States. Non-Hispanic Whites, about 60 percent of the 2020 US population, are about 75 percent of health-care crowdfunding users. Latinos, the next largest group, are about 18.5 percent of the population and 13 percent of health-care crowdfunding cases, and Black Americans, who make up around 12.5 percent of the population, appear in less than 9 percent of campaigns. Asians, almost 6 percent of the population, make up less than 2 percent of crowdfunding cases. Members of Indigenous groups (Native Americans) constitute almost 1.5 percent of the population, but appear in around 0.5 percent of cases in our dataset.

In Canada, Whites of European ancestry make up about 70 percent of the population according to the 2021 census, yet they create around 85 percent of health-care crowdfunding appeals. In contrast to their US counterparts, Black Canadians, who stand at roughly 4 percent of the population, are the second-highest health-care crowdfunding group by race, with about 4.5 percent of appeals. Latinos, about 1.5 percent of the Canadian population, account for 2.5 percent. We consider these numbers as suggestive evidence that Black and Latino Canadians are roughly as equally represented in crowdfunding as they are in the general population. Asians, on the other hand, are about 17 percent of Canada's population but only about 5 percent of its health-care crowdfunders, and the roughly 5 percent of Indigenous/First Nations peoples are significantly underrepresented, at just 1 percent.[12]

All told, White people in North America dominate health-care crowdfunding. In the US, White users are responsible for about 3 out of every 4 health-care campaigns, and in Canada that rate rises to 85 percent. These rates are markedly higher than we might expect based on population share. Most strikingly, when we look at combinations of race, gender, and age, we find that in both the US and Canada approximately 3 out of every

5 cases benefit a White adult man or woman. All other racial and ethnic groups are underrepresented, with the exception of Black and Latino Canadians, who appear about as frequently among health-care fundraisers as they do in the general population if not slightly more often. This is the case even though we might expect minority ethnic groups' financial needs related to health care to be relatively higher compared with the White majority.

Unpacking the Motivations of Welfare Crowdfunders

The "who" dictates the "why" in welfare crowdfunding. The two aren't separate. Where we grew up, where we live, our race, our class, and our gender all figure into our social trajectories. This is basic sociology: the path we follow is in part one of our own making and in part channeled, shaped, and opened or obscured by the social forces and structures that surround us. The reasons that people crowdfund are as diverse as the populations of the United States and Canada. But we've found patterns. Individuals within certain communities need more help than others.

It's also clear that when you do need help, crowdfunding is now the place to go. The word is out, and everyone knows or has heard of someone using crowdfunding to seek support. As Jessica recounted in an interview, "I felt comfortable using the platform because ... I've seen that a lot of people use it." Or as Hope told us, "I think a lot of people know that crowdfunding can be quite effective when it works. It can raise millions of dollars sometimes. ... I just thought, 'Who knows?'" And GoFundMe is the gold standard according to Julia: "I figured it couldn't hurt, but it might help. ... I did GoFundMe specifically just because I knew it was a well-known platform. So I knew that might make it more likely for people to donate [to] it, because they didn't have to worry about [credit] cards getting scammed or whatever." Today, crowdfunding is common and holds little up-front risk. Why not try it?

And to be clear, the front-stage reason for asking for money isn't always the whole story. Appeals frequently mask a much more complicated situation, a back-stage if you will. We don't see this because crowdfunding pages are marketing tools. They sell stories. A very sick child tugs at the heartstrings. A poor, hard-working young person with a shot at going to Princeton piques interest. Covering hospital parking costs for a month or paying for a run-of-the-mill school field trip? They're less compelling.

We do our best to present the front-stage, bold-headline reasons people crowdfund. Almost 40 percent of the crowdfunding cases on GoFundMe can be sorted into health-care and educational—and there are some good front-stage reasons for them. But we also try to provide a glimpse at the far messier back-stage of welfare crowdfunding. The triggering event, say a cancer diagnosis, doesn't tell the whole story of these hardships.[13] We start with a consideration of crowdfunding for education, including individual stories to provide a richer picture, and then move to medical and health campaigns.

Education Needs

We all know that education can be expensive. Public funding makes it more accessible in Canada than in the US, but it nevertheless takes a chunk out of a family's finances, and the resource needs of public school systems can outstrip the means of their cash-strapped communities. People and classrooms fall through the cracks in public education funding, and they need help climbing out of them.

One of the most significant front-stage reasons for setting up an education crowdfunding page is in response to a death. These fundraisers are common and among the most successful in total dollars raised. Usually triggered by tragedy, either these appeals benefit children who've lost one or both parents or they create a scholarship fund in memory of a child or young adult. Among the tens of thousands of education cases we observed, many of the highest-earning campaigns were one of these two types.

Few people can imagine the emotional and financial devastation when a family loses a parent (or two). Michael from Spokane, Washington, is diagnosed with terminal pancreatic cancer, and the family, knowing there's no way his young daughter will be able to afford college when it's time to be without her father's financial support, sets up a GoFundMe page that opens with the heart-wrenching line "Sometimes lightning strikes too close to home." Or an Edmonton man dies unexpectedly, and his brother launches a GoFundMe campaign to create an education trust for the six-year-old son left behind. Or a young aspiring dancer dies suddenly in Florida, where her heartbroken family sets up a fund to support the education of future dancers. Or a pair of Texas teens die in an accident, and their friends and family rally to create a GoFundMe for scholarships in their memory.

It's natural when we lose someone to try to find meaningful ways to express and channel our grief. This is the engine that drives the creation of crowdfunding pages for education funds. "In lieu of flowers" is now a common line in obituaries, and GoFundMe provides a mechanism for channeling mourners' goodwill. This might be welfare crowdfunding at its best.

Education crowdfunding is also powerfully motivated by the rising costs of higher education, especially for those who have overcome adversity just to get in. Being accepted is one of life's most exciting—and daunting—moments. Exhilaration quickly gives way to financial anxiety. Though American students can pay multiple times what Canadian students do and Canada provides far more support to cover the costs of university attendance, this scenario plays out in both Canada and the United States. Tuition, room, and board are still real money in either country, and if you don't have it, you don't have it. Most people don't.[14]

The unaffordable Harvard acceptance is a mainstay of GoFundMe appeals. Tonika, for instance, is the woman of color accepted into Harvard for graduate studies (you met her in the Introduction). That's not something you turn down. No, you make it work no matter what. But Tonika, a Canadian, didn't have enough money and federal and provincial governments don't provide support for students seeking education outside Canada. She turned to the only option available—GoFundMe.

Jane from Alberta escaped decades of intimate partner violence and went back to school as she raised six children alone. Her son Michael created a GoFundMe campaign to raise money so that Jane could attend law school in the US. He wrote:

I am the twenty-year-old son of a hero; a single mom of six children
... a victim of domestic violence who went back to college at age 42;

earned a 4.0 GPA at the University of Alberta; and was recently admitted to a highly ranked law school in the US. Please help me help her achieve her dream of becoming a lawyer.

Like Tonika, it's easy to root for Jane. When you read their stories, you want them to make it. And there's also a little frustration—why is it sometimes so hard to move forward even when you've worked and worked to get a chance at change? If we can't fix that big problem, donating can help us feel that at least we can help one person achieve the next step in their education.

Marsha, a woman from Virginia who responded to our survey, is another eye-catching case. She became a flight attendant with a top airline in 2019, where she quickly noticed that the people in the cockpit were overwhelmingly White men. She wrote in her GoFundMe appeal that she flew with "a few White women [pilots] but NEVER a black woman or woman of color. After many flights and much thought, it didn't take long for me to see where I truly belonged. The cockpit!" Marsha enrolled in flight school, despite the fact that earning a certified flight instructor's license can cost up to $80,000 and there are few available scholarships. Determined to make her dream happen, Marsha tried crowdfunding.

Our interviewee Hope didn't need as much money as Marsha when she was accepted into a top Canadian university several years ago, but it might have been millions.. "Well, money has always been fairly tight in my family," she began,

> I come from a single-income home, because my parents are divorced. And so based on my mom's salary and what she was able to afford for us, I figured, because we didn't have significant savings for a university necessarily, that [a crowdfunding campaign] might be something to help chip in towards those costs. Especially with my brother also starting university.

This kind of story isn't new, but it resonates. And GoFundMe offers a different way to solve the problem of a motivated young adult who doesn't have the resources to cover all the costs of college. Hope said she'd heard crowdfunding could be effective: "Who knows?" So she set up an appeal. "I wasn't asking for very much. I set the goal for the campaign . . . around $2,000." That's pretty normal—most students don't ask for very much, a few thousand dollars at most.

An anonymous University of Virginia (UVA) student set up a crowd-funding page with help from a student support group called UVA Mutual Aid. Caught in a perfect storm of struggle, they wrote about the seemingly insurmountable challenge of paying for and going to school during a pandemic:

> I am a first generation immigrant kid. I am financially independent currently. My parents cut off ties with me due to my sexuality and mental health issues. I am seeing a therapist at the Women's Center. I am working a part time job but am hesitant to pick up more shifts during the pandemic due to my autoimmune disorder along with asthma issues. I am taking on a full semester of classes as well as working an unpaid internship. I am trying my best but I am afraid that I might run out of funds for rent and tuition. I have some saved up from working in retail since I was 16 but again I am afraid I'm running low.

This wasn't someone who has spent their life waiting for handouts, and we all know hard work isn't always enough.

Both Canada and the United States have significant public education systems. But there's tremendous variation in government funding levels across states and provinces. Some school systems come up short on the basics, let alone technology, field trips, or teacher salaries to help reduce class sizes. In our data we found many pages set up to help teachers and students cover education-related costs. For example, one California man set up a page to benefit an old college friend, writing: "She's a teacher in an underprivileged area and wants to take her students on an overnight field trip." He added that few of her sixth-graders had ever traveled outside of their immediate neighborhoods.

Small gaps also nagged at a new teacher in Washington, whose Go-FundMe page was titled "Please Help My Students!" She began the story like this:

I am beginning my first year of teaching under some very unique circumstances. Just this week I have started teaching my own fourth grade class. Sadly, I am the fourth teacher this class has had this year. The students are used to being walked out on and have experienced emotional trauma that makes it very hard for them to bring their best selves to the authority figures in their lives. These kids deserve a fresh start and I am really hoping to give it to them. I'm trying to get to the root cause of how this classroom has come to be so chaotic, and it has become clear to me that the reason is lack of organization and resources! The students have not been provided any systems for navigating simple tasks like finding their notebooks, or keeping track of school supplies! When kids are not able to do something as simple as find their work from the day before, lots of time is wasted and they are set up for failure. So, this brings me to why I am asking for money. The students need simple organizational tools such as cubbies, notebooks for each subject, clearly labeled cabinets with supplies, individual desk caddies, and even basic supplies like pencils, pens and lined paper!

We aren't talking laptops or smart boards here, just notebooks, paper, pencils, and a place to put it all. Teachers' crowdfunding appeals often focus on money for the small things that might make a big difference. Community fundraisers and tax initiatives aim to fund big stuff like renovations, but what about the tiny gaps? Principals have limited discretionary funds in budgets stretched to the breaking point. And school boards, typically elected political bodies, don't want to answer for anything that smacks of excess and they may not understand what matters in classrooms. Teachers know, and they do what they have to do because they care about their students.

Students, parents, and community members see these needs and try to address them. Sometimes the needs aren't about material things like computers or books but opportunities. Students are under relentless pressure to differentiate themselves, to participate in activities and take up hobbies and score well on tests—anything and everything to rise above their fellow students as they angle for college admissions or first jobs.

On GoFundMe, these opportunities usually take the form of conferences, training, or study-abroad trips. Dana, who works at a nonprofit in Minnesota, told us she tried to raise money for local kids to attend a journalism education program. Her organization applied for a substantial grant and made it to the second round. To move forward, they needed $6,000 in matching community funds. The nonprofit grant sponsor required that applicants raise this money (as evidence of strong stakeholder support) on the crowdfunding platform CrowdRise, so Dana set up a page hoping her organization would eventually get the grant and so fill a gap in the public school system, which lacked robust journalism and media education programs.

Among the students who tried to fund such opportunities on their own, we found a young woman from Missouri who knew that a high school field trip for future business leaders would enhance her education experience. But as she explained, "the cost of my trip was over $3,000. I have only one parent and I worked part time. No matter how much I saved I couldn't seem to make it. . . ." After failing to make thousands with a bake sale, she turned to GoFundMe. So did Michael, a California fifth-grader who was invited to attend a National Youth Leadership Forum, Pathways to STEM, at the University of California, Berkeley. In a family with six children, there was little hope of coming up with more than $2,000 to send the baby of the family to the forum. Thus the GoFundMe appeal stated: "The hope is [Michael] will be inspired to continue to love all things science, technology, engineering, and math, we hope that he will go on to enjoy his educational experience." College student Matt said in our interview that borrowing a high-quality digital camera from his photojournalism school was hampering his ability to do his work effectively, but broke and having lost his campus job in the pandemic, he had few options. His GoFundMe campaign aimed to raise money for his own camera.

We love stories about hardworking young people who want to do a little extra to get ahead in their education. The right equipment can make all the difference. Camps, workshops, courses, and travel are all potential boosts. They help build networks, add to knowledge and experience, and build character and confidence. Who wouldn't want their kids to do these things? A quick scan of GoFundMe, however, shows that these opportunities aren't available to all in equal measure. Some have to hustle to make it happen. Others just can't get the resources together and their plans fall apart.

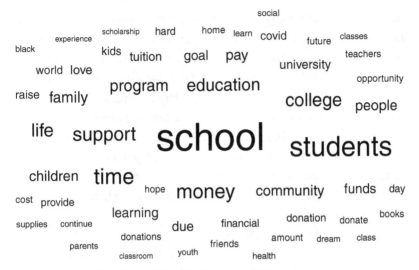

Figure 1   Keywords in GoFundMe education crowdfunding campaigns.

We created a word cloud from a random sample of education crowd-funding campaigns on GoFundMe. The bigger words appear more frequently across crowdfunding pages. The image illustrates what's going on in these pages. Notice the key word *school* at the center, followed by *college, time, support, life, education, money,* and *community*. And there are strong feelings here as well, from *love* to *hope, dream,* and *opportunity.*

These are basic and fundamental needs. We're talking about education. Without a robust education system, our society and economy falter. Our children can't flourish. Our future dims. As the proliferation of crowdfunding pages asking for help covering basic education needs and modest opportunities attest, we aren't doing enough. The same holds true for basic health-care needs, as we'll see next.

Health-Care Needs

The "who" and "why" of crowdfunding health-care needs are just as hard to separate as they are for education needs. For structural rather than individual reasons, we know that some populations just need more help accessing and affording medical care. In its absence, their health suffers. Take the Indigenous peoples in British Columbia. A recent report shows that their access to primary care and family doctors is inadequate, meaning that they simply aren't able to get the kinds of preventive care many of us take for granted. The result is that they're forced to turn to emergency rooms at disproportionate rates—we're talking about a 75 percent higher likelihood of an ER visit compared with the general population of Canada. That's a sobering statistic. Along with the systemic racism across Canada's health system, Indigenous peoples endure a host of illnesses attributable to the massive environmental degradation of First Nation reserves. This isn't solely an Indigenous Canadian story. It's also an African American story, a White working poor story. Some groups of people are worse off than others. They need help to get past the obstacles in their way.[15]

At the time of this writing, more than 19,000 active GoFundMe appeals turned up in a search for "domestic violence." This is heartbreaking. The physical and mental trauma of abuse derails lives, and the costs of treatment, recovery, medication, and therapy are often out of reach for victims who frequently miss days and weeks of work or are more immediately concerned with securing safety and a place to live.

Cassie, from Florida, titled her 2019 GoFundMe campaign "Please I'm in Desperate Need." She wrote: "I faced two of the most painful and disappointment [sic] challenges in my entire life, breast cancer and domestic violence from the person I was in love with." Cassie and her partner had only recently purchased a house when she was diagnosed with cancer. Her partner began to emotionally abuse her, cutting her off from communication with her medical team and making it clear that he would offer no support. Things got so bad that Cassie had to go to court and was granted a temporary restraining order that forced her partner out of the house. Still, temporary protection is temporary. Cassie explained: "The judge doesn't think that the harassment and the nightmare I am living is [enough] reason unless they see blood or bruises. . . ." When her partner tried to have Cassie evicted, she got a friend to help her set up a GoFundMe appeal: "Now I am facing major medical bills, and [it] is really hard to support myself with no income and possibly facing legal costs [not to] mention uncertainty [in the] future with no home. Not having family here makes this even Harder."

A Colorado woman from our survey "was seriously injured in a domestic violence situation," and a family with whom she was close got together to raise money to support her in her recovery. A woman in Alberta and her children "were victims of domestic violence which left them homeless," according to a close friend who set up a crowdfunding page, updating it two weeks later with the sad news that the same woman had been diagnosed with inoperable stage 4 breast cancer. A pregnant woman in Oklahoma was brutally beaten by her boyfriend, and her friend set up a fundraiser, telling us: "There is a long uphill battle coming. From medical bills, baby necessities to the upcoming court battle for parental rights." There are thousands and thousands of similar stories on the GoFundMe platform alone. Again, we keenly sense that something in our society is broken when we read these pleas, when people victimized by others have to beg (sometimes revealing intimate details of their lives) to get the help and safety they need and deserve.

By far, cancer is the most common reason for health-care crowdfunding. And this makes sense: well above the age-standardized global rate of about 200 per 100,000 in 2018, the US and Canada have rates of more than 300 cancer diagnoses per 100,000. The fight against cancer is global, and we're making progress. Still, we have a lot to learn and treatment options aren't always clear. Expensive and experimental treatments, as well as holistic alternatives, all figure into a common "all hands on deck" approach to fighting cancer. But this kind of mobilization costs time and money, and it can be all-consuming.[16]

For those without resources or family and friends who can gather round in support, it can feel like they're heading into their battle with cancer without armor. GoFundMe is full of such cries for help. Hannah from Texas told us in her interview that she felt "lethargic and tired all the time," having "issues that were all signs towards cancer." However, she didn't have insurance coverage or enough money to pay out of pocket for an emergency screening. Previously, Hannah had raised money for her dog's surgery on GoFundMe, and her family suggested she crowdfund for her own medical needs. As she told us, "it worked so well for the dog that I was like, okay, surely it'll work for me." And it did—boosting her campaign on Facebook, she was able to raise enough money for the screening. "Come to find out," Hannah said wryly, "I actually did have cancer." Her troubles were just beginning.

Ellen from New York City told us in our survey that she found out her nine-year-old son's father Kirt had throat cancer just before the two were set to go on a Disney vacation. After chemo and radiation, Kirt thought he had beaten it but it had only spread. He had surgery, losing his voice box, tongue, and parts of his cheek and mouth but still couldn't shake the disease. As Ellen recounted, "a month later and devastation again when he learns they missed a large cancer mass and it had now spread beyond fixing. My son looks up to his Daddy like his daddy is God. . . . I just wanted to raise some money to send them both somewhere very special before it was too late." Ellen's GoFundMe appeal raised $3,000, and a bottle drive earned a bit more—not to pay for the direct costs of her ex's cancer battle but to help him and her son make the most of the time they had left together.

Sonia from Saskatchewan also witnessed the tremendous tension between the desire to spend dwindling time with loved ones and the need for money to keep the lights on when her dear friend was diagnosed with cancer:

> So I sat back and said, "Okay. I've got to do something. I can't take his cancer away, I can't take his pain away, but what I can do is turn around and take away some of his stress." So that the time he has left isn't spent being stressed over being a financial burden or about his children having to bury him and who's going to pay for that, but that time left is spent with your family, enjoying the time you have left instead of, like I said, worrying about where the money's going to come from to pay your bills.

For Sonia, that meant setting up a GoFundMe appeal to make her friend's final days easier.

Cancer disrupts lives in all sorts of costly ways. One woman in our survey shared that her aunt in urban North Carolina "has throat cancer and is elderly. Her husband is taking care of her and has a hard time affording all of her medications and working while taking care of her." At roughly the same time, Alex, a musician in Montreal, told us in an interview that he was setting up a GoFundMe page for "one of my friends who got cancer. Colorectal cancer. He's alone. He doesn't have a lot of money and in fact he's poor. He needed support to go through all this." And Elisa from Alberta found out exactly one year to the day after her divorce that she had cancer. The divorce had turned her into the major breadwinner for her four kids, ages eight, ten, twelve, and fourteen. The primary care-taker for the kids as well as a part-time writer and historian, Elisa was just getting a handle on the change when her cancer diagnosis arrived: "I had to stop my work, which was measly income anyway, and go into full-time treatment." She was ineligible for a host of potential govern-ment supports, telling us, for example: "I couldn't apply for [Employment Insurance] because I hadn't been working and because I was on contract work, so I was self-employed anyway. . . . There weren't really a lot of places to turn to." This was "a big emotional change."

The front-stage appeal of Cree elder Cecil Redstar's GoFundMe story was his 2017 colon cancer diagnosis. His campaign detailed his cancer's rapid spread to his lungs and lymph nodes. Doctors told him that he didn't have much time left, and he decided to take traditional Indigenous medicines. Too ill to work and with no family support, he lost his hous-ing. Community members stepped up to fundraise for his basic needs. As one supporter put it, "Cecil has served his community and many others and now we must take care of one of our own." The back-stage story is more complicated. Cecil's struggles weren't new, but were exacerbated by his cancer. He had endured a lifetime of discrimination and abuse that started when, as a young child, he was forcibly separated from his family and culture and sent into a racist residential school system de-signed to make a "socially respectable" Canadian gentleman of him. In a large random sample of Canadian health-care cases that we investi-gated more closely, Cecil's was one of only two examples of Indigenous crowdfunders.

It may be that Indigenous Canadians and Americans ask for and receive help in ways that aren't immediately legible to social scientists or non-Indigenous people. Our earlier analysis in the first phase of our research suggested instrumental reasons for this paucity in welfare crowdfunding, including the digital divide and the relatively small In-digenous population share. But particularly because social indicators show that Indigenous people in general need more financial and social support than they're getting, we suspect that we really need to worry about why they ask for help less often than other social groups do.

Inadequate insurance and inaccessible appropriate care are additional back-stage reasons for appeals in which cancer is the front-stage explanation. More specifically, the price tags attached to these issues lead to crowdfunding. Note, for instance, that we said "inadequate." Costly problems crop up even for those who have health insurance, as Carrie, an Indigenous woman from Nevada, told us:

> I was recently diagnosed with a condition with my lungs that requires multiple types of specialists including rheumatologists, hematologists, oncology and respiratory in order to even begin assessing how much damage there is and where to begin as far as trying to treat it. I have Medicaid and where I live hardly any specialists accept [it] because of many problems in the past that physicians have had . . . so they chose to no longer accept Medicaid entirely.

In other words, in Carrie's community, past problems with government insurance led doctors to create a two-tiered system. Those on Medicaid get limited help, while those with "better" insurance or the ability to pay cash get all the help they need. Carrie decided to crowdfund "to cover costs for office visits, testing, et cetera, until my social security is approved which will allow me to receive Medicare."

A White Ohio man in his early sixties told us of his struggles after he fell and broke his leg: "I'm a veteran but the VA has no bed for me. Medicare covered some of the expenses but I owe $10,000." A woman from North Carolina told us she was crowdfunding to help with IVF treatment, which is often not covered by US health insurance (though it's covered by most Canadian provincial plans). Some medical interventions, as it happens, simply aren't covered by existing health insurance plans. Maybe they should be, maybe not. But the stress takes a toll on anyone who finds they can't afford the health care they need.

Take the case of Alexis, a student from Orlando, Florida. They work part-time for a consulting firm that advises on green building practices.

(For some, gender identity can't be pinned down by a simple binary of he/she pronouns, so we use "they" deliberately here.) Alexis was looking to have what is commonly known as gender confirmation or sex reassignment surgery. They described it as a physical transition made possible through surgery that would align their body and being. "Just about every person I know who is seeking [gender confirmation] surgery has a GoFundMe," they told us, because there just isn't much support for trans health care. "I'm very lucky that [my insurance] covers any of my trans health care, but there are a lot of hoops to jump through. . . . They require you to get letters and signatures from multiple gender therapists. . . . A lot of the time the surgeons require that as well. Like, even if they're not taking insurance, they require that." Pointedly, Alexis noted that "a surgeon wouldn't expect a doctor's note if someone . . . went in to get a breast enhancement." Here, persistent stigma felt more acute amid the high-bar burden of "proof" that Alexis's gender confirmation surgery was medically necessary (even after insurance confirmed that the costs would be covered).

Natalie, a self-employed aesthetician in New Brunswick, Canada, and a cancer survivor, was diagnosed with new stage 4 breast cancer. The fallout included a double mastectomy, treatment for a brain tumor, and the removal of half a lung. In her case, as the GoFundMe campaign set up by her brother explained, Natalie needed donations to cover ongoing medical expenses above her insurance caps as well as the basic expenses of daily life: "Medications will be over $1,000 per month. [Natalie]'s insurance is capped at $1,000 per year. . . . Your generous donation will help Natalie afford expensive cancer medications and help to offset living expenses."

Natalie's story leads us to the catch-all category of people who can't make ends meet amid health emergencies or while managing chronic diseases. Often, the need is tied to back-stage issues like those we've mentioned: insufficient insurance coverage or too high deductibles, lost wages, ongoing costs of care that loom over budgets as tight as drums. Robert and Lisa, whom we met in the Introduction and revisited at the start of this chapter, found that most of the medical treatments Lisa needed for her brain cancer were covered by their fairly comprehensive provincial health insurance. Robert scaled back his hours, though it meant foregoing income just when they learned Lisa, now quadriplegic and requiring breathing assistance, would need twenty-four-hour care if she were to come home (they were quoted $492 a day for personal nursing care, Robert remembered). In the event that Lisa came home, their financial situation would be untenable. Robert could work, but his salary would only cover Lisa's care. There wouldn't be enough for food and rent and utilities. Or Robert could stay home as Lisa's primary caregiver and make no money at all. Women who have to choose whether to do paid work that barely covers the cost of childcare or give up professional lives to become stay-home-mothers will recognize this dilemma.

By and large, the people we spoke with were proud and independent. They didn't want to ask others for money. Lewis, a 59-year-old from Georgia, told us: "It's not like I've got a ton of money, but everything I have, I've made. Nobody's ever given me anything." Still, the tidal wave of insurance bills and the lost income from his wife's liver cancer were too much. At one point, the hospital called and told him he needed to bring a check for $10,000 when he brought his wife to her next appointment. He couldn't; he'd already committed $15,000 for additional treatment and medication, and his wife no longer had an income. Take the woman from urban Texas who needed life-saving kidney surgery: "I have three daughters who I need to keep a roof over their heads. I can't work because of the kidney cancer." She put a lot of hope into the crowdfunding appeal she set up to try to cover the family's rent. Or consider the woman from South Carolina who created a fundraiser for "her best friend in the whole world [who] had to have emergency surgery and their children had no food or electricity so they needed the money." Or Alex, whose Montreal-based musician friend had great insurance but few other resources to deal with the consequences of his cancer: "It's a bit of everything. . . . I told you he's pretty poor. So lodging and eating is a bit of a struggle every time. He has an old car. He has to put it back in shape to go to the hospital to get his treatments."

Sonia from Saskatchewan described a vicious cycle in which her hard work was never enough to provide real security:

Not one bar job of any sort or any hospitality type of job I've ever had offered health and dental benefits. [In a] lot of those you're making minimum wage. The tips are good, don't get me wrong, but without having any dental or health coverage, most people tend to not look after themselves. You wait until your teeth are really bad before you go spend $2,000 getting a root canal because you didn't have $1,000, $1,500 every year to spend on cleanings and check-ups. And same with their health. You don't turn around and put a whole bunch of money into prevention because that's not an option. You wait until you're sick and figure it out at the time. You don't turn around and put a whole bunch of money into gym memberships and eating properly, et cetera, et cetera.

Without the time or money to get yourself out of such a vicious cycle, asking friends, family, and strangers for help may be the only recourse—and that can be humiliating.

A word cloud, generated from a random sample of GoFundMe's health-care crowdfunding pages, paints a clear picture. Right in the middle, at the heart of things, is *family*. Some of the specifics make it into the cloud, where we see *cancer, surgery, hospital, treatment, chemo, heart, bills, insurance, support, care,* and *mom*. And everywhere you look are strong emotions: *love, pain, difficult, appreciated,* and *recovery*.

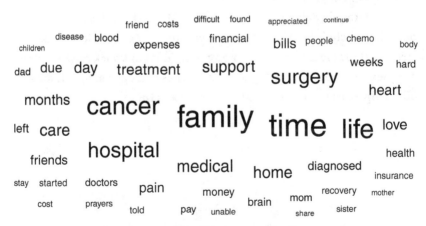

Figure 2   Keywords in GoFundMe health-care crowdfunding campaigns.

A Well of Sadness?

This general look at welfare crowdfunding's demand side gave us an understanding that some types of people open this door more often than others. We considered who asks and who doesn't and why they make those choices. One major finding is that online fundraising is primarily a tool of the relatively privileged in terms of age, class, race, ethnicity, and social capital. White people do the most crowdfunding. Education trust funds either to benefit children who have lost one or both parents or to create a scholarship fund in memory of a child or young adult are the most common appeals. Tuition and a need for extra learning materials drive a significant number of appeals as well. Cancer is the most prevalent front-stage reason for setting up health-care appeals, with the back-stage realities of insurance, job loss, and general financial troubles underpinning most of them. Given that non-Whites are more likely to get cancer, have less insurance, and have less job security than similarly situated Whites—well, all this should cause some concern. The most precarious, marginalized, and prone to illness among us may be asking for help somewhere, but they're not doing it through crowdfunding.

The struggles we documented—welfare crowdfunding for education and health care—are, as our respondent Mark from the Introduction put it, truly "a well of sadness" where people put their biggest challenges out in the open. They describe brutal abuse, devastating losses, school shortfalls, and unaffordable prescriptions. And these struggles are generally not self-inflicted. They're the social symptoms of our society's massive structural problems—too big for any individual to knock down and too complex to avoid. But we try to address these struggles, to ask for and offer help, because, really, what other choice is there?

Three

A Very Daunting Task

Based on our presentation in Chapter 2, you should now have a better sense of who uses welfare crowdfunding and also know some of the main reasons they do. In this chapter, we consider what happens next. We focus on the mechanism of welfare crowdfunding, trying to show how it operates and what the process is like for users. The bottom line is that some people have an easier time than others. This chapter primarily considers the former—those who figure out how to move forward with a crowdfunding campaign. But some people can't even get started, or are significantly disadvantaged, because they're staring across the digital divide. Others can't move forward because of their immigration status. We think it's worth brief consideration of the inaccessibility of welfare crowdfunding for some; then we'll turn to the work of hustling for help.

A Road Not Taken

People considering crowdfunding come to a fork in the road. One way is for those who aren't comfortable with—or don't even own—computers and smartphones. It's entirely possible they've never seen a crowdfunding page. The other is for those who live with computers every day. They know what they're doing on the internet and think setting up a basic online account is a piece of cake. This fork in the road is linked to the digital divide.

For people who are technologically literate and internet savvy, setting up a crowdfunding page can feel totally intuitive. GoFundMe makes it seem fairly easy—a hunch most of our respondents confirmed. Sherice from Washington State told us she hadn't needed any help and called the process of setting up an appeal "really easy and straightforward," and Lorie from Florida said, "Oh, it was great. It was really easy and it was simple."

It wasn't at all like that for Brett from Michigan. Reflecting on his experience using GoFundMe, Brett said, "It wasn't super easy. . . . It's hard to send to others, it's hard for people to contribute. It was hard to set up a link thing for people to follow." He saw the hope crowdfunding represented, but trying to access it was beyond frustrating for him—Brett figured out how to cross the digital divide, yet his experience demonstrates that there are serious consequences when people have different levels of access, comfort, and ease with technology. You may remember the early COVID-19 vaccine rollout in the US and Canada, how thousands of eager seniors were unable to connect to registration systems. An innovative volunteer network emerged just to help people find and secure appointments through the patchwork of online systems. Should digital prowess really be the determinant of who can access help?

Another vivid example of the obstacles to crowdfunding presented by the digital divide comes from a *Washington Post* article written by Theresa Vargas in 2018. Vargas tells the story of immigrant Ista Jalloh, who had worked at Dulles International Airport for twenty years, all the while sending money home to support her children in Sierra Leone. When Jalloh, who helped passengers with mobility issues get around the airport, allegedly asked for a tip, she was fired. After the article came out, Vargas was deluged with emails—at least a hundred different readers went out of their way to contact the journalist to try to help Jalloh. But there was no mechanism set up to get funds to her. She didn't know what GoFundMe was, let alone how to set up a page. As Vargas pointed out in a subsequent column, "the difficulty and time it took for Jalloh to get her GoFundMe page in place speaks to how disconnected her life is from the wired world many of us take for granted." Jalloh had no smartphone, no laptop, no social media accounts, and no digital photos. Luckily, Beverly Duran, a union organizer with connections to Jalloh, helped her create the ultimately successful fundraising appeal.[1]

So the digital divide means that we always have to be aware of the pool of people who aren't even trying to use crowdfunding as a way of getting the help they need. As we saw in Chapter 2, minorities are underrepresented among crowdfunders. Non-Whites, older adults, and poor people are most likely to face the biggest challenges stemming from the digital divide. You can connect the dots, but so can the US Census Bureau.

The bureau concluded in two separate studies that Black and Hispanic households in the US as of 2018 were much less likely than White households to have internet-connective devices and/or internet services. Black-White inequalities are particularly substantial: about 90 percent of White households have access to some kind of computing device compared with 84 percent of Black households (because Black households are also least likely to own a desktop or laptop computer, these devices are skewed toward smartphones). Whatever the device, about 83 percent of White households but only 73 percent of Black households are able to use it to connect to the internet—in real terms, that's 1.5 million more Black than White households missing out on internet connectivity.[2]

Education and income inequality are other interrelated keys to the digital divide. Over 93 percent of households headed by someone with a bachelor's degree have internet access compared with just 56 percent of those headed by people who didn't finish high school. About 60 percent of households making less than $25,000 a year have an internet subscription, but 80 percent of households earning just a bit more ($25,000–$49,999) are connected. Further, the richer you are, the more likely you are to have different devices available for completing homework, applying for jobs, or setting up a GoFundMe page. The poorest households are disproportionately likely to only access the internet via smartphone.[3]

Even if you do have access to an internet-enabled device and are able to connect—perhaps via a library's or fast-food restaurant's Wi-Fi— numerous obstacles remain. These get at the digital inequalities scholars tie to people's social positions: some people are better at using the internet than others, and these differences are patterned by social groups. It makes sense. When you're trying to keep your head above water, working more hours for less pay, there might not be much free time to use the internet, let alone get good at it—racialized working mothers bringing home a minimum wage come to mind. Also, we know that having a disability impacts internet access and use. Adjusting for age, Americans with disabilities are about 30 percent less likely than others to use the internet daily, and nearly 20 percent of Americans live with disabilities (potentially amplifying their need for crowdfunding but hampering their access to its platforms).[4]

Ista Jalloh wasn't an outlier. Millions of us are unable to access or effectively use the internet. And let's not forget that when it comes to welfare crowdfunding, the fork in the road is more like a forced exit for undocumented people living in the US and Canada. Just to set up a Go-FundMe campaign, you need to provide a US Social Security number or a Canadian Social Insurance number. For noncitizens to get these, the US requires the in-person presentation of visa documents and proof of permission to work from the Department of Homeland Security; Canada requires permanent or temporary resident status, with temporary residents further needing proof of a work or study permit issued by Immigrant, Refugees, and Citizenship Canada (IRCC). Informed estimates suggest that about 3 percent of the US's total population are undocumented (roughly 10 million individuals, two-thirds of whom have lived there for more than a decade) as are 1.5 percent of Canada's (about half a million people). Undeniably, people without legal status are among both societies' most precarious: few have insurance, few make even minimum wage (and many experience wage theft), few have completed formal education. In real need of social welfare support, these millions are entirely excluded from GoFundMe.[5]

Getting Started

For those not blocked by immigration status or scared off by the challenge of tech, the next step in bringing a campaign to life is to find and select a crowdfunding site. GoFundMe, the proverbial 800-pound gorilla, shows up at the top of Google search results for "Crowdfunding," so for most it's an easy choice. Click through, and a prominent green button tempts "Start a GoFundMe." Click, and you're prompted for a name and phone number to create an account. The last of the initial hurdles is two-factor security—so long as you know how to verify using a code sent to your phone or email, the process is now in motion.

Next for the potential crowdfunder, after telling the site whether they're fundraising for an individual or an organization (we focus on individuals in this book), is to "start with the basics," as GoFundMe describes it. Question one "Where are you located?" right off the bat may give pause: there are only twenty choices in the drop-down menu for country. As we discussed earlier in the book, these are all wealthy democracies, almost exclusively in Western Europe and North America. GoFundMe is clear: "If your postal code isn't recognized by our system, your campaign cannot be created." But for discussion, let's assume they choose either Canada or the United States and provide a postal or ZIP code. When we did this process ourselves, the postal code suggestion was within a kilometer of where we live, based on identifying our location through our IP address. Convenient for most, but perhaps also concerning.

Next up, the crowdfunder must indicate their reason for fundraising, selecting from twenty categories. There's some overlap, meaning that, for example, either "Emergencies" or "Medical, Illness, and Healing" (which we refer to under the catch-all of "health-care crowdfunding") covers injuries sustained in a car accident. The most common choice is the GoFundMe medical category which, according to our data, accounts for about 30 percent of welfare fundraising appeals originating in the US and Canada. Broadening the scope, we find that three in every five crowdfunding campaigns are for health-care costs, including accidents and emergencies, or funeral costs. Therefore, the majority are for help coping with some kind of misfortune (the marketplace in this case functioning like a sort of capricious insurance company). Education costs, another pillar of welfare crowdfunding, are the fifth most common fundraising category, making up about 7 percent of all cases.[6]

The rubber meets the road when it's time to choose a title for the campaign. GoFundMe prompts the crowdfunder " . . . to include a person's name and the purpose" and says on its support page, "This is your chance to stand out." No pressure there. Oh, and GoFundMe allows only thirty-five characters and spaces for this marketing pitch, a high-stakes bid for attention. Folks in our study chose titles like "Beating Cancer with Mike J."; "Smith family education fund"; "Save the testicle"; "Oliver Williamson's journey to Duke University"; "Please help John fight Stage 4 cancer"; and "Alan's heart surgery." After choosing a title, the crowd-funder is prompted to set a fundraising goal (in their country's currency).

So far, the assumption is that the applicant is setting up a welfare crowdfunding page for themselves. But in many cases crowdfunding appeals are set up by people other than the beneficiary, for a number of possible reasons: the beneficiary might be too unwell, too young, or too inexperienced in using the internet. Or perhaps they're reluctant and need a little nudge to get the help they need. (In some of our inter-views, beneficiaries had no idea they had a crowdfunding page until it was active.) At the time of writing, GoFundMe offered three responses to the question "Who are you fundraising for?": yourself, someone else, or charity.

When Lisa received her diagnosis, it was Robert's friends, not Robert, who suggested the couple needed a GoFundMe page. Remember that Robert told his close friends that he didn't yet know whether Lisa's illness would be totally devastating or "we just go back to a normal life after eight months." He listed the ways he could "make ends meet." To us, Robert confessed to a welter of conflicting emotions that included pride and the need for privacy. Lisa understood, but when things got worse she asked Robert to accept help. Again his friends asked, and this time Robert agreed—they quickly got a GoFundMe page up and running. Robert's reluctance is common across our data—not everyone is willing to put their vulnerability on public display no matter how difficult their situation.

The begrudging beneficiary is one reason creating campaigns for others is so common in welfare crowdfunding. According to our three-year dataset, about 26 percent of all campaigns in the US and Canada are created by someone other than the recipient. This is almost cer-tainly a low estimate, since we were only able to count campaigns that explicitly state they're raising money for someone else. Health-care campaigns do this more often, with around 36 percent—more than one in every three—created for someone else compared with just about 12 percent of education campaigns. This makes sense because we expect a meaningful number of health-care campaigns intend to help people who, simply due to their medical condition, are unable to make a campaign for themselves, a situation that doesn't readily apply to educational fundraisers.

Family, close friends, and people with shared characteristics make up the majority of those creating campaigns for others. These are the stalwarts, the people you turn to at your lowest point, knowing that if you ask they'll do whatever it takes to help. A respondent from New Jersey described his efforts as "other veterans trying to help a brother," and a man in California told us about helping a coworker whose son had been in a horrible car accident: "My boss and I started the fund to assist the family with their medical expenses." Amanda from Ontario told us that she and her neighbors raised money to help the well-liked concierge in their apartment building during a medical emergency. Religious connections forged in churches, temples, and mosques also seem to matter in these moments. In our data, we saw a number of references to crowdfunding teams made up of congregation members, particularly in midwestern US states. The more secular pursuit of group sports was also a natural foundation for team crowdfunding. Maybe it's that person who plays second base on your softball team, your hockey team's backup goalie, or the person on the next mat over in your community center's yoga class—you know them and want to help.

Still others meet and form ties through adversity, and these connections lead to future support. Jane, for instance, told us that she had befriended a couple during her cancer treatment a few years back; one of them was going through the same treatment, a time-consuming chemotherapy regimen, and so they were spending hours together. Fast-forward, and the other survivor's partner has been diagnosed with cancer. Jane and the survivor set up crowdfunding for the newest member of their club—and they went out of their way to promote it. As Jane told us, "it took time to convince my friend that this is the way to go. As I live far away from her, I had to travel. Then we did a lot of flyers and [went] door to door in their community to dispense [them]." This is true friendship in action.

Recall divorcee Elisa from Alberta, who had the help of a great group of friends as she navigated the first year of single-parenting four young children. They stepped up again when Elisa was diagnosed with cancer, setting up childcare rotations and creating a GoFundMe page, which Elisa indicated she might not have set up for herself: "Having it be a third party also made it possible, I guess, because I couldn't have done that. I might have been able to send out an email, but then having the responses would have been overwhelming." With the ability to post updates on Elisa's condition on her GoFundMe page, her close friends raised money and lowered the burden of communicating individually with concerned people like family and community members.

Whether a neighborhood or a religious congregation, many of us belong to something bigger than our family and friend groups. We're connected to people we don't necessarily know. "Our community," one Missouri respondent noted, is made up of "many people who just care about a person in these types of situations and we want to help out." When a woman in the respondent's community had a baby and the next week lost her husband to a car accident, a crowdfunding page was among the first help she was offered: "She needs help financially in caring for the baby until she can get on her feet again." And as a student from Pennsylvania learned, people can step in when they recognize there may not be anyone else ready to offer assistance. The student was helped when a church group boosted her effort to raise money for tuition. In the words of a group member and respondent, the student "needed help because she has no one and does not qualify for tuition assistance." Those in the helping group identified themselves in the appeal as "fellow Christians. A group of church members and leaders who have put it upon themselves to support education."

It's a comfort to know that even when we feel very alone there are still lots of people who will come to our aid. A friend, a family member, or potentially a stranger can help ease the burden directly or can ease the effort of seeking others' help. When his wife's sudden liver cancer diagnosis threw him for a loop, Lewis from Georgia remembered: "I guess by the time I came out of the hospital, my friend had done the GoFundMe page, my life was moving too fast, I was almost embarrassed at it by that point, too much was coming up and I couldn't even process—all I could think about was her health at the point, what am I supposed to do? I can't even spell the name of the freaking stuff, am I right?" He was reeling, yet people who cared had already anticipated the needs Lewis and his wife would have in the coming months.

We were amazed how often our interviews revealed GoFundMe pages set up without beneficiaries' knowledge. When Tom, the personal trainer, went into kidney failure (see Chapter 2), Mary admitted, "No, I didn't tell him. . . . He didn't know because he was in the hospital and so much was going on; to be honest he wasn't very cognitively aware of what was happening." We know that Tom is a fairly proud person, so it's likely he wouldn't have agreed if Mary had asked his permission. Sonia from Saskatchewan said of her friend Sid, as he was losing his battle with cancer: "[H]e was a very prideful man," so when she set up the crowdfunding effort for him, "I didn't say a damn word. Went ahead and did it all." In Manitoba, Kate benefited from a friend who started a fund to help her handle medical expenses when she broke her back in a biking accident. Grateful, Kate still pointed out that a third party "might not really know what our needs are."

Further, when someone else sets up a page for you, they can push the boundaries of privacy and personal comfort. Sean from Alberta was falling into a spiral of depression and pain when his sister stepped in to help. He spoke to us of his struggles with chronic testicular pain. He was in agony, couldn't work, and had to go on long-term disability. This was a great help to be sure, but it didn't cover his full lost salary, so Sean's family budget took a major hit. And because of the nature of his problem—and taboos about discussing genitals—he found it embarrassing and isolating. That was abundantly clear when his sister, who didn't tell him she was setting up a campaign titled: "Help Sean Wilson be pain free—no more ball pain." Sean told us:

> Like I said, she basically started it without having talked to me about it before. . . . If I recall correctly, I think I had seen her the week prior and was talking about what was going on. And she of course expressed concern or whatnot, but she wasn't throwing out ideas like "what if we do this or what if we do that," whatever. She just digested it and I guess thought about what to do and eventually came up with the idea. I think . . . the first time I knew about it, by that time she had already posted it. [She said], "Hey I started this for you." . . . There was a very

brief thought that I wish I'd kind of been consulted or whatnot. It really kind of exposed a lot of what was going on to a lot more people than I was initially comfortable with. That very quickly was replaced just by a feeling of humility.

Initially, Sean was embarrassed—the issue was serious, but the tone of the campaign was irreverent—and some of his friends and family seemed annoyed to learn about his struggles through GoFundMe. Regardless, by the time we talked he was grateful for the help that it brought his way.

There's a clear social mechanism at work here, with well-intentioned friends, family, acquaintances, and community members looking to find an outlet for feelings of helplessness. Setting up crowdfunding gives them a way to roll up their sleeves and actually do something. And doing something, offering help, is often how family and friends and communities sustain themselves and thrive. Yet it can still be tough. Recall our respondent from California who set up a page to help a coworker's son:

> The instinct to help came naturally but it is a very daunting task to recruit people in your life, and the people in their lives, to stop what they're doing, see what's possible and hope that most of them make some attempt to help. Inevitably, the people I expected might help have not and the people that seemed to have been a lost cause due to their own issues, have stepped up in a major way. No way to know where the source of kind-hearted giving might come from for this sort of endeavor.

By stepping up for another person, you're now involved. And it can be a lot of work, even just to set up the page.

Setting a Goal

Once setup of the GoFundMe appeal has begun, the site points out: "Your goal is important but you'll want to make sure it's attainable." Simple advice for a very complicated decision. The site then prompts you with the question "How much do you want to raise?" How much money does the crowdfunder need to overcome their particular set of challenges?

Is it possible to put a dollar amount on it? What does "attainable" even mean? What will others think is reasonable? The crowdfunder doesn't want to seem greedy, especially since the first donors are likely to be people they already know pretty well. Yet GoFundMe's homepage features stories of people in need receiving thousands upon thousands in donations. Looking at more than 830,000 health-care and education crowdfunding campaigns in the US and Canada, we know that people mostly pick round numbers for their goals. The most common amounts are $10,000 (more than 15 percent of cases), $5,000 (just under 15 percent), and $2,000 (6 percent), whether in Canadian or US dollars. Rather than precise estimates of true financial need, we believe the goals reflect uncertainty and urgency: unexpected medical incidents, for instance, frequently mean immediate need and wholly unpredictable bills. A round number is a quick way to get through the setup process and start raising money.

In general, people creating health-care campaigns ask for larger amounts, with a median ask of $10,000 (after currency conversion, about US$7,500 as a Canadian median), while education campaigns hover around a $3,500 in both countries after conversion.[7]

To put these numbers into perspective, we can compare them with those in other countries. Among the five countries with the largest overall numbers of crowdfunding appeals, users in the US and Canada on average ask for the largest sums of money, in that order. For health-care campaigns specifically, Australian fundraisers come in third, setting their goals at an average $6,900. Why then do users in Ireland and the UK, the next countries on the list, ask for substantially smaller amounts ($1,600 and $1,300, respectively)? Both are known for their comprehensive national health-care systems that significantly reduce residents' out-of-pocket health-care costs. If their governments, by design, leave people on the hook for much smaller amounts when it comes to health care, it's logical that their welfare crowdfunding would involve significantly smaller amounts—about six to eight times lower than the US average.

Education campaigns are less variable in terms of goals, though US, Canadian, and Australian welfare crowdfunders lead again, seeking about $3,500. The average goal in the UK is about $2,500, with Irish users asking for about $1,700 on average. That halving is another strong hint that the magnitude of crowdfunding use is directly tied to the politics and social policies of various geographical regions—less need means lower fundraising goals.

How much money a crowdfunder asks for also depends on who they are. Our data on demographic characteristics shows differences even when people are asking for money for similar reasons. In Canada, health-care campaigns for men and women tend to have similar goals, with a median of around US$6,500. Campaigns for transgender and non-binary fundraisers ask for significantly less, about $2,800.[8] In the US, those amounts hit medians of $6,000 for men and women and $4,000 for trans and nonbinary campaigners. Of course, medians are different from means—the former is a middle value, with half of campaigns boasting higher amounts and half lower, and the latter is an average. The mean goal of health-care campaigns for Canadian men and women is US$12,800; for US men and women, it's US$15,700. For trans and gender nonbinary people in both countries, whose fundraisers nearly always focus on trans health-care services that include gender affirmation, the mean is around $3,200.

Trans and nonbinary campaigners consistently ask for smaller amounts in their fundraisers, though there's plenty of data to suggest that their financial needs are greater than those of their cis-gendered peers. Notably, trans and gender-nonconforming people experience exceptional barriers to health-care access, including far higher out-of-pocket expenses. Women likewise tend to pay more than men for medical services. That their fundraising patterns show women asking for amounts similar to those of men attests to inequality in crowdfunding before we even look at how the campaigns actually end up doing.[9]

All this variation aside, welfare crowdfunding goals are expressions, however rough, of the financial need arising from an unexpected medical bill or an educational opportunity. They give us a sense of the overall scope of hardship. According to our three years of data, US-based health-care campaigns asked for approximately $21 billion; education campaigns, more than $8 billion. In Canada, which has about one-tenth its neighbor's population, health-care campaigns sought $857 million; education campaigns, $158 million.[10] We argue that these tallies of the struggles and needs of those using welfare crowdfunding are a measure of the gaping holes in the countries' frayed social safety nets.

Roughly one-third of welfare crowdfunding pages aren't created by the beneficiary. How do other individuals make these determinations about goal setting? Our interviews helped us understand the difficult calculation involved when goals aren't easy to choose—when there isn't a specific procedure, device, or fee to pay—and when people are setting up fundraisers for others. The California respondent mentioned earlier had a tough time choosing the amount to fundraise for his coworker whose daughter had been in a car accident. He wrote in his appeal: "Despite the relatively young age and hope for full recovery, there's no way to know if the planned target amount will make a significant dent in the family's expenses."

Kate, an interviewee from Manitoba, made this point so clearly: "I think the challenge with it being run by somebody else is they might not really know what your needs are." Her friend set up the campaign after Kate's traumatic back injury left her paralyzed. Kate quickly added: "I would have felt bad if my friend had ended up asking for a lot more money. I think that the amount we had was good and sufficient . . . . But I guess the person running it doesn't necessarily know that, and I also don't know what percentage of people would really cap it off, and say, 'Oh! That's good, I'm able to buy everything I need now, and anything beyond this . . .' I would want it to go for what you're donating it for, right?"

Mia from Ontario referred to goal-setting as "arbitrary." Henry from Florida, when asked whether he had met his crowdfunding goal, responded: "Not quite, but we didn't really have a set goal. We, of course, typed in something, but we didn't really know exactly how much we needed." In the end, he recalled, "we were able to get by with what we got."

Beyond converting needs to dollar amounts, welfare crowdfunders suggested that they were engaged in a complex set of mental calculations and competition. They used rudimentary game theory as they tried to anticipate how much was too much and how potential donors might respond to one goal or another. This kind of mathematical modeling is used by social scientists to understand behavior in everything from nuclear proliferation to car shopping, but it's also familiar to anyone who's tried to set prices at a yard sale.

Diana from British Columbia reflected on her GoFundMe goal of $3,000:

> It seems like a lot of money, and it is a lot of money, but in the grand scheme of things, I've seen GoFundMe's for hundreds of thousands of dollars for medical bills, and there's no way to say that everyone will have a fair chance. I mean if everybody . . . the whole concept of it is built off of an idea that you go and donate to whoever you feel pity for, but not everybody is going to donate to everybody. It's already a weirdly competitive . . . system. I wouldn't directly call it competition, but I don't have a better word for it.

And it *is* a competition: fundraisers are operating in a marketplace, jockeying for a limited supply of financial help. As a young woman from Texas told us, "there are so many people these days having a campaign, even for things that are very small."

Amid the competition for scarce resources, you can imagine the goal-setting moment feeling difficult, uncomfortable, or a bit gross for many people. Krista from Montreal talked about her emotions during the page setup: "I just needed to be a bit vulnerable and maybe that was the biggest hurdle in all of that. And just asking people for help isn't always the easiest thing." But like so many others, she'd come this far, so she picked a number. The number gives the crowdfunder something to reach toward.

The Hidden Costs

Goal-setting is frequently the point at which people start thinking about what's "in it" for the crowdfunding platform. Platforms try to put users at ease up front. For example, GoFundMe is clear: "There's no cost to an organizer to create a GoFundMe, but a transaction fee (which includes debit and credit charges) per donation applies." More recently, it altered the language: "Keep in mind that transaction fees, including credit and debit charges, are deducted from each donation."

Seems fair enough. Essentially, you're assured that there's no cost to you now, as you set up your fundraiser, so you can worry about it later. (And you will.)

Another thing we noticed early on was GoFundMe's tip mechanism. It's never mentioned during page creation, where we read about debit and credit card transaction fees (though not in real terms, which turn out to be 2.9 percent of all funds raised plus $0.30 per donation), which GoFundMe says, "go directly to our payment processor and help us keep GoFundMe a safe place to donate." It's important to know that every donor will be asked to indicate both the amount of their gift *and* the amount of a tip for the platform. The slider bar under "Tip GoFundMe Services" defaults to "15 percent," though it gives options in increments from 0 to 30 percent as well as a "custom" hyperlink that allows a donor to enter any value, including zero. If you do decide to slide the bar to nothing, you get a guilt trip from GoFundMe in the form of a message: "Adding a GoFundMe tip means being a key part of improving the service for donors like you and the campaigns you support." We should also note that when we first started writing the book and exploring how the service works, this process involved a drop-down menu that defaulted to 12.5 percent but could only be changed in increments of 7.5–15 percent. It was only when a donor selected "Other" that they could manually enter a zero tip.

The tip is tacked on to the donation total, like a tip for meal delivery. The company frames it as a way for donors rather than fundraisers to cover the site's operating costs. In 2018, GoFundMe's Rob Solomon pitched tips this way: "A lot of feedback over the years has been . . . 'we want all of the money to go to the cause.' And in hearing about that, we decided that there's such good sentiment around GoFundMe the brand that we could remove the platform fee, and rely on the generosity of our donor community." It sounds great, but let's remember that corporations only do things that improve their bottom line. There's little transparency about tips on the GoFundMe site. According to *Slate* in 2020, "GoFundMe has a dark side," while *Atlantic* reporter Rachel Monroe quipped, "It seems strange to me to think that you would be tipping a corporation."[11] But the practice has obviously worked well enough: multimillion-dollar for-profit corporations don't keep doing things that aren't profitable.

People already making donations aren't inclined to pass along costs to their beneficiaries, so we can see why they may balk but agree to suggested tips, and beneficiaries are just so relieved that they don't have to pay more fees that they're unlikely to dig deeply into how fundraising platforms make their money.

Indeed, many of our respondents were unaware of the tipping mechanism. Sadie from Toronto used GoFundMe to raise funds for her teenage daughter, who was being treated for cancer. "I was a little surprised that the default on GoFundMe was a 15 percent tip," she said, and that made her wonder whether she had tipped when making her own crowdfunding donations in the past. "Maybe I gave with the 15 percent on top, I don't know." Because the donor-facing checkout pages are tailor-made to safeguard the tip income, she probably did.

Robert was particularly put off when several people who donated to his wife Lisa's GoFundMe page brought up tipping. He went looking and, sure enough:

> [T]here is no zero, you have to click "other amount" and physically type in zero, it's the only way to prevent leaving them a tip. So, I've got a lot of people that found that to be disingenuous which I agree with, there should definitely be an option of zero. Some people, a lot of people, probably would have tipped, but the fact that they felt like they had to almost, was—I wasn't a big fan because . . . they made thousands more dollars directly off of us—just because of how they set up their tipping process.

For Robert, the issue wasn't that those dollars could otherwise have supported his family in a really tough time. It was that the tips seemed *sneaky*.[12]

The seeds of GoFundMe's profits are planted in the goal-setting step. With built-in, opt-out tipping, higher initial goal amounts suggest higher potential income. Mark from Wisconsin, who used GoFundMe after his catastrophic chiropractic injury, captured our tip trepidation: "As a business person . . . I can understand it, but at the same time when someone's life has just been torn apart and you're sticking your fingers in that cookie jar, it just does not feel right."

Marketing with Pictures and Stories

The process is still not complete once the goal has been set. Next is the moment to plead the case: writing a story and selecting a picture that goes at the top of the page. It's a huge deal. If a picture is worth a thousand words, those words had better be the same words the story is trying to "sell," said Indiana resident Andre, "I spent a lot of time. I'm a very visual-oriented . . . person and so I think that images can tell a lot about the story. So if you look at the statement and the pictures together, they kind of should say the same thing." For example, does the crowdfunder select a picture of themselves in a hospital bed, showing how hurt they are, even though all the pages are public and this feels awfully personal? Or how about choosing a picture of a smiling and healthy person in a family photo—something aspirational, showing how much better the crowdfunder will be if the fundraiser works out?

GoFundMe's prompt to "tell your story . . . explain who you are and why you're fundraising" comes with a minimum-length requirement. You can write whatever you want, even include videos, but the copy has to be more than a couple of words. The site encourages people setting up a medical fund to "explain what happened" and "describe recommended treatment." Fair enough: we wouldn't expect people to give without knowing some personal details. But this can get uncomfortable fast. Beyond privacy concerns, medical conditions or education challenges can be embarrassing. So too is talking openly about money—why it's needed and when, how it'll be spent or why it'll be saved. The crowdfunder needs a plan and a willingness to open up about the personal finances and struggles motivating their ask.

In our research, we found a link between the quality of pictures and stories and the success of crowdfunding campaigns. We'll talk about this more in Chapter 4, but as you might imagine, there's a lot of variation when it comes to the quality of these elements of GoFundMe appeals. Poorly lit photos and those taken at unflattering angles garner less sympathy (and likely fewer donations). Stories can be too short or too long for donors' tastes, spelling and grammar errors may be off-putting (or build a sense that the beneficiary is "just a regular person"). Photos and stories that seem disconnected or incoherent are a worry too. It's just that a lot can go wrong and there's hardly any information about what works best.

Among what we call the "happier times" photographs, we saw many that, especially in tandem with tear-jerking stories, were truly affecting. An Edmonton page has a photo of a father and son walking away hand in hand. The young boy is clearly excited, pulling at his father's hand while the dad wears a faint smile, taking pleasure in the moment. Below the picture, potential donors learn that the father died recently and his survivors are fundraising for the son's future education (when last we looked, the page had nearly met its $25,000 goal). A page based in Philadelphia shows a man, his arm slung around a woman, smiling—maybe a vacation shot. Turns out, the man needs a double lung transplant. While he waits for a donor, he has to remain within two hours of the hospital at all times; his family is fundraising to cover the costs of relocating to be close to the transplant center. These two photos are typical of the most common crowdfunding images: "happier times," which seem to connect with potential donors. We can relate. We can see ourselves in those photos. And we want to help people get back to their happier time.

A second effective photographic theme in our categorization scheme is "struggle and pain." Typically, these pictures are taken in hospital rooms. We see infants in NICU facilities hooked up to electrodes and oxygen. We see accident victims hooked up to ventilators. We see emaciated and hairless adults in hospital beds, clearly battling cancer. These are designed to shock, to draw back the curtain and show the urgency of a person's need. Like the gritty video montages nongovernmental organizations use to raise money for people living in severe poverty, they're a call to action.

There's no good reason to spend time on the crowdfunding train wrecks—the campaigns with ineffective photos and stories. It isn't nice; nor is it necessary. You can imagine them: photos that look like family trip outtakes and stories that read like junior high first-draft essays. Such poor-quality pitches tend to founder. Again you may be thinking, "fair enough." Some people are just better at putting themselves out there. Why shouldn't they benefit? Yet it's concerning because crowdfunders whose native language isn't English or who have developmental disabilities are at a disadvantage in writing stories, and those who don't have the equipment to take good pictures are at a disadvantage in illustrating their plights. It takes only a moment's effort to come up with evidence that this is unfair.

At present, it is what it is. We all know that marketing—clever images and turns of phrase—can garner millions. But people aren't commodities. Why should their marketing capabilities dictate whether or not they get help? This brings us to the next step in crowdfunding, where the passive marketing of setting up a crowdfunding page turns to the active marketing of getting the word out.

The Page Goes Live and the Work Starts

Making the fundraising appeal go "live" is a moment pregnant with possibility, with beneficiaries, friends, and family ready to watch the donations pour in. Not so fast. You still have to hustle. Without promotion, few crowdfunding campaigns succeed.

GoFundMe knows this. When you set up a fund, you're immediately instructed to send the page to three to five friends, sharing it by email or through social media like Twitter and Facebook. If you created the campaign to benefit someone else, GoFundMe tells you that "teams raise 3x more funds" and encourages you to add to your "team" by entering email addresses for those who might want to join the fundraising effort. It's hard to turn down, but if you haven't yet consulted with friends and family, it might be awkward. Even so, following this step is actually good advice. Sherice from Washington state told us: "I get texts from GoFundMe with links to share it, and then it gives advice. . . . Within the first week and a half, it was sending me a text every couple of days from GoFundMe saying, 'Here's how to increase the visibility. Here's the link to share.'" (That this freely and frequently given advice is effective doesn't make it any less annoying, of course.) "Friendfunding" is the emerging term for this stage of campaigning.[13]

Earlier in the book, we talked about "weak ties" that extend our social circles beyond friends and family. Friends of friends are actually quite likely to donate or share a page with other prospective donors. Amanda from Ontario understood this from the start: "You can't just launch a campaign and hope that people find it. I think you have to be able to let your circle of people know that it's there. So, I think a lot depends on how good you are at publicizing it."[14]

It's gratifying when the effort to use connections pays off. As Alice from California told us, "I shared the link with . . . some of our friends, and they've passed it on, so it's kind of interesting to see. Like some of the donations came from people I don't even know, and I don't know exactly where they got the link." In Florida, Henry was just as surprised by the extent of the connections he, his wife, and his friends had: "Between all of us, we had more than 5,000 friends [on Facebook]. So we figured it was a good way to get the word out. . . . There were a lot of old high school friends that [my wife] had and, by posting on Facebook, she got to reconnect with them and found a lot of donors that way." Twitch, a livestreaming platform designed for gamers, proved similarly useful to Lucas, who had had a heart attack just after relocating to British Columbia to be with his partner. Rather than just playing Fortnite or League of Legends, the partner's daughter used Twitch, one of the biggest social media platforms in the world, to spread the word about Lucas's GoFundMe.

Crowdfunding with social media can also be helpful in building a sense of connection with a caring community. Taylor from Utah set up a GoFundMe appeal for an exercise bike to help with her husband's medical recovery: "I tagged his family members in that post just saying, 'Hey, this is what my plans are for his birthday. If you want to help us get there, that'd be super cool.' And then it just turned into something way, way bigger than I expected."

"It made me feel good that at least people were willing to share it, even if they weren't financially able to donate," said New Yorker Matt. Numerous online sites allow you to communicate with your supporters and family, making it easier to give updates and reducing burdens for those who are sick or otherwise unable to do so. Shay from Illinois, looking to get the word out for a friend, came across the private, ad-free, nonprofit site CaringBridge "that's kind of like a blog platform that you can use to just inform people and so invite people to campaign" for the appeal at the same time.

Sharing on social media isn't the only way to hustle; it's just the easiest—the low-hanging fruit. People who want to do more keep creating new avenues. TikTok didn't exist when crowdfunding first started, but today it has hundreds of millions of users. Not only can it help get the word out about GoFundMe appeals; it can also help creators make extra money via ad revenue should their creative videos gain an audience. In one example, a young woman sings along to a dramatic indie-pop song in her car before the scene shifts and we see the same woman, Jane, lying in a hospital bed. A scroll at the top of the screen tells viewers: "We can't do this on our own." Family pictures and finally a screenshot of a Go-FundMe page follow. Within a week of posting the TikTok, Jane died and her older brother converted the crowdfunding appeal:

> I know that initially this was a fundraiser . . . for her medical needs but now at this point I have decided to turn this fundraiser into a grievance one for me and my family. [Jane] didn't have life insurance before she passed, and I am asking for assistance to help our family with things like: unpaid medical bills, funeral costs, a coffin, [mortgage] payments, rent, travel and lodging expenses as well as food, [Jane]'s car payments (she had just bought a car) and much much more.

When we saw this clip, it was only a few weeks old and had more than 350,000 likes, nearly 40,000 shares, and $20,000 in donations.

In the year or two after this book is published, there will doubtless be even more technologies that welfare crowdfunders can leverage to market their campaigns. By intuition or trial and error, those who learn to effectively use the latest popular media can rise above the fray.

For supplementing and amplifying welfare crowdfunding, the internet is king. But there's also the "bricks-and-mortar," old-fashioned way: face to face. Mark, the man from Wisconsin suffering after a chiropractic injury, reached out to a few professors of marketing at the local college for advice about his GoFundMe. The experts told him: "You've got to build your credibility, because, again, this is such a tough story to pitch." For Mark, that meant an in-person event: "And we did a town hall. My hometown actually stepped up. They gave us the city hall." Fundraising for her friend Sid, Sonia decided to supplement her online efforts with posters supplied by the GoFundMe app. "[I] posted them at all the stores in town, the post office, everywhere . . . especially in a small town with a lot of older people, they don't use social media, they don't use online banking, stuff like that, so the GoFundMe limits a bit of your audience. Although it expands your audience, it kind of limits it." Recall the picture of the Edmonton man who died unexpectedly, leaving behind a young son. His brother placed a link to the GoFundMe page for the boy's education trust fund in the obituary, telling readers: "Friends and family can donate online." It might make some readers cringe, but the idea of responding to grief by supporting a child's future success makes more sense than sending flowers. The point is that people use all kinds of media to get the word out, from posts to posters to obituaries.

Even negative attention can occasionally turn into donations. As the old adage goes, "any press is good press." Remember Alexis and their efforts to get help with gender-affirming surgery? Well, the trolls came out on Twitter, mocking their campaign. Alexis told us: "Because it's controversial, I feel like you have a chance to get your campaign noticed a lot more easily. . . . I've had several people post screenshots of my campaign to make fun of me on Twitter. . . . I've actually gotten more donations after that because donors see these people making fun of me. . . . I mean, thanks, guys. I don't know what to say about that." For the record, we do: it's a shame that anyone in need has to face online abuse in addition to the suffering that spurred their fundraising. We're pleased that others, put off by the cyberbullying, stepped up to help Alexis.

Alexis isn't the only person we heard about when social media promotion didn't go as planned. The Westhoff family from British Columbia includes two daughters, ages eleven and thirteen. Both have a rare brain condition called pontocerebellar hypoplasia type 2, which typically results in death before age eighteen. A family friend wrote the family's crowdfunding story in the voice of one of the girls:

> We live in a rural area in the Okanagan and all of the medical specialists that we need to see are a 6 hour drive away in Vancouver. We need a vehicle that will enable us to travel more comfortably. The long drive to Vancouver does not have proper accessible washrooms anywhere along the route. So we could really use a vehicle that is large enough to handle our full-size changing station with a ceiling lift to help us onto the change table. I am a teenager now and have grown. It is no longer safe for a two-person lift-and-carry technique to be used to move me

from my chair onto a change station. We need a van that has a ceiling
lift to keep our staff safe from workplace injuries.

This is where things get complicated. As told to the *Toronto Star*, when
the friend tried to post the link, Facebook flagged it as suspicious and
wouldn't allow her to share it." Mother Cathy was devastated: "It was
so disheartening to hear that Facebook was hiding her post regarding
our fundraiser." The algorithms just weren't working properly. And
because this happened during the pandemic, Facebook's response was
slow. Being at the mercy of online platforms piled frustration upon
frustration. Luckily in the Westhoffs' case, the problem was eventually
fixed and several thousand dollars came in, likely because of the media
attention.[15]

For some, this cautionary tale might be enough to convince them
that crowdfunding—at least the friendfunding portion—isn't worth
the trouble. Anticipating problems, fearing pushback, or perhaps just
too uncomfortable to promote an appeal, some crowdfunders don't do
much beyond setting up a page and crossing their fingers. As Lorie from
Florida told us, "I haven't really promoted it or anything. It's just been by
word of mouth. So I've just kind of left it up there, but I'm not pushing it.
If someone happens to see it and they want to help, that's fine. But yeah,
I'm not . . . pushing it." Fellow Floridian Alexis cut their promotion efforts short: "I have stopped promoting my campaign as much because of
the Black Lives Matter movement right now. I think that people's money,
if they have disposable income, should probably go towards mutual aid
funds and bail funds and stuff like that." Indeed, we heard several people
speak about their discomfort as they sought help for themselves while
understanding that there are bigger, broader issues facing the world.

Though it's hard to prove a negative, we know that some users can't
promote their crowdfunding pages simply because they don't have
strong social networks, on- or offline. Crowdfunding research offers evidence that people with weaker and less robust social networks—who
tend to be disadvantaged in other ways as well—aren't successful at
crowdfunding.[16] This appears to have been the case for Tasha, a woman
from Texas who was raising money to cover insurance co-pays for her
kidney cancer treatments. Her husband had recently been incarcerated,

and her online business wasn't paying the bills. Talking about her efforts to spread the word about her GoFundMe campaign, Tasha said, "Look, I only use Facebook and I don't [even] really use that, so I don't actually have a whole lot of friends. I mean, I sometimes do. But my daughters, they do, so they posted on theirs. They're getting a lot of feedback . . . and a lot of people have shared it from their social media to others that they know." Still, her campaign didn't get a single donation—only comments wishing her well. Again, we see how the setup of welfare crowdfunding can shut out some of the people most in need of help.

Since GoFundMe's potential returns are uncertain, and few people want to put all their eggs in one basket, it's common for fundraisers to supplement their crowdfunding campaigns with what a woman from New York described as "side hustles." Mark, whom we heard from earlier, used a town hall event to tell his story and direct people to his GoFundMe. A young man from Ohio told us he was raising money for a former neighbor who had had a stroke by creating flyers and donation boxes to leave at local gas stations. A man from Missouri said that his friend, forced to retire when he was diagnosed with stage 4 throat cancer, was in a "very dire situation," so a group of friends set up a Go-FundMe page and held a trivia night with more than 400 attendees—that's a lot of people coming out for a cause.

Religious institutions have provided an offline platform for significant fundraising since the early days of philanthropy in the US and Canada, when congregations worked to support newly arrived immigrants squeezed by the Industrial Revolution. In our data, many respondents relied on the church, the synagogue, and the *masjid* (mosque) as an organizing base for bake sales, raffles, and suppers. Friday night services at a *masjid* are an opportunity to call for help. Sunday morning prayer at church can be a time to pass the hat and collect funds. Religious communities make a difference—just as they always have.

Yard and garage sales are another popular method of raising additional funds, as are car washes. Selling handmade bracelets to coworkers at her office worked for one respondent, while a Texas woman described raising funds for her fellow teacher whose breast cancer treatments required her family to endure extended hotel stays by organizing a Go-FundMe and selling catered meals before a Friday night football game.

While the woman described the GoFundMe process as easy, "... the meal catering and getting stores to donate took a lot of time." Setting up, managing, and promoting a GoFundMe page, are often far less labor-intensive than old-fashioned fundraisers and can reach a lot more people, so it's easy to understand the appeal of crowdfunding. But it's also easy to understand why many people do both online and offline. You never want to think that you could have done more to help someone you love.

A Very Daunting Task

Our California respondent who described getting started with welfare crowdfunding as a "very daunting task" is clearly correct. The situation that gave rise to your need—or all the other demands of daily life—might make it hard for you to find the time or energy. The digital divide and other structural inequalities accrue additional disadvantages to non-Whites, elderly adults, those living with disabilities, and those living in remote and undeveloped regions. Some of the most disadvantaged have the hardest time seeking help via welfare crowdfunding.

Assuming you have the time, access, and internet savvy to set up a crowdfunding appeal, you have to market your struggles and your story (or a friend or family member's, which may or may not involve uncomfortable talks). Privacy goes out the window because it's crucial to select emotive, high-quality pictures, write engaging text, put a dollar amount on your need, and, if you have them, activate your social media and community connections. And then, no matter how strong your network ties, no matter how much enthusiasm and energy you have for promoting the cause, there comes a moment when you have to let it ride. Wait. Hope.

"There's really only a few folks—me, his family, and his friends," said a young man from Georgia trying to help a coworker through GoFundMe. "They're sharing the links with family and friends, and we are hoping for the best." It's a funny thing, this moment. You're out there in the public hoping to get attention, and you have little control over the outcome. What if no one really notices?

Delilah, a teacher from Ohio, took the wait in stride: "The only thing that can happen is nobody donates to your campaign and it just ends, you know what I'm saying? So it's not a big deal." Plus, said Tasha from Texas,

"With [asking for help] on the internet, I would say it's a little bit easier because you don't have to actually ask somebody face to face. You have to deal with either the rejection or them saying okay, they can. And online, you don't have to do that. You just click what it is that you're trying to do and what it's for, and you just sit there and wait and see what happens."

Others were more like Tom Petty, agonizing because "the waiting is the hardest part." When our survey asked welfare crowdfunders to write about the highs and lows, the wait was frequently mentioned as a low point. It took months for some to get their first donations; others never got them at all. In Chapter 4, we focus on results. What happens to welfare crowdfunders once they've reached out for help?

Four

Queen for a Day?

In the late 1950s, a US radio game show called *Queen for a Day* leapt to television and became a hit (at the time, it was America's most watched daytime show). On each episode, female contestants took turns telling the host, Jack Bailey, about their struggles and needs. The audience eagerly awaited the moment when Bailey asked each contestant to pinpoint her most critical need—typically, one after the other, the women burst into tears. Their pitiable stories, communications scholar Susan Douglas tells us in *Where the Girls Are*, detailed "financial deprivation and physical and emotional loss, about the isolation and sense of helplessness of many bereft housewives." The game was decided by audience applause, with the titular queen for a day receiving a bevy of prizes to help with her struggles, and the runners-up taking home consolation prizes. It was a feel-good hit with viewers. As Douglas points out, "there was no problem, no catastrophe that couldn't be fixed." Sound familiar? What we've revealed thus far about welfare crowdfunding feels a lot like this game show. But in the real world, as we show in this chapter, most people don't become Queen, even for a day.[1]

The book thus far has chronicled what might be understood as the prologue to welfare crowdfunding. The public story we're most familiar with begins (or quickly ends) once welfare crowdfunding pages are up and running. What happens next? Do most welfare crowdfunders reach their goals? Our data offers a pretty clear, simple answer: no, they don't. Those waiting anxiously, hoping for help, are nearly always disappointed at this stage. Few people meet their crowdfunding goals. Few crowdfunders get the help they need. The data is littered with runners-up.

In this chapter, we show what all of this looks and feels like, both the bird's-eye view and the personal, up-close experience. We start with the exceptions—that minority of welfare crowdfunders who raise most if not all of the funds they need. We then turn to the vast majority who raise little or no money. By the end of this chapter, we will have made our case: welfare crowdfunding with GoFundMe fails to live up to the hype (and to the featured stories on its own home page). What seems like a fruitful space for supporting hopes and dreams is actually, in Mark's memorable phrase from Chapter 3, a well of sadness, full of disappointments big and small. The process is an emotional meat grinder.

The Winners

Some people do get the financial help they need on GoFundMe, and it can be wonderful. Inspirational. One headline-grabbing story from the media is that of Theodis Ray Quarles. When the Tennessee man died of COVID-19 in early 2021, he was survived by a heartbroken wife and five daughters, none of whom could be at his bedside in the hospital. A friend of the family set up a GoFundMe page "in support of [wife] Vicki and her girls to offer financial relief and [freedom from] worry from things associated with basic immediate needs as well as for their continued growth, goals and aspirations." Music star Taylor Swift, also from Tennessee, personally donated $50,000 and sent along a "sweet personal note" that Theodis's widow said "warmed" her heart. The media picked up the story and it went viral. Another $10,000 in donations poured in overnight. It turns out, Taylor Swift has a sort of Midas touch when it comes to supporting a GoFundMe cause; every time she chips in, it becomes international news (and a windfall). Her generosity in this respect is so well known that back in 2015 Swift was the one who prompted the platform to increase its maximum individual donation limit from $15,000 to $50,000 so that she could send that amount to a girl battling leukemia.[2]

Robert and Lisa, who you've met throughout these pages, are another success story. In large part due to the social network Robert developed during his time as a professional hockey referee, the GoFundMe page his friends created took off like a rocket. As Robert tells it, "all of a sudden we woke up, and after like 20 hours, it was at $30,000. And I think by 24 hours it was at 40 grand or something crazy like that. . . . Somebody must have sent it into local news and our local radio station." In fact, Robert and Lisa raised nearly $50,000 in the first twenty-four hours. When a newspaper article closed with a link to their GoFundMe page, another $20,000 in donations rolled in. Robert figures people from the hockey community recognized his picture and wanted to help.

At the time of our interview, the tally was about $70,000. That's a lot of money but not enough to make their problems go away. Robert was still missing work. Lisa was still sick. Remember, Robert did the math when it came to Lisa coming home and it totaled $492 per day for twenty-four-hour nursing care: "Over 145 days, that's $70,000 . . . so we're definitely not out of the woods financially." The money they raised crowdfunding might cover five months of at-home care for Lisa. It wouldn't cover the lost wages, and it couldn't guarantee they'd be relieved of financial stress. Their story—one of the more successful in terms of dollars raised—is bittersweet. Despite raising tens of thousands of dollars, the disheartening fact is that still wasn't enough to meet Robert and Lisa's ongoing needs.

Jamison, a talented dancer in New York, died unexpectedly at age fifteen. Her devastated friends and family thought the best way to honor her memory would be to establish a scholarship to help kids realize their dance dreams at the academy Jamison attended. The initial crowdfunding goal was $5,000, but they were surprised to raise nearly $58,000 from almost seven hundred donors. In a GoFundMe update post, Jamison's mom explained how the funds would be distributed: "Six students will receive a full-year scholarship, totaling $36,000, three students will receive partial-year scholarships, totaling $9,000, and four students will be given scholarships for the summer intensive, totaling $3,100." After distributing the funds, Jamison's mom told supporters: "Handing out these scholarships was a gut-wrenching experience, but I have to believe Jamison was watching over her beloved studio today with that megawatt smile. Thank you again for all of your support in making this possible."[3]

News media also picked up on the crowdfunding campaign of Mary from Oklahoma. Mary was brutally beaten by her boyfriend while pregnant, and the picture at the top of her crowdfunding page showed the severity of her situation. There, next to the goal of $65,000, was Mary, swollen and bruised. As we draft this book, Mary's fundraising total has hit $65,265, with contributions from more than 1,800 donors—sorority chapters at Oklahoma University and across the United States chief among them. Donors' messages were supportive and angry. A $150 donation from a local sorority was annotated: "We donated to show our respect, thoughts and prayers to [Mary], and to all individuals who are survivors of such heinous actions," while a $5 donor simply wrote: "Fuck domestic abusers." Following the link from the GoFundMe page to Mary's mother's Facebook page, we learn that Mary gave birth to a healthy daughter and is moving forward with the next chapter of her life. Even so, we can't escape the uneasy sense that this "success" story is hardly a success at all. Mary never should have gone through this. Healing from intimate-partner violence (and from giving birth) is a slow process, and Mary's future will include a potentially nasty custody battle with her abuser. The donations, at least, are a start.

These stories from our data are the sort that makes the news. And they're good for our society, showcasing the kinds of reciprocal social relations that strengthen the fabric of our democracy. The back and forth of connecting with and helping our neighbors and fellow citizens is what Alexis de Tocqueville famously called "habits of the heart." They bolster good feelings about our community, acting as a rising tide that can potentially lift all boats. Good actions beget more good actions, is the idea.[4] Typically, in the most successful cases a catalyst leads to an eruption of free media coverage and the fund takes off (who doesn't like to see someone who deserves it get the help they need?). It's not quite like winning the lottery, but it's winning nonetheless. These are the kinds of stories GoFundMe makes sure we see on its main page. And they inspire other people in need of help to give it a go. Why not? What's the harm?

The Losing Majority

Unfortunately, such stories provide false hope. The news, not to mention the crowdfunding platforms themselves, tell us about the winners because the failures aren't the sort of thing people want to read about over their morning coffee. Appeals that blow through their goals and raise tens of thousands of dollars are incredibly rare. Of the approximately 1,750,000 crowdfunding campaigns created in the US and Canada between 2018 and 2021 and included in our analysis, fewer than 300,000 (or about 17 percent) met or exceeded their stated goal. Let's put that another way: *Only about one in every six campaigns meets its fundraising goal.* Fewer than 600,000 campaigns (36 percent) raised half of their stated goal, and only 54 percent raised at least a quarter. The average campaign closed after bringing in less than one-third of the original ask.[5]

Certainly, we define welfare crowdfunding "success" in terms set by the fundraisers; those who set up a GoFundMe page decide how much they need and choose a goal amount, so we call it a "success" if they meet or exceed that monetary amount. As we noted in Chapter 3, these goals actually tend to be modest, particularly against the kinds of costs associated with health care and education. Partially, the goals seem low because they're so often associated with an unexpected bill that becomes a major obstacle for someone living paycheck to paycheck. Only 5 percent of the campaigns we analyzed asked for more than $70,000; 95 percent asked for less than $50,000; 80 percent, for $10,000 or less. The median goal was $5,000 or less, and around 50,000 campaigns had goals of just one dollar.[6]

If anything, success across the full range of crowdfunding cases presents an unrealistic picture. Many campaigns seek very small amounts; others set perhaps unrealistic goals. Some people meet their initial goal and raise it to a more aspirational level. To deal with some of these concerns, we can look at success not across this enormous set of campaigns (which, remember, totals one in six successful campaigns) but across a more typical set.

To avoid the influence of very low or very high goals in our analysis of crowdfunding success, we cut out the extreme cases. When we narrow them down to those with goals in the middle two-thirds of all campaigns, our dataset tallies 1,200,000 campaigns. This subset's goals range from $1,001 to $15,000—amounts that should be neither too easy nor too difficult to attain. Yet the chance of success is even lower among these more typical cases. Now only about half make at least a quarter of their goal amount, one in three gets to the halfway point, and fewer than one in eight (about 12 percent) meets or exceeds its goal. No matter how reasonable the goal, the chances of any single crowdfunding campaign succeeding are slim.

It's worth emphasizing that we observed the cases we're talking about over a long period of time. Specifically, among the cases we discussed earlier, the average time between a campaign's creation and the date on which we last checked its success was thirty-three weeks, or about seven months. As we detail in the Appendix, our data collection involved revisiting crowdfunding cases regularly over many months, systematically recording information about each campaign and its progress. This data let us calculate how long each campaign had been live whenever we checked on its progress. On average, we tracked campaign progress over half a year. Removing the relatively small number of short-duration campaigns at the time of observations barely improves the success rates. In other words, it's not that we didn't wait long enough to see campaigns succeed—most fell short in their fundraising campaigns, no matter how much time they had.[7]

Comparing across countries and campaign types reveals some differences when it comes to fundraising success. For one, campaigns in Canada are more likely to meet their fundraising goals. Among our "typical" campaigns—those with goal amounts neither too high nor too low—we find that 17 percent of Canadian campaigns meet or exceed their goal and about 40 percent get to the halfway point. In the US, only about 12 percent make their goal and 32 percent make it at least halfway. The median Canadian campaign makes about 38 percent of its goal; the median US campaigns make 29 percent. Neither of these numbers is particularly impressive.

Comparing across categories among the full range of goal amounts, campaigns for charities and nonprofits tend to do the best in both countries, with about 27 percent meeting or exceeding their goals. Education campaigns do relatively well, with about 21 percent in both countries making their goals. Campaigns for health care, accidents, and funeral costs—the majority of all campaigns—have lower success rates, with around 17 percent meeting their goals. The least successful category is animal and pet-related, with 11 percent success.

When we turn to our subset of typical cases, removing unusually low and unusually high goals as before, these rates plummet. The middle two-thirds of all health-care campaigns by goal amount (between $1,500 and $20,000) see success only about 11 percent of the time; 33 percent make at least half. Typical campaigns for funeral costs and memorial funds (between $2,300 and $11,000) tend to do slightly better (15 percent fully funded; 39 percent at least half-funded), but typical education campaigns (between $500 and $10,000) do worse (13 percent fully funded; 30 percent at least half-funded). Finally, 91 percent of typical pet or animal-related campaigns (between $750 and $5,000) fall short of their aims.

Perhaps leaving goals out of it will tell a happier story? When we switch to measuring success simply by counting dollars, we can report that the vast majority of crowdfunders make *something*. Less than 1 percent of campaigns make zero. Across both countries, the numbers are fairly consistent: In the period we observe, we find that two-thirds of campaigns make at least $500 and about half reach $1,000 or higher. The drop-off is steep from there: only a quarter bring in $3,000 or more and only a tenth reach $7,000.

Put differently, the good news is that the median welfare crowdfunding campaign brings in at least $1,000—that's real money. But recall that this is five times less than the median goal amount ($5,000). By category, health-care campaign median fundraising is $1,900; the education campaign median is $600. Given that the average goals for these categories are $7,400 and $3,000, respectively, that means that their goals are at least four and five times higher than the amounts they eventually bring in. There's a sizeable gap between what people say they need (which they may downplay or underestimate) and what crowdfunding provides.

At the same time, some crowdfunders make *a lot* of money. Each of the top 5 percent of the highest-earning campaigns in our dataset made over $12,500. The top 1 percent topped $35,500, and the top 0.1 percent—roughly 1,700 in the period we cover—brought in more than $120,000.

Certainly, many of these high-earning campaigns benefited entire groups of people like victims of natural disasters and mass shootings or broad social movements like Black Lives Matter. But plenty were for individuals or families seeking to cover common crowdfunding costs, such as expensive cancer treatments, rebuilding a home after a fire, or starting a college fund for a child who's lost a parent.

Once again, our data points to the fact that inequality is central to welfare crowdfunding. This is apparent at multiple stages of the process, from the decision to start a campaign to how it's set up, how many friends the campaigner is able to share it with, and how much those friends can help. The money ultimately raised is in part a result of the choices made along the way, in part a result of the advantages and disadvantages that each of us carries and in small part a result of luck. The final dollar sum is what we get when these complex processes shake out. Looking at the dollars spread out across campaigns lets us see how different sources of advantage and disadvantage add up, as well as the key tendencies in the big-picture operation of welfare crowdfunding.

The unequal distribution of crowdfunding dollars is, in a word, staggering. The bottom 50 percent of all campaigns created between 2018 and 2021 received only *5 percent* of all dollars raised in that time. The bottom 75 percent together claimed just 20 percent of the dollars raised. The view is different from the top. The highest-earning 5 percent of campaigns (those that made more than $12,500) claimed half of all the fundraising dollars; the top 1 percent (earning over $35,500) took in a quarter; and the top 0.1 percent (earning over $120,000) received a full tenth of all funds donated to all campaigns in this period. There's an astounding concentration of funds donated to a very small group of crowdfunders. The tiniest sliver, the roughly 160 fundraisers in the top one-hundredth of one percent (campaigns making over $508,000) earned over 5 percent of all funds—the same total dollar amount spread across the roughly 780,000 fundraisers in the bottom half of all campaigns.[8]

Do these statistics make you think of the "1 percent"? It should. For context, in the United States, which has infamously high income inequality among advanced industrialized countries, the top 10 percent of income earners (families with annual incomes above $134,900) made about half of all income in 2018. The top 5 percent made almost

40 percent; and the top 1 percent, about 22 percent. Looking at the highest earners, the top 0.1 percent (approximately 170,000 families with annual incomes above $2.2 million) had about 10 percent of all income and the top 0.01 percent (incomes above roughly $11.5 million) shared 5 percent of all the money Americans earned that year.[9] At the very, very top, in the highest fractions of the 1 percent, crowdfunding earnings edged out the unequal concentration at the top of US incomes. Half of all crowdfunding dollars are claimed by the top 5 percent of fundraisers; half of all US income is shared among by the top 10 percent of earners. This means that welfare crowdfunding is considerably more unequally distributed than income in the US.

Social scientists studying income and wealth also use summary measures that capture inequality in a single number. One of the most common is the Gini index. This is a scale on which zero refers to perfect equality (everyone has the same share of total income) and one hundred refers to perfect inequality (one person or family has all the income). In 2017, the Gini index for disposable income in the US was around 40—one of the highest among industrialized democracies (Canada's Gini was around 30; the UK's, 35; Norway and Finland's, 25).[10]

To measure the overall inequality in crowdfunding incomes, we can follow the same procedure, producing a GoFundMe Gini. For the US and Canadian campaigns that we observed between 2018 and 2021, the Gini is 74. This means that the alarmingly high-inequality US economy still does a better job of evenly distributing income than crowdfunding does distributing donations. So does South Africa, one of the most unequal countries in the world, where the Gini in 2014 was 63.[11] In fact, we can't find a Gini index in any country at any point in recent history as high as the one we computed for GoFundMe.[12] If GoFundMe were a country, and campaigns' funds raised were its people's incomes, it would boast the world's highest income inequality.

Understanding the broad trends in welfare crowdfunding contextualizes the individual stories we heard during our research. Remember Jane, the Alberta mother of six who decided to go to law school? Like Mary, she was a victim of domestic violence looking for a new way forward through crowdfunding, and we found her story quite inspiring. Well, crowdfunding didn't unlock her future. Nearly six months after her son created the GoFundMe page, it had raised just $870 of her goal of $14,131 (tuition for one year). The page listed nine donors and forty-nine shares on social media.

Thanks to our quantitative analysis, we know that Jane's disappointing outcome is common. Though the total dollars she raised came close to the median amount for Canadian education appeals ($990), her campaign is among the quarter of those that failed to bring in even 7 percent of their goal. And, of course, Jane is just one of the roughly 80 percent of Canadian crowdfunding users who don't make their goals either. Elder Cecil Redstar, the Indigenous man who was fighting cancer, had only raised $1,860 of his $8,000 goal before he died on June 2, 2020. His lack of success is disheartening, yet our analysis tells us that it's a totally normal outcome for Canadian health-care campaigns, one-third of which raise no more than a quarter of their ask.

Crowdfunding platforms have gained a tremendous amount of goodwill in recent years. They have a reputation for successfully connecting people in need with people who are able to help. They cultivate and market this rosy ethos. GoFundMe has produced a podcast called "True Stories of Good People." Since 2018, the episodes have profiled people who help and get help.[13] The stories are inspiring, heart-wrenching, and true; they demonstrate what's possible when crowdfunding works out just right. But by focusing on the successful cases, platforms like GoFundMe also promote the idea that crowdfunding is a good way for everyone to get help and that it does a good job at brokering connections between donor dollars and those in need.

This reputation is undeserved. However we split up our data, we found extremely unequal outcomes across crowdfunders and their welfare campaigns. GoFundMe bills its services as "trusted fundraising for all of life's moments." The data shows that the trust we have in this for-profit company to help us with our problems is misplaced. The fundraising happens for a select few, and the rest have to deal with their "moments" on their own.

This is perhaps one of the most important points in the entire book, so it bears repeating: *most welfare crowdfunders do not get the help they need.* Only a small few succeed. We don't doubt that the people who work at crowdfunding companies are by and large well-intentioned; we simply find the inordinate attention they lavish on the most successful campaigns misleading. As we explored in earlier chapters, studying crowdfunding reveals pressing equity concerns at every point: access, technical ability, and outcomes are all rife with inequality. In the end, these platforms don't do a particularly good job at what they claim to do. They have an abysmal track record in actually facilitating fundraising for those who need it. Contrary to their public relations efforts, we've demonstrated that crowdfunding platforms have created a shockingly unequal system of winners and losers. And that has emotional repercussions.

The Emotional Cost

Money is money and every little bit helps. Even if people don't meet their goals, the funds they do raise can make a difference. As stay-at-home mom Hannah from Texas told us, the money she raised (in large part through donations from Facebook shares) enabled her to pay for an emergency cancer screening. It wasn't all she needed, but it helped her detect her cancer and she beat it. Martha from Newfoundland said, "I didn't quite reach my goal but whatever is there, it helped. But I'm not going to be reposting it again and just keep continually begging people for money or waiting for those people who didn't see it in the first place to see it then. I'm not going to keep begging. . . . I just don't like the feeling of it. I don't like being the person to ask for money. I would so much rather give people money than ask for it." Small amounts were better than nothing, she said, in a voice saturated with emotion.

Adam, another Texan, was upbeat about his welfare crowdfunding experience, telling us: "It's actually made me feel hopeful there are good people out there that'll help." In Florida, Lorie recounted how she was glad she overcame her shyness to give welfare crowdfunding a try: "I was happily surprised and didn't really expect to get that much at that time. So yeah, it was a very good, positive experience." Julia, a New Yorker, said raising money was "uplifting because it was a fundraiser for my education, for me. I saw that every person donating was essentially investing in my future and saying that they believed that I could do something with that education. That was a nice feeling." And Martha insisted that her welfare crowdfunding campaign was not just about receiving money but about receiving support during the unprecedented hardship of the COVID-19 pandemic:

> That was probably the thing that helped me the most over the money, actually—the fact that people are willing to reach out and especially when everybody is having a hard time. Everybody was out of work, everybody's strained financially or physically or emotionally. So, it's not just a regular time on our planet when people are reaching out to help when everybody is working. This is a particularly odd time in our history. So . . . the fact that even during this time, they are able to reach out and help with words or financially or whatever, that was very touching.

Not a single donation is taken for granted. Our respondents typically appreciate the tangible and symbolic dimensions of every contribution and message that comes their way through crowdfunding.

Sean, the man who was incapacitated by serious testicular problems, became quite emotional during our interview. Marveling at the support he received, he wondered whether he deserved it:

> I still feel very unworthy of not just the donations, but [the] outpouring of support or whatever. I spent a lot of time thinking about who I am and what I've offered the world and the people around me.

Uplifting, hopeful, and touching. To be clear, all these people received some amount of financial support and their positivity was palpable. It felt good to hear, and it feels good to share. Yet the emotions spurred throughout the welfare crowdfunding process are complicated. Obviously, the small number of "winners" who bring in a lot of money feel good about their success. The donations help ease real burdens. Knowing people out there are willing to help provides its own significant boost. Unfortunately, though, the majority of welfare crowdfunders are unsuccessful and that creates a lot of bad feelings.

As we showed in the previous section, most people who try crowdfunding end up falling short. This failure forces them to grapple with complicated, largely negative emotions. Jeremy from Oregon wanted to raise funds to get a service dog for his autistic son. He raised just over $8,000 on GoFundMe. Pretty good money (based on our data, only about 15 percent of US health-care crowdfunding cases are as lucrative), but the average service dog costs between $30,000 and $50,000 and isn't covered by insurance. As Jeremy told us, "I want to help this boy, and I'm dead set on doing so, to the point that I'm going to put myself and my business out there for the world to see. That makes me feel. . . . It's confusing how it makes me feel. Embarrassed. Hopeful. Now that's pretty much done. I have no choice [but] to accept any embarrassment that might've come, because that's just kind of what it is."

Jeremy was blunt about the amount raised through crowdfunding: "I don't know how that's going to work." It's just not enough to meet their goal, but there's no way for Jeremy and his wife, each burning the candle at both ends, to bring in more money. The strain—and their efforts to get the bills paid—is clear when Jeremy says, "I wake up at 1:00 in the morning to go on duty at 3:00, to get home at 2:00, because mom goes to work at 2:30, because if we don't . . . then daycare is more than what I make." And the $8,000 didn't come free and easy. A local news program interviewed Jeremy at the start of his GoFundMe campaign. As he mentioned, he found it nerve-wracking to put his family's story "out there," and some of his worst fears had come true. Over a hundred "cruel and pretty mean" messages flooded onto his GoFundMe page and the news program's website: "Go to the dog pound and get a dog. You're stupid." "He needs his ass beat. Autism isn't even a thing." "You can go to the shelter and get an animal, and so what the fuck is your problem?" Frustrated and embarrassed but still in need, Jeremy tried reaching out to celebrities for help, but no one stepped up.

A young woman from Colorado told us: "We live in the United States, where health care isn't a right but a luxury for people who can afford it," describing crowdfunding for her father. "It was to try and earn money to help him out with the rising costs of health care. He has cancer. . . . I posted every day and begged everyone I knew for help. I got none and felt even more discouraged." The woman's goal was $1,000, and her campaign fell short.

Recall Mark, whom we introduced earlier as someone who had a terrible time with the entire experience of welfare crowdfunding. He said of his 2017 campaign, "My first attempt belly-landed." After the first week, "there hadn't been a single donation, and only my sister and one other person had shared it with anyone. So we just ended up giving up and taking it down." Several years later, Margaret, a local high school student, became aware of Mark's plight and offered to help. When she suggested they try GoFundMe again, Mark told us: "I'll be honest, I was not ready to do it again. Margaret's the one that really pushed the gas pedal down and said, 'Let's do this.' I was so dejected by the previous attempt."

When the second attempt languished, Mark was devastated. He and Margaret tried hard to get the word out via social media and other avenues, but by the time of our writing, their campaign had brought in a paltry $70. Mark felt unsupported and exhausted as he faced his disability:

> It's an awful thing to go through something this terrible. . . . You can't begin to comprehend the thousands of hours of just hellish, nightmarish symptoms that go along with an injury like this. It's difficult to put it into words. So, to go through all of that and then be told, "Well, you might not get any money, and you might not be able to start your life over, because you're not good enough at pitch marketing," it's insane. Nobody should be in that position.

Like a number of our respondents, Mark believes that something is wrong when people are put in positions like his. Few good emotions come out of such struggle.

In New York, a Latina respondent fundraising for a sick family member confided: "I want to sometimes just die. The stress level is massive and I often have sleepless nights." In Nevada, a woman who had only raised 10 percent of her goal amount told us: "We haven't had any real support or communication from anyone interested in trying to help, thus far. It has been quite disappointing honestly." And the niece of an elderly North Carolina cancer patient said of raising less than $1,000 toward her $25,000 goal: "It was all pretty much low because no one wanted to help her."

These stories, the sad ones that never get much happier, are no outliers. These are no isolated experiences. They're the norm. Welfare crowdfunders overwhelmingly feel despair, stress, anger, disappointment, discouragement, and sorrow. GoFundMe is indeed a well of sadness.

Fraud and Bad Behavior

GoFundMe is also a space for bad behavior. As with any kind of program involving lots of money, there's fraud. Occasional news stories reveal swindlers using the platforms, and a website called "GoFraudMe," created by Adrienne Gonzalez, accepts tips, investigates malfeasance, and reveals fraudsters (work Gonzalez does on a volunteer basis at night when she isn't working at her job for a beverage company).[14]

In one attention-grabbing instance that appeared in the media, a small community north of Manhattan came together to help a new resident in their midst. The woman, who had two teenage sons, told several prominent community members she had terminal cancer, and soon everyone was helping. There was a GoFundMe page and a spaghetti supper—and then there was an anonymous tip. The FBI got involved. The whole town had been fleeced. Far away in Detroit, another scammer was charged and sentenced to prison when she faked having breast cancer, raised more than $50,000 on GoFundMe, and then—when police began investigating and shut down her crowdfunding page—solicited direct donations via PayPal. Sometimes crowdfunding fraud is a sin of omission. When Oluwatoyin "Toyin" Salau, a Black Lives Matter activist in Florida, was sexually assaulted and later brutally murdered in 2020, a GoFundMe page popped up quickly. Just as swiftly, though, one of Toyin's friends publicly challenged it. Not only did the friend say the page creator "was not a friend of the family"; they requested that no one donate money to any of Toyin's family. Why? Because allegedly the same family members who stood to receive donations via GoFundMe had abused Toyin, forcing her out of her home and making her even more vulnerable. The page was subsequently taken down.[15]

Fraud stories bring suspicion down on legitimate welfare crowdfunding efforts. When asked about his crowdfunding experience, a young man from Illinois told us his low point: "When people think we're faking and don't want anything to do with us." It's hard enough to go through the whole crowdfunding experience without being doubted and distrusted when you share the deeply difficult reasons you need help.

Quentin Fottrell's advice column, *The Moneyist*, revealed another sticky situation—not fraud but a crowdfunding case in which scarce resources flowed to someone who didn't need them.[16] This person, nicknamed "Ask Before Funding Me" (Ask) in the column, had been in a terrible accident that left them comatose. While Ask was in the ICU in a coma, a friend set up a GoFundMe page. More than three hundred friends, family, and strangers quickly donated approximately $15,000. The problem, Ask wrote, was that "most of the expenses are covered by insurance and a couple months before that, I received almost $1 million from a relative. I had not told anyone about my good fortune nor made any purchases (yet!) that would indicate a change of status." Ask felt terrible and wasn't sure what to do. Fottrell advised giving all donations back. This particular case is truly unusual, but given that many crowdfunding appeals are crafted by people other than the beneficiaries, and that few of us have serious, in-depth conversations with others about our finances, misunderstandings are bound to happen.

We saw no evidence of widespread fraud in our data. In today's wired world, it's possible for people to triangulate data and verify stories. Plus, it isn't in the best interests of crowdfunding platforms to allow fraud—it undermines confidence and results in profit losses. But clearly some fraud exists. With a lack of oversight and transparency, it's possible to misrepresent yourself and create a scam. That's nothing new, though. Charity organizations and social work evolved in the nineteenth century in part to combat perceived fraud and malfeasance. What was to stop someone from knocking on doors to ask for money, telling the same story over and over? That there was little credible evidence that this was happening with any regularity was no match for the calls for oversight. To systematize the provision of help, charity organizations created central registries for the needy and sent volunteers ("friendly visitors") out to their homes to diagnose actual need. The "worthy" were given help. The point is that we've been here before, with needy folks asking for help from others directly, and we've rejected that model.[17] Yet to us the world of crowdfunding, with its weighing of worthiness, feels pretty similar to the unregulated world of nineteenth-century charity. It's clear to us that purposeful fraud isn't a significant part of welfare crowdfunding—most people then as now simply want help. But the presence of fraud does speak to the need for increased oversight.

Privacy and Profits

All of this—the good, the bad, and the ugly—is happening in the public eye. None of the crowdfunding experience is private. Once you launch an appeal, your story and situation are out there for all the world to see. In the sense that you need people to learn about your struggles and offer help, you *want* the world to see. But it can upend your social world and it can mean a lot of unpleasant emotions, including anxiety and disappointment. While Robert and Lisa exceeded their fundraising goal, according to Robert:

> I'm not comfortable. . . . I'm avoiding social situations. . . . what I haven't enjoyed about it is the publicity of it all—and it's good to give people updates and she has a million friends and people want to know what's going on, but it's just like a lot of people coming up to me in public that would have otherwise waved from across the store, you know what I mean?

Similarly, Krista from Montreal felt like she was living in a fishbowl:

> Asking for help is something I have even more struggle with than telling people about the health private details just because, I don't know, you sort of go through these insecurities of looking needy or not able to take care of yourself or irresponsible with your money or anything like that. . . . It sort of circles through your brain whenever you're allowing yourself to be vulnerable in a very public way.

Dana from Minnesota described feeling a mix of accountability and vulnerability when people who had donated to her campaign later asked, "So, what's going on with that?" As social beings, we spend much of our time thinking about what other people think of us and then altering our behavior to suit. Who we are is influenced by what we think others see in us. Charles Cooley called this the "looking-glass self."[18]

Crowdfunding turbocharges the instinct. Suddenly, some core elements of your existence are open to public comment and validation (or rejection). One Illinois respondent told us she tried to put up a barrier between her crowdfunding and her personal life: "I personalized my social media accounts where it was hard for strangers to find it." That's because welfare crowdfunding isn't just a matter of raising (or not raising) money. It's also about how we socially construct our sense of self. And, based on our data, the process is harmful to most. The public spectacle aspect of welfare crowdfunding is a significant concern. People are looking for help with the most intimate of problems, and they lose some of their dignity chasing an elusive and scant payout. We think this is problematic on its own.

We're also worried about the data that welfare crowdfunders and their donors freely and often unwittingly give to for-profit crowdfunding platforms. Millions of people use sites like GoFundMe, and along the way they reveal personal details that become the property of these platforms. This data is another way for corporations to turn a profit. It allows them to refine their services to squeeze out every last dollar. It helps them understand human behavior and bring more money through the digital door.

We have no idea what else this data might do for its new owners. GoFundMe, for example, certainly has profit-making plans. Its privacy statement makes clear that the company actively uses all the data it collects in order to make more money: "We use the information we collect to analyze data usage trends and preferences in order to improve the accuracy, effectiveness, security, usability or popularity of our Services." It's definitely keeping track of your computing behavior, including "the type of internet browser or mobile device you use, any website from which you have come to the Services, your operating system, and location data through an IP address that identifies the city and region where you logged into the Platform." Elsewhere, GoFundMe explicitly reveals that it may sell your data at some point in the future, at its discretion: "As we develop our business, we might sell or buy businesses or assets. In the event of a corporate sale, merger, reorganization, dissolution, similar event, or steps taken in anticipation of such events (e.g., due diligence in a transaction), user information may be part of the transferred assets."[19]

GoFundMe and other crowdfunding platforms also wrangle profits from tips and fees. You may remember that GoFundMe, which has a virtual monopoly on welfare crowdfunding, buries its tip mechanism in the crowdfunding process. As we write, the default tip amount is 15 percent; throughout our research, the amount and how it's asked for have shifted slightly, but the mechanism has stayed constant. As it reminds its users, "[We rely] on the generosity of donors like you to operate our service" and it doesn't charge fees to its fundraisers. So the tip, as we wrote in Chapter 3, is meant to be an extension of the donor's generosity. Yet it requires attention and extra steps for a donor to avoid accidental generosity—in our interviews, very few fundraisers or donors were aware of the default tipping, which suggests that many, many users never notice they've paid it. Your generosity is assumed and becomes the default. By our numbers, we believe tens of millions of dollars flow to GoFundMe per year through donor tips. Not bad. Further, GoFundMe passes along credit card and operating costs to customers in the form of transaction fees, taking an additional 3 percent or so from each donation, on top of the tip, depending on regional interchange fees.[20]

There's nothing inherently wrong with corporations turning a profit. It's what they're designed to do. Still, the vague language and presentation around tips feels a bit underhanded. It's part of a broader trend of "dark pattern" design—a subtly ominous term for a fairly insidious practice. Harry Brignull, a self-described UX (user experience) specialist, coined the term in 2010 to describe "tricks used in websites and apps that make you do things that you didn't mean to, like buying or signing up for something." The practice is everywhere now, and it's bad enough that *Consumer Reports* has created a website for you to report any "manipulative designs that impact real people." And the Federal Trade Commission published a report in 2022 expressing serious concerns about dark pattern practices. Dark pattern design takes advantage of our impatience—who among us hasn't clicked "agree" on an Apple or Amazon user agreement without actually reading it?—as well as our psychology.[21]

Lab research shows that dark patterns are effective at getting people (especially the less educated) to pay for things they might not otherwise.

It's a commonplace business practice as old as commerce, an expression of what Adam Smith called the "propensity to truck, barter, and trade" updated by technological advances. GoFundMe's tipping interface is an example of a dark pattern known as obstruction, where the option of tipping nothing is hidden away so that users must manually type in different numbers to avoid the default. It isn't illegal, but it feels intuitively unethical, particularly in welfare crowdfunding.[22]

Elisa gave a typical response when we asked about the tipping and transaction fees: "I knew that [the tipping process was] there, but I never really considered it. The fact that it's for-profit. . . . So, the people would say, 'Okay, I'm going to send you money,' and I would . . . get $94.16 or something like that. Obviously, they donated $100, right? And if I stopped to think about how much was going to GoFundMe, I [would think], 'Bye,' a little bit." Jeremy from Oregon, on the other hand, gave another common response: "Yes, it's a for-profit organization and I'm okay with that. If it was half of the proceeds, then I would [think], 'Whoa, hold on here. This is a little excessive.' But it's such a minor amount that I'm just fine with it."

Indeed, relying on transaction fees and donor tips is a brilliant system. GoFundMe only makes money from people who are making money (transaction fees) and from people who have money to give (donor tips). And the idea that it might profit from the personal data of users in the future is abstract compared with the pressing needs of the now. Welfare crowdfunders are focused on the donations coming in and the problems they're dealing with. GoFundMe might say that it's free (well, other than the transaction fees) for crowdfunders and that the company runs on donor tips. It all seems to add up, but we're doubtful that this tangle of profit and acquiescence, made possible by the corporatization of welfare fundraising, is the best way of helping.

Understanding Success

So now we know how GoFundMe, as a corporation, became a success. It's important to understand how companies make money, but we're focused on the people asking for help and it's time to get back to exploring how the small percentage of successful crowdfunders become successful.

Some success is tied to the profits GoFundMe stands to make. Like choosing contestants for *Queen for a Day*, it picks "winners" to feature on its site. Unless a potential donor knows the particular cause or person they're searching for, they end up using the "Discover" link to browse. That's where the company's choices of which campaigns to feature become self-fulfilling prophecies.

We spent countless hours browsing. It was rare in our three years of research to "discover" a cause that had raised zero dollars. All the pages shown to us were well-done, compelling, and on their way to meeting goals. The company stacks the deck in its favor.

As Susan Adams reports in *Forbes*, beyond promoting promising cases on the front page, members of GoFundMe's communications team—at one time led by a former senior communications advisor to President Obama—"filter through the flood of campaigns and pick the ones to amplify . . . pitch[ing] feel-good GoFundMe stories daily to national and local media and promot[ing] them on social channels." The platform is throwing its weight behind perceived "winners," which makes sense now that you understand how the company makes its money. Pages that are more likely to get donations are more likely to bring in lucrative tips. Chasing that 15 percent cut, it makes sense to back likely successes. That's good money.[23]

The GoFundMe Discover page is another example of dark patterns in website design. It's difficult to systematically search the platform. It's been designed this way. You can search and browse, but ultimately you see what GoFundMe wants you to see. And it's naïve to think that what they present isn't tied to profit-making.

A number of our respondents spoke as if their causes depended on the whims of fate. A Tennessee man fundraising for his sister's medical needs said with resignation, "In the end, all you can do is hope someone notices, or you get lucky and go viral which never really happened." What's overlooked is that, in addition to the structure of GoFundMe, there are particular social structures that combine to limit some and privilege others. Inequality isn't easy to see, whether in the "real world" or online, so we chalk up our outcomes to luck rather than call out the overlapping inequalities of race, class, gender, age, and social capital, as well as the digital divide that move some people to the front of the crowdfunding line. Handily for the status quo, those who have trouble getting help are socially conditioned to see themselves as "unlucky" rather than structurally disadvantaged.[24]

Along the way in this book, we've pointed out various practical elements that can lead to welfare crowdfunding success. We like the term used by one of our respondents, a "careful chemistry" that needs to happen for people to feel compelled to follow through and donate. A number of circumstances need to hold true at once to make the campaign resonate. To some extent, it seems like these conditions can be manufactured. The "marketability" of a page matters for crowdfunding success. Those with high-quality pictures and well-written copy typically do better. And we've talked extensively about how marketing yourself online requires digital skill and savvy. Those on the far side of the digital divide are probably out of the running on that one. Also, the specific nature of your problem or challenge can drive what help you get. Discrete and specific problems that can be directly solved by money seem to garner more donations.

Crowdfunding is a social media phenomenon: all of our stories hinge on the social ties of those trying to get help. The more connections you have, the more you hustle and tap into them; the more resources your social contacts have to give, the more money you're likely to raise.[25] This isn't rocket science. Our respondents certainly knew this. "I mean, it depends on your contacts, on your community, your friends and everyone that's around you," said John from Montreal. "It is not what you know, it is who you know," added Lucas from British Columbia. "I guess it would depend on their connections and how they share it. Someone with 10 friends probably isn't going to get very far when they try crowdfunding," said Henry from Texas with the certainty of someone who knows he's right.

Donors, like a platform's profit mechanisms, aren't the prime focus of the book, but they're undoubtedly part of the social media–related success or failure of welfare crowdfunding. When you follow a link to a GoFundMe page, pop-ups say things like "Help by sharing" and, as we mentioned, "Fundraisers shared on social networks raise up to 5x more." The page doesn't say where that number comes from, but it sounded about right to our respondents. When a Colorado woman and her family teamed up and exceeded their fundraising goal of $10,000 to benefit a friend dealing with domestic violence injuries, she correctly said, "Luckily I have a rather large social media network where friends shared and donated." In Washington State, Sherice explained the magic of social media and crowdfunding to us:

> With being able to share it on Facebook and other social media platforms, it's a really easy way to get the word out . . . our world is so online and internet nowadays. . . . It's a way for people to not feel pressured, it's not [that] you're asking someone face to face or contacting them directly and saying, "Will you donate?" It's more of an anonymous platform where someone can not feel pressured, and they can donate if they want to.

Social media is a space that warps distance and proximity. You have an immediate connection to others through it, and you maintain that connection through an electronic device from a physical distance. Sidestepping the exposure and pressure of a more dynamic face-to-face encounter, an online ask can feel easier and it can spread like wildfire. Eloise from Texas was astonished: "I put it on my Facebook page and then I had some family members share it. . . . I got people that I didn't even know to donate to my GoFundMe." In New York, Matthew was pleasantly surprised at the spread of his campaign too: "Everybody who had actually spoken to me about it, or done something with the Facebook posts that I had used to spread awareness of it was supportive. So if they couldn't donate, or if they saw it they would share it, or they would reach out and say, 'Hey, I can't, but I shared it.'"

Research shows that the majority of crowdfunding donors are the friends and family of beneficiaries, though an estimated third of donations come from individuals the crowdfunder doesn't know. By and large, donors aren't wealthy—nearly half have household incomes below $60,000 per year.[26] A review of thousands of donor comments corroborates our interview data: at least half of donations come from family and friends. Who you know matters for crowdfunding, and friends and family do a lot of the heavy lifting.

But it's also clear that you need to go beyond your strong network ties to get at the other half of the potential donor pool, those weak ties we talked about earlier in the book. Rishi from Pennsylvania said his friend's donors really stepped up: "They were all the university students who were new for the fall semester. . . . All the money he received from his friends. While being a grad student, you know how they work in one lab? So they make friends in that lab. So all those lab members also helped him a lot." Interestingly, Rishi implied that his friend's donations *didn't* come from family members but from fellow graduate students living on tight budgets. This is a really tricky situation. We know our own world of friends and family. Think of yours. You probably know which people you think would help you out if you were in need. When the reality doesn't match those expectations, you can be left with a mix of emotions. Jeremy from Oregon felt a bit overwhelmed seeing where his donations came from:

> My heart almost breaks and I almost feel bad that people are giving, and I know that's the point of GoFundMe. But what I've found to be very interesting is a lot of family and friends have given. I know how these people are doing in their life, whether they're doing pretty well for themselves or they're barely making things work. What I've come to realize is the people that were barely making things work were the first ones to give. The ones that have [money] to give, have not. . . . I have a different mindset towards these individuals. I don't know, good or bad, it just kind of puts things into perspective [regarding] who your true friends are, if that makes any sense.

Fair or not, donations become a proxy for friendship and loyalty in the minds of some crowdfunders. That complicates feelings when you learn who your "true friends are" on top of an already difficult situation.

Donations that come from anonymous people or unfamiliar names are consistently surprising to crowdfunders, though they can be impactful. In Alberta, Elisa told us about receiving a donation from someone outside her network: "She gave me $500 and I [thought], 'I don't even know who you are,' and she [said,] 'I've had cancer before.' She came across [my page] on GoFundMe and she just [thought], 'I need to pay it forward.'" It must have felt like luck or magic to Elisa. Others noticed donors with whom they had ties but distant ones. Taylor from Utah said of her donor pool, "It ended up being the majority of . . . my coworkers. But because we work from our homes, I've never met any of these people other than on Facebook. . . . And so it ended up being mostly people we've never met in person, but who know my name and my family from our work trade pages on Facebook."

In our interviews, we heard that asking friends, acquaintances, and strangers for money through social media usually feels easier than asking them in person. Crowdfunders we studied still had very different tolerances for how far they were willing to go in their asks. Martha from Newfoundland was reluctant when her sister created a GoFundMe campaign to help her after her breast cancer diagnosis: "I despised the idea of putting it out there and saying, 'Can you please help me?'" It was hard enough to think about telling anyone beyond close friends and family about the diagnosis, let alone posting it on Facebook. She went along with the campaign, but after sharing it once and getting some donations (but not meeting the campaign goal), she refused to continue. Martha felt a visceral aversion to asking people for money, online or otherwise: "Ugh, I just don't like the idea."

Dana, who works at a Minnesota nonprofit, had a very different approach. She had been discouraged by previous attempts to use crowdfunding for community initiatives, but when a youth education program at a local high school needed money, she gave it another try. By this time, she had learned that she couldn't just put the campaign up and hope for the best, so she decided on a new strategy. She would contact twelve people she personally knew and who, given their jobs, wouldn't have a problem donating a few hundred dollars each. Jump-started by her in-person and telephone appeals, Dana's crowdfunding campaign soon took off and the money came together, largely on the back of her personal network. In this case, she was able to engineer some of that "careful chemistry" to get noticed and succeed.

The strategy someone uses to crowdfund—if they have a strategy, that is—certainly depends on what they're raising money for and whether it's for themselves or someone else. Each comes with a different level of discomfort, mediated by individual tolerance for putting themselves out there, often in a desperate circumstance, and asking personal contacts to donate.

Donors, it must be said, are crucial. They make up the "crowd" and provide the "funding." Knowing who they might be can help welfare crowdfunders, like professional fundraisers, become more strategic about seeking help. But it doesn't matter who the donors are if you can't reach them. You may be ineligible to crowdfund because of your citizenship status, or you may be staring across a yawning digital divide, or you may be blocked because of your social position and networks. The welfare crowdfunding machine allows only a select population to reach out to donors, and an even smaller population will have any success when they do.

In any case, most people don't end up mining a rich vein. Brenda from Florida reminded us of the emotional consequences of a crowdfunding effort, including for her self-image: "It definitely makes me concerned, worried, stressed, anxious, and upset that some people get so lucky. . . . Is it because they're a social influencer or something, that they just had a lot more followers and it was doable for them? I'm just not as recognized or noticed in this world." Sure, some people have plenty of friends and relatives willing to broadcast their campaigns across social networks, but even then their success hinges on whether their friends and family (and their friends and family) have resources to spare. If your friends are broke, there's nothing in the vein to mine. We end up right back at persistent inequality—inequality in network resources is reproduced as inequality in crowdfunding success.[27] Brenda asked plaintively, "How do you have such a successful fundraiser when you're not so known?" The short answer is: You don't.

Helping a Select Few

There are pockets of joy in welfare crowdfunding. You only have to think back to the support Robert and Lisa received from friends, family, and strangers. Looking over our data, talking with people who sought and sometimes got the help they needed through crowdfunding, we're left with the inescapable sense that this is like the *Hunger Games*, where patron-sponsored parachutes drop down with lifesaving supplies but you're still locked in a death match. We love Taylor Swift,[28] but when you're struggling, should you have to wish for a pop star to be your fairy godmother?

This may seem overly dramatic. But recall that after removing out-liers, only 17 percent of Canadian and 12 percent of American crowd-funders make their goal. This means that somewhere in the range of 80 to 90 percent come up short (often by a mile).

The welfare crowdfunding process on GoFundMe privileges a select few. Those at the top, the highest-earning 5 percent of campaigns, claim more than half of all fundraising dollars. The successful often receive a boost from GoFundMe when they're featured by the platform. Pro-motion leads to more visibility and donations, which lead to more tip income and profits for GoFundMe. But this can't happen for every cause. The select few with more robust social networks and marketing know-how rise to the top; the others languish at the bottom. Overlapping real-world inequalities seep in, resulting in the campaign earnings on Go-FundMe being more unequal than incomes in any country in the world. The cost of failure is as high as its incidence. Those who "fail" are over-whelmed by despair, stress, anger, disappointment, discouragement, and sorrow. They gave up time and privacy to put their problems in front of the public and got little or nothing for their trouble—unless you count all the awful feelings. Heck, the data on their suffering becomes the property of GoFundMe, which can use it to make profits in the future.

If welfare crowdfunding is so bad, why do so many people do it? It turns out sociologists have long understood this dynamic. As individu-als, we tend to look down at our shoes and ignore the bigger social forces swirling around us. C. Wright Mills wrote about this in his pioneering book *The Sociological Imagination*. We see our actions and our troubles as personal, of our own making, and we don't link them to larger structures or understand them as public problems. For example, if we can't get a job, we tell ourselves we're at fault rather than the structure of the econ-omy and the biases of hiring managers. So rather than try to address systemic bias or pursue social change, we work hard to solve our own problems. And when we can't—when our GoFundMe campaigns fail, for instance—we say, "It's us, not them." Discussing *Queen for a Day*, scholar Susan Douglas suggests that Americans in particular like to think that any person can be helped and any problem can be fixed.[29] We don't want to believe that people are trapped in their social circumstances, utterly tied to the whims of profit-seeking corporations and their feel-good slogans; instead we opt for the less realistic but sunnier worldview in which people who work hard win.

Welfare crowdfunding today feels a lot like *Queen for a Day*. It makes for great entertainment, but it might not be our best expression of how to help each other in our society. The crowdfunding platforms love it, of course, because welfare crowdfunding is a massively profitable venture. The rest of us are right to be a bit unsettled. When GoFundMe and other sites crown queens (and kings), those people's lives may be materially and demonstrably bettered. For every person crowned, though, there are many, many more runners-up. Social responsibility demands that we find practical ways to move forward and help these people too.[30]

Five

What to Know Better, Do Better, Help Better

What are we to do with a system that feels more like a game show than a process for truly helping those in need? Can we do better?

In this concluding chapter, we ask and answer this question, offering some possible paths forward. By revisiting our findings, we isolate and emphasize the massive potential and positive contributions of welfare crowdfunding. We also underscore the significant problems we've uncovered in for-profit welfare crowdfunding. Throughout, we urge you to consider what you might do if *your* partner needed surgery but insurance refused to cover it, or if *you* got into your dream school's most selective program but couldn't afford the tuition. These are ordinary misfortunes that most of us will face in our lifetimes. Tornadoes level towns, medical bills add up to bankruptcies, opportunities are too big for our budgets. Regardless of all you've read in the previous chapters, it's quite possible you'd turn to the internet. Most people can get access to a computer, tablet, or phone, either at home or at a local library. Appeals can be made from home, and stories of need—ones just like yours—can spread quickly. It doesn't cost much to crowdfund—just a little bit of time. And haven't we all heard about someone getting thousands of dollars through crowdfunding? *Why not?* you think. *What do I really have to lose?*

The Potential and Problems of Welfare Crowdfunding

This book isn't a call for scrapping welfare crowdfunding. It's here, it's impactful, and it's enormously popular. Nearly 20 percent of Americans gave to a health-care crowdfunding campaign in 2020.[1] Crowdfunding has become part of our culture, so let's lean in and consider its benefits first.

Hope is a major selling point. When you use crowdfunding, there is a sense at the start that you might get help, that things might get better. This is powerful. And while our analysis of nearly 2 million crowdfunding campaigns created in the US and Canada between 2018 and 2021 turned up fewer than 300,000 (or about 17 percent) that met or exceeded their stated goal, and the average campaign closed after bringing in less than one-third of its original ask, the vast majority of crowdfunders make *something*. The median welfare crowdfunding campaign brings in at least $1,000, which is nothing to scoff at. At the same time, some people make *a lot* of money using crowdfunding. The top 5 percent of highest-earning campaigns in our dataset made over $12,500. The top 1 percent topped $35,500, and the top 0.1 percent—roughly 1,700 in the period we cover—brought in more than $120,000. That's a lot of helping in absolute terms, and it might not have arrived without crowdfunding.[2]

Obviously, the small number of winners feel good, and that too is one for the pro column. The financial support helps ease real burdens, and knowing people out there are willing to help is a real lift.

A third win for welfare crowdfunding is that it streamlines and simplifies the process of getting help. As Xavier, whom we introduced in the Introduction, put it, "it's something that was not there before, and if that platform [weren't] there, I mean, it [would] be much harder . . . asking for help or anything like that." Adam from Texas agreed: "It's easier to have something you can click on if you want to donate money and it can get transferred and go over right then, instead of calling somebody that's 200, 300 miles away and having to explain over the phone and *then* asking." The process highlights the best the internet has to offer: instant communication to millions of potential donors, with pictures, videos, and text providing information transparently. This is such a far cry from the days of knocking on doors with hat in hand.

GoFundMe can be a stage for showing and building the good in us. Helping others is heartwarming and infectious. The incredible potential of our family, friends, and community to step up and reach out is there for all the world to see. Connecting with others through acts of kindness and care can create a more durable and democratic fabric that provides resilience for our society during times of strain. People helping people can be contagious and lead to other good social behavior. In this positive aspect, we see the democratic promise of the internet in the "habits of the heart" it facilitates (see Chapter 4) and the transparency it brings to the need in our communities and the helpers around us. You can see who gets help, how much, and from whom. It's possible to get some sense of an individual's plight and if necessary verify it with some digging. This is a good thing if we want to foster trust and reciprocity. And it can build empathy and the impetus to fight inequality online and off.

Perhaps GoFundMe has done our society a service. It serves as a diagnostic tool, showing us our problems and neutralizing some of the stigma of asking for help. If it actually does teach us that everyone is vulnerable to an array of setbacks, GoFundMe suggests that the individualistic American narrative that says you're a moral failure if you need the government's help has always been a red herring, a way to divide us and keep us from demanding that governments do more. In this way, GoFundMe's existence and popularity implore support for a broader social safety net.

Like the vase between the faces in the famous optical illusion, GoFundMe's welfare campaigns are a negative-space portrait of our countries' teetering health-care and education "industries," a repository for the costs that students, patients, and underwriters can't or won't cover on their own.[3] Government "welfare" in both Canada and the US is usually given to people invisibly—their stories and life circumstances remain outside public scrutiny—but recipients are nonetheless stigmatized and subject to callous stereotypes. Mindful of this, many of our interview participants talked of the shame of having to ask for help. GoFundMe does away with privacy and, when it works, gives aid in a highly visible manner. It shows us who needs help, what their struggles actually look like, and how close we may be to needing help ourselves.

GoFundMe lifts the veil of secrecy covering the struggles of families across North America and helps us see how shared our vulnerabilities really are. What we see is that many of those who ask for help using crowdfunding are seemingly successful and middle class, defying the stereotypes and assumptions of who struggles and who asks for help. GoFundMe has laid bare the widespread insecurity of Americans and Canadians in the contemporary economy, and we hope this will create greater appreciation for the fact that most of us, even when we've made all the "right" choices in life, are financially vulnerable. Scandinavia's flourishing universal welfare states work in part because they have the support of the middle classes who see themselves as also benefiting from services that maintain high living standards, received in return for high taxes, thus creating a broader coalition of support for such policies. Along these lines, we hope that welfare crowdfunding creates a greater recognition of the shared economic risk borne by Americans and Canadians and inspires new efforts to explore alternative, public solutions to mitigating such risk.

We're sincere when it comes to the good in GoFundMe. But the good is inescapably outweighed by all the problems we've traced to its current iteration. To start, digital acumen and access determine whether or not some people can use GoFundMe. Once you know about the digital divide, you can't overlook its consequences for those on the far side of it.

Millions of people are also shut out of crowdfunding because of their immigration status, though we know that undocumented workers perform some of the economy's most dangerous jobs and form the backbone of the supply chains that keep goods and services flowing. Few have insurance, few make even minimum wage (and many experience wage theft), few have any formal education. As we wondered in the Introduction, does anyone *really* believe there is no way around these access issues? Churches and immigrant aid groups seem to be able to provide undocumented workers with financial and material help regardless. And it's not beyond our countries' abilities to digitally connect our populations (rural electrification campaigns of the past stand as evidence). If GoFundMe is going to continue as a major vehicle for getting help, we need to think seriously about unequal access.

Additional, significant inequalities accrue when we actually dig into the system of welfare crowdfunding for those who can access it in the United States and Canada. The digital divide, that is, doesn't end at internet *access* but continues into people's *differing ability to effectively use the internet* when they do have access.[4] Race, age, and social capital, as well as technological and marketing skills, largely determine whether or not you succeed. Older people, those who aren't White, and those lacking the necessary skills and connections just don't do as well. This points to inequalities in social network access and technical skills and perhaps also to discrimination in this new online marketplace. There is a disconnect between the assurances given by crowdfunding platforms that anyone can raise money using them and the reality that only a small fraction of funding campaigns ultimately meet their goals.

White people dominate and minority groups are underrepresented among welfare crowdfunders. For example, Whites make up 73 percent of Canada's population and approximately 85 percent of health-care GoFundMe appeals, while Asians respectively account for 15 percent and 5 percent. In the US, Indigenous groups are 1.5 percent of the population but only 0.5 percent of cases in our welfare crowdfunding data. The Whiteness of GoFundMe should be a concern for anyone who believes in racial equality and social justice.

Inequalities exist beyond race and ethnicity. We might expect seniors to be overrepresented in health-care crowdfunding, relative to their share of the population, because of their greater demand for health care combined with the likelihood of their having a low income. Instead, we find the opposite. Seniors are disproportionately underrepresented, likely because of the digital divide and weaker social media "marketing" skills. Based on our data, welfare crowdfunding is primarily a tool of those who are relatively privileged in terms of age, class, race, social capital, and so forth. Privilege shouldn't determine who gets to ask for help and who doesn't.

The determinants of success continue to tip the scales toward the relatively privileged once a campaign is launched. For instance, the problems that drive you to seek help may make it harder for you to craft the high-quality appeal that tends to succeed. Even if an undocumented immigrant could ask for help on GoFundMe, they might have trouble telling an organized, tearjerker of a story with passable spelling and punctuation in English. Or a person struggling to pay medical bills might not be able to afford a cell phone that takes high-quality photos (or have the tech to make sharing them straightforward). Photos and stories matter for fundraising success, but it's easy to forget that they aren't available to everyone.

Those with weaker and less robust social networks are not as successful at crowdfunding either. This is a problem, as social ties vary by race, class, gender, geography, and a host of other social factors. There is inequality in the social networks that form one cornerstone of welfare crowdfunding.

From a campaign's inception to its often disappointing close, inequality is central to welfare crowdfunding. The money ultimately raised is a result of three things: our personal advantages and disadvantages, the choices we make throughout the process, and, well, luck. How donor dollars are ultimately spread out across campaigns lets us see how different sources of advantage and disadvantage add up, as well as key tendencies in big-picture crowdfunding operation.

The unequal distribution of crowdfunding dollars is jaw-dropping. We broke it down in a granular way in Chapter 4, finding that the level of inequality in funds raised among campaigns on GoFundMe would rank at the top of a list of the world's most unequal countries. The bottom 50 percent of all campaigns received 5 percent of all dollars raised in our study period. Tallying the bottom 75 percent still adds up to just about one-fifth of the funding total. Meanwhile, an astounding concentration of funds accrues to a very small group of campaigns. The tiniest sliver, the roughly 160 fundraisers in the top one-hundredth of one percent (making over $508,000) earned *over 5 percent* of all funds. In terms of hard numbers, median health-care campaign fundraising is $1,900; median education campaign fundraising is $600. However, the average respective goals are $7,400 and $3,000. People are getting help but rarely as much as they need.

Getting the help you need through GoFundMe is unlikely. As a Tennessee crowdfunder told us: "in the end all you can do is hope someone notices, or you get lucky and go viral, which never really happened." This is in part due to a fair bit of behind-the-scenes manipulation by the platform. Algorithms bring bias into supposedly neutral decision-making, and GoFundMe's are no exception. They help pick winners and losers and contribute to a sensation of riding an emotional rollercoaster. GoFundMe promotes cases that will bring in the most donations and consequently provide the most revenue. What a way to run a system meant to help people.

In the end, the feelings our interviewees and survey respondents expressed about the whole experience correlated with the outcomes of their campaigns. Most campaigns don't succeed, and most crowd-funders end up feeling bad. They blame themselves. Why? Because our society teaches us to blame ourselves for any lack of success. Welfare crowdfunding dresses us up, and then we have nowhere to go. In this respect, we're concerned that the negative emotions and the sense that we have no control over what will happen—which are enormous parts of welfare crowdfunding—may increase our "learned helplessness."[5]

GoFundMe users may walk away with a bitter taste in their mouth, though GoFundMe's owners and investors are probably delighted because their operation is incredibly successful and highly profitable. This is in large part because of its tip mechanism and what's known as dark design. As Rachel Monroe noted in the *Atlantic*, it's an unusual practice to tip a corporation, but GoFundMe makes a big deal out of the fact that it doesn't charge fees to its fundraisers (well, other than a processing fee taken from each donation). That builds goodwill that can make tipping on top of donating feel like a double good—*we're so generous!* The bigger problem is that our respondents and their donors, assuming they knew about the tipping at all, usually thought that GoFundMe was a nonprofit, which certainly made the tip more palatable.[6]

A second profit driver is GoFundMe's sneaky practice of picking campaigns to feature on its home page, in its searches, on its Discover page, and on its own social media. The algorithms promote already fairly successful campaigns to the front page, where strangers come across them and make them go viral. It's not about the cream rising to the top, at least not in the way we might imagine it. Home page features aren't the neediest causes, but, through opaque choices they turn out to be those already raising blockbuster sums (thus bringing in huge profits to GoFundMe). It's not unlike a bouncer letting famous, attractive, and stylish people cut the line while the rest of us wait outside. The company's choices become self-fulfilling prophecy and profits spiral upward.

The value of the data freely provided to platforms like GoFundMe by welfare crowdfunders and their donors is incalculable, though privacy statements make it clear that the platforms intend to monetize that data if the opportunity comes up. From addresses to pictures of patients in hospital beds, the data supplied belongs to them, whether or not a campaign earns a dime. We don't think we need do more to explain to you why this is concerning and probably shouldn't be part of our system of helping others.

Charity and Cultural Conundrums

Many of the problems with GoFundMe are deeply rooted in welfare crowdfunding's origins. Recall that crowdfunding was originally an efficiency-seeking market tool for funding innovative ideas. That market logic stayed embedded when crowdsourcing inspired crowdfunding. Profits and helping don't mix, however. The logic and principles of the former are antithetical to social citizenship and basic social welfare. Companies like GoFundMe are not the natural outcome of helping's evolution but the result of intentional decisions aimed at maximizing capital. And we can't believe they're the best expression of the potential of the internet or the "crowd."

Meanwhile, crowdfunding promotes the already American idea that individualized charity is the solution to problems that in fact are much bigger than the individual. The stories we see on GoFundMe draw attention away from our systemic problems and toward the idea that our inability to meet basic costs is the result of not marketing ourselves well enough—a failure to hustle, not a failure of democratic policymaking.[7] It's possible that the individual accounts of suffering laid bare in crowdfunding campaigns may open more eyes to the extent of hardship in our societies and spur community organizing, yet the faulty solutions crowdfunding provides make us suspect they do more harm than good.

Mind you, it's not a coincidence that people in western democracies like the US and Canada believe they bear individual responsibility for their well-being. Governments and companies have encouraged us, *taught* us to think this way. Since the 1980s, governments around the world have chipped away at the strength of public services through economic policies favoring privatization and deregulation. In this way, they've reduced their role in the economy and society and increased the role of business. Such large-scale economic and social policy changes—most closely associated with Ronald Reagan in the US and Margaret Thatcher in the UK—fall under the banner of neoliberalism, which shifts risk to the individual: it's up to us to sink or swim, and asking the government to provide help is downright impudent. *Don't want to be bankrupted by medical bills? Buy some insurance or stop whining!*

The consequences of neoliberalism are still dramatic today, mediated by Canada's relative generosity when it comes to social supports as well as the ways companies are allowed to take advantage of the gaps left by retrenchment. This is illustrated, for instance, by the rise of the so-called gig economy—jobs stripped of benefits and worker protections and sold as ways to earn as much as you want, to be your own boss, to chart your own path. Corporations thus make operations cheaper, responsibilities lighter, and risk anything but their problem. Welfare crowdfunding follows this individualist hustle philosophy in meeting some of our most basic needs. In this sense, we need to think of GoFundMe alongside companies like Uber, Lyft, and DoorDash, which ask us to be entrepreneurs for our own well-being.

Short-Term Changes

The promise of today's digital world is that we can fix almost any problem with internet access and the right software. From that perspective, welfare crowdfunding makes sense. It's just that it's inadequate to meet our needs. This is a social problem we can't ignore. Maybe, though, we can fix it, reconstruct it, take it apart, and put it back together with some tweaks here and there to help it do its job better.[8] To begin this reconstruction, we have to tear down a lot. From the start, we have to reject the idea that crowdfunding failures are due to personal shortcomings rather than problems with the system itself. The "pull yourself up by your bootstraps" mentality of nineteenth-century charity was cruel and ineffective then and remains so now. On the basis of our data, what would we say otherwise? *We know you're fighting cancer, but could you possibly get more friends or learn Photoshop or be your own brand?*

Still, we believe there are some short-term, fast-acting changes that will make things better. Our book is part of an effort to get under the hood of GoFundMe and other crowdfunding platforms, but we need a lot more. Watchdogs like *Consumer Reports* might build on their dark pattern monitoring to provide honest and unbiased information on how sites like GoFundMe actually work. This would likely dissuade many potential users, but it would also discourage the public from thinking of the underlying social problems behind individual need as best solved by individual solutions. GoFundMe itself could provide outside researchers like us greater access to its operations. We urge GoFundMe to create an API (Application Programming Interface) that would make it easier for researchers to pull data for analysis, as one exists for Twitter and which scholars use to study social phenomena like the spread of fake news. GoFundMe, like Twitter, could generate tremendous goodwill—no matter how regularly Twitter is blamed for the political and social problems of the day, it's lauded for having shared its information with scholars and the public, and its valuation has done fine to boot.[9] What are you waiting for, GoFundMe? This is an easy fix that would make it possible for researchers and the general public to have a more accurate sense of what you're offering prospective crowdfunders.

Government oversight should be increased significantly as well. Around the globe, governments are summoning the CEOs of tech companies like Google, Meta, Amazon, and Apple to account for allegedly monopolistic practices that harm consumers. Let's add GoFundMe to the list given that they're profiting off the public's problems. Speaking of which, it's possible the only thing that will motivate companies like GoFundMe to change is a threat to their profit margins. What is the quickest and simplest way to get their attention? Boycott. If you can't boycott, change your behavior as a donor. Stop tipping. If donors stop donating and/or tipping, GoFundMe will take immediate notice. Donors can also comment when they give, telling the platform its current system isn't equitable and asking for greater transparency. We know that GoFundMe has detailed information about crowdfunders' success and lots of data about individual users because they selectively shared some of it in the past. If GoFundMe is serious about trying to help—as its executives have claimed in op-eds and interviews decrying the popularity of health-care crowdfunding—and serious about its bottom line, it will embrace the opportunity to actively help connect more people to more money and enjoy the good press that comes of the change.[10]

We often forget that the internet isn't literally "in the cloud" or some autonomous force buzzing over our heads. The internet reaches us through physical cables and switches, and our data is stored on computers in physical data centers. In writing this book, we've brought the internet back down to earth. We've introduced many of the real people inside the "well of sadness." We've also mapped welfare crowdfunding and shown how it happens in real places. We tend to forget these connections while swiping and scrolling our way through digital space, but making it all concrete shows that we can and should make these spaces work for people in ways they currently don't.

For instance, there's obvious bias in the way the GoFundMe machine operates. The solution? Make the system more equitable by reorienting the algorithms.[11] The evidence in this book (and elsewhere) shows that GoFundMe isn't equitable, but its algorithms could be redesigned to promote campaigns that benefit floundering members of marginalized groups. How about it, GoFundMe? Why not get rid of the sneaky behind-the-scenes stuff on your platform?

If GoFundMe turns some of its central, individualist questions on itself—*How can we take control and become our best self?*—it may find fruitful avenues forward. Its current strategy is diverting some profits to charity via its separate charitable organization (GoFundMe.org). This is what it calls developing society's "giving layer."[12] This layer is pretty damn thin, and in our view it's a smokescreen. It's time to change the way the *for-profit* machine runs. It might help GoFundMe's stakeholders to stay true to their stated principles.

In a similar vein, GoFundMe could easily address the lack of access for undocumented immigrants. If you don't have legal status, you can't crowdfund through GoFundMe, which self-describes as the "world's largest social fundraising platform." And we know that the undocumented in our society are some of the neediest. It wouldn't be difficult to partner with charitable organizations to promote a fund for undocumented immigrants and feature it on its main page. GoFundMe could still take its cut through fees and tips while making sure those who can't access their services can still benefit.

We can also focus immediate energy on closing the digital divide, particularly in rural areas. Not just so more people can crowdfund but so they can access essential parts of society. We learned the importance of internet access during the pandemic as schools closed their doors and moved instruction online. Stories of kids without access sitting in library parking lots to get Wi-Fi or getting homework printouts delivered by school buses do not speak well of our infrastructure. According to a recent estimate, more than one-third of households in Baltimore are without high-speed internet.[13] How can we expect all people to compete in the race of life if the starting line is not the same for everyone? This is an issue of distributive justice. With political will, we can build digital infrastructure and provide low-cost internet access to those who need it.

Big Fixes

So far, what we've talked about are Band-Aids. Real change needs to move beyond government hearings and come through government action or changes in the nonprofit sector. Our social history isn't marked by major social welfare changes brought about by private-sector, market-based solutions but rather by moments when we realize that we need more than what the market provides. Somewhat surprisingly, Tim Cadogan, the CEO of GoFundMe, agrees, writing in an op-ed that "our platform was never meant to be a source of support for basic needs."[14]

Nora Kenworthy, a top scholar of health-care crowdfunding, points us to Audre Lorde's words: "The master's tools will never dismantle the master's house." That is, relying on existing structures (particularly those created by business) is not the way to solve pressing social problems. As we explained earlier, the crowdfunding model wasn't created to connect personal struggles to financial help. It was about streamlining business solutions and boosting profits. There are good reasons that we have Medicaid and Provincial health plans and public education. The free market won't provide them on its own, despite their inherent value. Journalist Moya Lothian-McLean writes in *The Guardian*: "Although private philanthropy can complement state support systems, it should never be plugging holes that were once filled by the welfare state. Victorian paternalism is a relic of our past that belongs in academic journals. Trickle-down charity didn't lift the poor of the 19th century, deserving or not, out of poverty, and it's not about to start doing so 200 years later. Those in need deserve much more than the fluctuating whims of charitable benefactors."[15] It didn't work then, and it doesn't work now.

Again, we aren't calling for an end to GoFundMe or for banishing crowdfunding from the internet. Even if that were possible, the most direct way to deal with financial need would be to give people money. (This is why pandemic stimulus payments were so consequential for child poverty.) But there's a problem when this becomes a private rather than a public function. In the US, where crowdfunding has become a backbone of social support, it's damning that the process is inequitable and only helps the better-off among those in need. If instead we fix the underlying circumstances that drive people to crowdfunding, the practice can flourish as a way to fund the optional things in life, like a business venture (as on the platforms Kickstarter and Indiegogo). GoFundMe's practices would be a lot less problematic if, say, a third of its campaigns weren't to fund life-saving medical care.

If we're pretty sure that the market, left to its own devices, won't solve the problem, we might look to promote mutual aid groups. This is a catch-all term for extra-market alternatives to GoFundMe—both volunteer and more organized community efforts to help fellow members of society. As legal scholar Dean Spade puts it, "Mutual aid . . . is based on a shared understanding that the crises we are facing are caused by the system that we're living under, and are worsened by those systems. Mutual aid focuses on helping people get what they need right now, as we work to get to the root causes of these problems." The dynamic is no longer one of the better-off giving to the needy. Mutual aid is nonhierarchical and typically happens at the neighborhood, street, block, or even building level. We saw the rise of mutual aid groups during the pandemic, and they made a difference.[16] We could tap into this zeitgeist and involve mutual aid societies in crowdfunding in their communities.

Jane Addams, the Nobel laureate who founded and operated Hull House in nineteenth-century Chicago, is seen as the mother of social work. She knew how to help people. We're big fans of Addams and think her work might show us how to do a better job of helping each other today. Addams saw neighborhood relations as key, writing that we could only figure out what to do and how to do it by "mixing on the thronged and common road where all must turn out for one another, and at least see the size of one another's burdens."[17] In your own life, you likely have a pretty good sense of what your neighbor across the hall or down the street needs—you've seen her and exchanged pleasantries for years. And if you haven't, it might be time to get acquainted. Locally situated mutual aid based on ties with neighbors can be powerful in providing a nongovernmental, nonmarket direction for channeling our crowdfunding enthusiasm.

Recent history shows that government can and should step in to make a major, immediate difference in terms of social need. The various relief plans offered by Canada and the United States during the 2008 financial crisis and the COVID-19 pandemic kept many terrible situations from getting even worse. The idea here is to "go big" with policy changes, reducing need by adding government support. People standing on a solid foundation of basic support are less likely to need welfare crowdfunding (but more likely to get it, as our data showed). With legislative action, we can lower the rates of crowdfunding in the US and Canada to levels observed in the eighteen other countries where GoFundMe operates. Of course, less demand for the product that crowdfunding platforms provide isn't good for business. But it's good for society, where capitalism collides with the public good.

In the US in particular, distrust of the government is a hurdle. We've been socialized to prefer slick, market-based solutions over legislative and regulatory wrangling, just as we've been trained to figure out what a bootstrap is rather than demand basic protections. Given this, perhaps we should look to the public-private partnership known as Obamacare (the Affordable Care Act), which brought private insurance under greater government purview without entirely undoing it. Obamacare has been wildly popular—more so since the coronavirus began its ominous spread—like most programs whose benefits people get used to, enjoy, and as constituents ultimately support.[18] Perhaps something similar can be done with donations, where people have some control but government regulation ensures equitable outcomes?

Creating a federal emergency help fund that taxpayers could tap into a few times over the course of their lives might be the place to start. It could even be means-tested to ensure that those who have adequate funds don't take more than they need. Or it could be a universal basic income, a regular payment from the government to all citizens to enable an adequate standard of living.[19] Relatively speaking, supporting citizens enough to make crowdfunding unnecessary wouldn't take a lot of money. As we told you earlier, between 2018 and 2021 in the US, welfare crowdfunding requests for health-care and education causes on GoFundMe added up to less than $30 billion . Let's round up and call it $50 billion. Compare this with the nearly $2 trillion in the 2021 US COVID-19 stimulus package and we're talking about a pittance. Welfare crowdfunding campaigns added up to just over $1 billion in Canada. Put another way, it is pretty cheap for countries like Canada and the US to use government policy to provide material help to a lot of people, saving them from the public shame and humiliation that comes with welfare crowdfunding.

These are just a few ideas. Not even the best ones, necessarily. We've shone a light on the operations and outcomes of a very popular mode of fundraising to cover needs that can be thought of simply as welfare concerns. What we've found is that the system is deeply problematic but not inevitably. It can be changed. GoFundMe's name is disingenuous, a smoke screen. Go fund me? More like go fail me. A system in which we publicly beg strangers, friends, and family for cash isn't the best we have to offer as a society. The welfare crowdfunding system needs to be changed. Now. We'll need all of us, and all of our best ideas, to do better for each other. Let's get to work.

Appendix: On Data and Methods

Some readers want details about how researchers collect and make sense of their data—what's known as our methodology (more often methodologies). Here, we discuss it all step by step, going into finer-grained detail about our four broad data categories: the internet, interviews, healthcare campaigns coded for demographics, and an original survey of crowdfunding users.

Internet Data

A certain amount of website data is publicly available to those who know where to look. We turned to GoFundMe.com's sitemap, its standardized directory of pages provided by the website's administrator. We browsed all of the fundraising URLs, recording key information from each, and repeated the process several times between Fall 2018 and Spring 2021. Combining and cleaning the sitemap data yielded a single comprehensive dataset for analysis.

Site-mapping is an internet protocol website owners and administrators use to make their sites easier for search engines to find and index in an ongoing process, providing useful, iterative results to users.[1] Large, sprawling websites can stymie the "crawlers" that continually scan the internet for data. To solve the problem of hard-to-find sites going undetected, administrators build text-based documents (the sitemaps) to document all of their pages, the linkages between them, and their most recent updates. Sitemaps therefore figure into search engine optimization (SEO), the process by which website owners make their pages easy for visitors to discover on search sites like Google.

GoFundMe has a strong financial interest in SEO. Its sitemap is located at https://www.gofundme.com/sitemap.xml. In this way, even campaigns that don't make it onto the vaunted home page have a better chance of being discovered.

What makes sitemaps useful for search engines makes them useful for social scientists too. For instance, as sociologists interested in digital inequality, we want to find the fundraising campaigns that don't "go viral" or aren't promoted to front pages. That is, we want to get beyond the methodological challenge of digital trace data and the algorithmic selection of featured cases.

Why? Because one of our major motivations is investigating claims that the internet, and crowdfunding specifically, are a uniformly democratizing force. To do that, we have to collect data on *all* crowdfunding campaigns—the good, the bad, and the ugly—rather than just the successful ones or those benefiting people and groups geographically close to us. Yes, that figures into the algorithms too. If you're in Los Angeles, you see different featured cases from those a user browsing the site in Toronto sees. Because visitors are only shown the cases that do well and are nearby, this phenomenon is sometimes called "algorithmic confounding."[2] As we've noted throughout the book, this makes it seem as though it's easy for anyone anywhere to successfully raise money on the site.

GoFundMe's sitemap allowed us to sidestep the algorithms. Given our research interests, at each sitemap review we chose to record information on a campaign's category (e.g., medical, education), title, and text description; the organizers' location; the crowdfunder's monetary goal; and the dollars raised. After removing duplicates, by the last update of GoFundMe's sitemap in our period of analysis, our complete dataset contained information on 2,634,932 campaigns.

It is almost certain that we didn't access every campaign created on the platform, though we have strong reasons to believe our set of cases is fairly representative. Not the least of these reasons is GoFundMe's financial incentives to make their pages as visible as possible by including them in a comprehensive and frequently updated sitemap. Further, though users have the option to exclude their campaign from search results (meaning only those with a direct link can see it), that too is counterproductive, and we suspect this option is infrequently selected.

To the extent that our data set is incomplete, this is due to technological and practical limitations. Short-lived campaigns of just a few hours or days didn't appear, for instance, if they fell between observation periods or never made it onto the sitemap. Deleted campaigns were slightly different. At the end of 2020, it was easy to delete your own appeal but only if you hadn't received any donations. Campaigns that garner funds, in what appears to be an accountability measure, are merely "deactivated" and their URLs direct visitors to a summary including their main image and the total amount raised. Users can delete at this point, but it requires personally contacting GoFundMe.[3] Other cases are deactivated or deleted because of inactivity over extended periods.

We recorded deleted zero-dollar campaigns whose URLs appeared in the sitemap (and were visited during our data collection) as missing data. This small number of cases was removed before analysis. But the fact that the cases most likely to be missing from our analysis were either very short-lived or deleted because they raised no money suggests that, among the meaningful ones (i.e., cases not created in error and deleted shortly after), we were primarily undercounting *unsuccessful* GoFundMe campaigns. In other words, because many campaigns that raised no money at all didn't end up in our dataset, *the situation is likely worse than our analysis suggests* when it comes to the likelihood of successfully raising money on the platform. Our estimates of the failure rate are thus conservative.

We can't be sure that GoFundMe doesn't condition sitemap inclusion, like homepage features, on factors associated with a page's importance or popularity, which would limit the representativeness of the cases in the sitemap. However, our method greatly improves upon those that rely on data selected by algorithms and mitigates many concerns about representativeness. The wider concern—the opaque practices by which websites organize, process, and make data available—is shared across digital researchers. Following others, we call for greater platform transparency and programmatic access to data through APIs (such as the one Twitter provides).

Overall, the quantitative data analyzed here overcame the limitations of earlier studies and went well beyond that used in previous research.

Interview Data

To hear the stories and perspectives of the people participating in crowdfunding, understand the emotions involved, and ask questions about specific parts of the process, we conducted interviews. The bird's-eye view, after all, is always different from the view at ground level.

The interview phase of our study built directly on our internet data collection, during which we discovered medical and education campaigns that were particularly informative and whose creators could provide insightful information. We contacted creators to solicit interviews touching on a variety of circumstances of need, campaign success, and geographic location.

In the end, we conducted fifty interviews (thirty with US residents, twenty with Canadians). We attended to geographic distribution, ensuring representation from each country's major regions (in the US, we recruited in the Northeast, Midwest, South, and West; in Canada, the Atlantic, Central, Prairie, and West Coast provinces). Interviewees hailed from California, Florida, Georgia, Illinois, Indiana, Kentucky, Michigan, Minnesota, New York, North Carolina, Ohio, Oregon, Pennsylvania, Texas, Utah, Washington, and Wisconsin; in Canada, from Alberta, British Columbia, Manitoba, Newfoundland and Labrador, Ontario, Quebec, and Saskatchewan. Thirty-nine of the campaigns associated with these interviews were raising money for medical or health-care costs; ten, for education costs; one, to cover rent.

Research assistants helped us conduct the interviews between April 2019 and October 2020. Because of our broad geographic distribution, as well as the arrival of the COVID-19 pandemic during our interview period, we conducted most interviews over the phone or via online teleconferencing. The average interview was just over half an hour, a focused period made possible by information already in hand via the interviewees' GoFundMe and social media pages.

We knew our respondents had tried to raise money using crowdfunding, and so our semistructured interview protocol focused on their own words about the course of each campaign (including inciting incident and decision-making), establishing the campaign, and waiting for funding to arrive. That is, the structure of the interviews largely followed the progression of the chapters in this book. We also sought reflections on the emotions associated with each stage, as well as thoughts on how people get help for unexpected costs like theirs, the role of governments, and whether crowdfunding was a good solution at the society level. Each interview participant was compensated for their time with a gift card.

We transcribed the audio recordings of our conversations and, with the help of research assistants, coded participants' stories for key research themes. Much of our analysis at this point involved finding patterns across respondents' answers to specific questions about decision-making, campaign creation, and campaign promotion. Interviewees also brought up many topics that we hadn't asked about but found fascinating and helpful in developing our understanding of the crowdfunding process. Additionally, in rereading the interview transcripts, we took note of key emergent themes, or those that respondents chose to emphasize, such as the role of faith and religious beliefs and new challenges and opportunities created by the pandemic. We don't quote all of our interview subjects in the book, but all interviews informed our analysis.

Health-Care Campaigns Coded for Demographics

A common challenge for researchers who study online phenomena and rely on data collected from the internet, like tweets and blog posts, is that such sources rarely include detailed information on the people responsible for them. This is what we really need since we understand that a person's *social location*, based on age, gender, race, ethnicity, and the like, powerfully shapes how they think and act. Although crowdfunding incentivizes users to publicly disclose more personal information than most online platforms (which we argue is problematic), a lack of demographic information is nonetheless a potential problem for the study of crowdfunding. Self-reported data is the gold standard, but a second-best for many researchers of online phenomena is rater-evaluated demographic data, which allows us to tackle important questions about the role of demographic traits in crowdfunding that we otherwise couldn't).[4]

To that end, we pared our full dataset down to campaigns created in the US and Canada for health-care costs between January 1 and June 1, 2020. These choices were driven by our research focus on these countries, our realization that health care is prototypical of welfare crowdfunding, and our desire to bound our analysis in a specific time period. From this subset, we randomly selected a thousand health-care campaigns from each country for demographic analysis. A pair of research assistants independently visited each campaign's page to determine whether it was in fact raising money for individual health-care costs. If yes, the coders classified each case on a set of attributes including beneficiary age (child, adult, or senior), gender, and race/ethnicity, as deduced through the organizer's campaign message and photos and videos. Raters noted cases that were without enough information to make a determination and those not fitting into established categories. On the whole, however, campaign pages contained more than enough information—as encouraged by GoFundMe during campaign setup.

Our use of two coders in the first round followed standard scholarly practice, allowing us to check their consistency in subjective assessments. Analysis shows that the category in which each campaign fell was highly consistent (more than 95 percent), as determined by standard measures of intercoder reliability. In other words, the two raters chose the same category for the same campaign (e.g., child versus adult) all but 5 percent of the time, lending credibility to their coding. In a second stage of analysis, the raters reviewed all instances in which their choices had diverged and, working together, reconciled them. We then merged the final demographic attributes into the objective online data for each case (e.g., number of donations).

Survey Data

Finally, we fielded an online survey of 603 welfare crowdfunding users in February 2020. This allowed us to ask questions about the crowdfunding process from a much broader pool of campaigners to determine whether the primary insights from our interviews fit with those gleaned from the broader population. We hired Qualtrics, a survey research company, to recruit a sample of adults from the US and Canada who reported using a crowdfunding site to raise money for individual health-care or education costs.

Companies like Qualtrics recruit from a variety of online research panels—groups of people who regularly participate in paid commercial or academic surveys. These participants provide detailed personal information, which is used to match them to a survey's eligibility criteria. All matching participants are randomly selected to take part in an approximately fifteen-minute online survey. In our case, we specified age, location, and previous use of crowdfunding as our criteria. Once we had an initial survey pool, we screened for type of crowdfunding and platforms used. Although our respondents shouldn't be thought of as representative of the full population of crowdfunding users, online samples of this kind are common in contemporary social science research and often used as an alternative to traditional survey approaches such as telephone interviews. Our respondents were compensated for their participation.

As in our interviews, we asked a variety of survey questions that couldn't be answered by our online data alone. These included basic demographic questions and various questions about the campaign they had participated in—for example, whether it was to their benefit or someone else's, what they were raising money for, and why they needed the help. We also requested their thoughts about how it had gone and who had participated. Finally, we asked about their political attitudes and thoughts about privacy and crowdfunding. To be clear, this survey involved significant opportunities for respondents to write in detail about their crowdfunding experiences. We made significant use of this qualitative data to supplement our more in-depth interview material.

In our analysis, we primarily drew on data from two open-ended survey questions. These questions, which to some extent overlapped with our interview questions, asked respondents to briefly reflect on the highs and lows of their overall experience and whether they had concerns about using crowdfunding in situations like theirs. Respondents typically wrote a few sentences, enough to allow us to compare emergent themes with those that came out of our interviews. We gained significant confidence in our conclusions upon learning that the interview and survey data largely converged. Some of the responses appear in these pages alongside interview excerpts to illustrate the experiences and phenomena we explore here.

This review of our data and methods is an abridged summary of a years-long, multifaceted, multimethod effort that involved thousands of hours of work by our research team. We hope that it demonstrates the unusually rigorous combination of data sources, both big picture and on the ground, we used to provide the most comprehensive, finely tuned lens possible for the study of welfare crowdfunding in this moment.

Notes

Introduction

1. We use pseudonyms throughout the book. This includes crowdfunding users from our interviews, survey, and online data. In a few cases, to honor the lives of specific people, we use real names. Robert is one of our interview subjects, as is Mark, discussed subsequently.

2. Unless indicated otherwise, we refer to US dollars throughout the book.

3. Tonika Morgan's story was featured by news outlets in both Canada and the US. We draw on reporting from Matchan (2015) and Seth (2015).

4. On the Las Vegas Victims' Fund and the challenging logistics of disbursing crowdfunding proceeds, see Mosendz and Woolley (2017). On the Humboldt Broncos' Fund, see Mattern (2018). On the Landsman family and gene therapies for rare diseases, see Regalado (2018). On the COVID-19 Frontline Responders Fund, see Etherington (2020).

5. We discuss the history of the safety net "going digital" in greater detail in Chapter 1. See Sisler (2012) and Berliner and Kenworthy (2017) as a place to start for understanding the contemporary use of crowdfunding to meet health-care needs.

6. See GoFundMe (2021) for a stylized statement of its recent revenues. Barrett (2021) provides a list of the largest US charities as of 2021; the revenues we describe apply to the most recent fiscal year reported by each charity at the time of writing and account for private contributions only. See United Way Worldwide (2020) and The Salvation Army (2021) for these charities' recent annual reports.

7. Internal Revenue Service (2021).

8. On GoFundMe's 2015 buyout by a group of venture capital investors, see MacMillan and Tan (2015). On the company's revenue and profit margins, see Adams (2016) and Harris (2017).

9. See GoFundMe (2020a; 2021) for two recent editions of the company's annual reports. Lunden (2017) describes how in 2017 GoFundMe abandoned its policy of charging a mandatory 5 percent fee on donations in favor of a tip-based model, likely to undercut competitors.

10. We provide only a brief sketch of the history of nineteenth-century charity and the rise of the welfare state here to help explain the context of our thinking and why we first became interested in crowdfunding for social welfare costs. For in-depth histories of nineteenth- and twentieth-century charity and the rise of the welfare state in the US, see Katz (1996) and Trattner (1998). For Canada, see Finkel (2006) and Tillotson (2008). For more on the connections between this book and earlier work, see Schneiderhan (2007; 2011; 2016).

11. Schneiderhan (2015) provides an in-depth discussion of the emergence of charity organizations and the resulting shifts in how we helped others.

12. See Keller (1998) and Lubove (1986) for accounts of the social and political currents that set the scene for the Social Security Act of 1935. See Amenta (2000), Piven and Cloward (1993), and Skocpol (1995) for analyses of the origins of US social policy and its subsequent development. In addition to the sources cited above on the origins of the Canadian social welfare state, see Boychuk (2008) and Tuohy (1999) for studies of the distinct directions that health-care policy has taken in the US and Canada.

13. The theoretical impetus for our investigation of crowdfunding comes from Swedberg's work on theorizing, Tilly's work on stories, and Mills's *The Sociological Imagination*, among others. Swedberg (2014) urges the sociologist to "find something interesting" and pursue it through data collection and theorizing. Tilly (2002; 2006) asks us to be skeptical of the neatly packaged "standard stories" that abound in the social world. He asks us to consider that most stories, once we peer beneath the surface, are messier and more complicated. And Mills (1959) shows that by using our "sociological imagination," we can see that seemingly personal and individual problems can be indicative of much larger "public problems" that point to structural inequalities.

14. In particular, see Snyder et al. (2017; 2016) and Berliner and Kenworthy (2017). Our own earlier work on crowdfunding appears in Lukk et al. (2018).

15. The onset of enduring public animosity toward large technology companies, including not only Silicon Valley social media giants like Twitter and Facebook but also Chinese companies like Baidu and Alibaba, since the 2010s has been termed "techlash" (Foroohar 2018). The string of incidents precipitating techlash include revelations of personal data harvesting and digital election manipulation via Facebook in the Cambridge Analytica scandal; Russian disinformation campaigns on Facebook, Twitter, and YouTube during the 2016

US presidential election campaign; and the incitement of genocide against Rohingya Muslims in Myanmar via Facebook. See Hao (2021) on how Facebook's drive to maximize user engagement with algorithms has rewarded inflammatory material and enabled misinformation and extremism. See Benkler et al. (2018) on the emergence and spread of disinformation in the current political media landscape. See Wylie (2019) for a whistleblower's account of the Cambridge Analytica scandal and Amnesty International (2022) for an in-depth report on Facebook's role in human rights violations against the Rohingya. See Vallas and Schor (2020) and Woodcock and Graham (2020) for introductions to the gig economy.

16. These findings and concerns appear in Berliner and Kenworthy (2017), Snyder et al. (2016), and Lukk et al. (2018).

17. See Ember (2019) on Bernie Sanders's long-term interest in Canadian health-care policy and how it has shaped his proposals for creating a single-payer national health insurance program in the US. See Soril et al. (2017) on recent challenges to affordability in the Canadian health-care system and how they compare with those in the US. See Banting and Myles (2013) for a characterization of recent trends in the Canadian welfare state and its various components.

18. The estimate of the prevalence of donating to medical crowdfunding campaigns among the US population is from a survey by the research organization NORC at the University of Chicago (NORC 2021).

19. The artist Taylor Swift is well-known as a regular contributor to welfare crowdfunding campaigns (see Aniftos 2021). Her generosity was once so large that it led GoFundMe to increase its maximum donation limit (Plucinska 2015).

20. See Covert (2019) on the "welfare queen" trope in US right-wing politics, including during Reagan's campaigns in the 1970s and 1980s. Numerous scholars argue that the US social welfare system systematically excludes Black Americans, thereby reproducing racial inequality, and that race powerfully shapes Americans' conceptions of who is "deserving" of government support. This happens, in part, due to misleading media depictions of who receives assistance. See Gilens (1999) and Quadagno (1994).

21. See DiMaggio et al. (2016) and Norris (2001) on the digital divide.

22. Social capital refers to networks of relationships and trust between people that enable different kinds of cooperation; having more social capital means having more useful social connections (Coleman 1988; Putnam 2000). If inequalities in internet access characterize the basic, first level of the digital divide, then differences in people's ability to effectively *use* the internet characterize what has been called the "second level" (Hargittai 2002). Scholars have shown that teachers and educational systems play a considerable role in shaping this aspect of the digital divide (e.g., Rafalow 2020; Puckett 2022). Igra (2022) shows that less privileged crowdfunding users often struggle with raising

money on GoFundMe in part because their most likely supporters—the friends, family, and acquaintances that make up their social networks—don't have much to give. This means that inequitable crowdfunding outcomes for members of marginalized groups can happen even when fundraiser organizers have strong technological skills and without explicit discrimination by potential donors.

23. Zuboff (2019).

24. The idea that full membership in a community requires a basic level of equality among members, in terms of economic welfare and security, is central to Marshall's concept of social citizenship (1950). Relative conditions of equality—which, notably, exist alongside some level of inequality generated by the capitalist economy—ensure a common overall standard of living and make a sense of community possible. States can achieve these conditions by giving their citizens access to public education systems, health care, and other social services and supports. Marshall identifies the emergence of social citizenship as the latest phase in the expansion of citizenship rights, associated with the twentieth century and the rise of welfare states, following the enshrinement of civil and political rights (at least for some) in the eighteenth and nineteenth centuries, respectively. Economists like Piketty (2014) and Stiglitz (2012) have warned that the growing concentration of income and wealth in many English-speaking countries threatens to provoke political upheaval and conflict as it clashes, increasingly starkly, with the professed meritocratic values of democratic societies. Other social scientists have traced the deleterious consequences of income inequality to wide-ranging areas of life (e.g., Pickett and Wilkinson 2009).

25. The notion that that internet might be considered merely "nice to have" rather than essential is epitomized by the well-known anecdote about Bush-era Federal Communication Commission chair Michael Powell, who downplayed concerns about the digital divide by likening the internet to a luxury car. During a 2001 press conference, he said, "I think there's a Mercedes divide. I'd like to have one, I can't afford one." Hargittai (2011) recounts this story and provides a broader discussion of how inequalities in access to various digital activities and resources can translate into inequalities in nondigital outcomes. Twenty years later, there can be little doubt that the internet, unlike a luxury car, is indispensable for many essential activities. By the early 2010s, scholars had found, for example, that using the internet for job hunting was basically the norm, and that those who searched online were much likelier to find a job and to find it faster, compared with those who didn't (Faberman and Kudlyak 2016). Related research has estimated that approximately 60 to 70 percent of all job openings at that time were advertised online and that online job postings overrepresented higher-paying, higher-status jobs (Carnevale, Jayasundera, and Repnikov 2014). Survey results reported by Smith (2015) corroborate these findings, but also find that a considerable number of Americans do not feel confident in their digital job-seeking skills.

26. We discuss the decline of welfare state supports in the second half of the twentieth century in greater detail in Chapter 1. See Hacker (2019) and Banting and Myles (2013) for why this has occurred and how it has resulted in shifting increasing amounts of risk and responsibility for individual well-being from institutions to individuals and families. The idea that GoFundMe and other welfare crowdfunding services are inefficient ways of supporting important causes is illustrated by cases like the one from 2020, where donors had given millions of dollars through GoFundMe to a group with "Black Lives Matter" in its name but which was not only unrelated to the popular social movement but opposed to its goals (Mac and Sacks 2020). GoFundMe campaigns for victims of the 2017 Las Vegas mass shooting and the Humboldt Broncos tragedy also showed that well-meaning amateur fundraisers are often ill-equipped for the major logistical task of efficiently and transparently handling fundraising proceeds, as described by Mosendz and Woolley (2017) and Klinkenberg (2019). See Spade (2020) for an alternative account of how to help others in times of need that rejects the charity model.

27. Clark (2012).

28. See C. O'Neil (2017) and Noble (2018) for more on algorithms and some of their pernicious consequences for fairness and equity.

29. Even before another round of acquisitions in 2018, GoFundMe controlled an estimated 90 percent of the market for personal causes in the US and approximately 80 percent globally. GoFundMe's CEO at the time suggested that such drastic market consolidation would be "ultimately very good" for the public (Harris 2018). See Srnicek (2017) on the emergence of "platform capitalism," a unique business model adopted by companies like Google, Meta, and Amazon that involves building hardware and software solutions—in other words, platforms—for others to use. The 2020s have featured some of the most aggressive attempts in decades by US and European governments to expand and enforce antitrust laws against technology companies. See Nylen (2022) and Espinoza (2022) for recent assessments of these ongoing efforts on both sides of the Atlantic.

30. See Marshall (1950) and note 24 on social citizenship.

Chapter 1

1. Hollis and Sweetman (2001) describe Jonathan Swift's loan fund as an early innovation in microfinance and part of the phenomenon of Irish loan funds—a network of nonprofit, bank-like institutions providing small loans to the country's poor without interest or collateral. These funds operated until the early twentieth century and at their height were among the most important financial institutions in Ireland. Kallio and Vuola (2020) provide a variety of examples in the history of crowdfunding.

2. de Tocqueville ([1835] 2000) observed Americans' seemingly unique propensity for forming voluntary associations in the early 1800s. See Harris

(1979) on the early history of Black benevolent societies in the US. Beito (2000) discusses the importance of such societies for many marginalized groups, including women and immigrants, in later periods. He also notes that their decline was in large part due to the expansion of the welfare state in the twentieth century.

3. McCullough (2018, 249).

4. O'Mara's (2019) wide-ranging history of Silicon Valley and its key players covers the early years of these and other social media companies. See Mezrich (2010) on the origins of Facebook specifically.

5. See Grossman (2006) for *Time*'s announcement of the 2006 Person of the Year.

6. Barack Obama's YouTube video announcing his 2008 presidential campaign can be found at https://youtu.be/H5h95soOuEg. See Miller (2008) for a discussion of the internet's role in Obama's election, which likens his use of the new medium to John F. Kennedy's successful use of television in his 1960 campaign. Smith (2009) provides a broader overview of the internet's role in the 2008 US election cycle. See Alvarez et al. (2009) on internet voting, Bail (2021) for an evidence-based account of social media's effects on political behavior, and Ravenscraft (2022) for a recent introduction to the metaverse.

7. See Allan and Thorsen (2009) for examples of citizen journalism in the 2000s from around the world.

8. Castells (2012) is often associated with the optimistic argument for the internet's ability to resist and topple repressive power structures and facilitate collective action. His work analyzes a number of prominent cases of social movements from this period, including Occupy Wall Street and the Arab Spring. Many others have demonstrated the considerable limits of the internet's democratic potential. Schradie (2019), for example, shows how powerful and well-funded political groups can leverage the internet for conservative ends, challenging arguments about the democratizing and equalizing power of digital activism. For other perspectives on digital democracy, see Bartlett (2018), Hindman (2008), Nyabola (2018), and Tufekci (2018).

9. Barbrook and Cameron (1996, 45).

10. Ferrari (2020).

11. Securities and Exchange Commission (2004); Ebersman (2012).

12. Nachtwey and Seidl (2020).

13. Howe (2006).

14. Platforms like YouTube and Instagram, which depend on user participation, can also be seen as crowdsourcing their product (i.e., videos or images) from their users, albeit without economic compensation. Other internet-based activities—distributed computing projects, open-source software development, open collaboration projects like Wikipedia, and so forth—are related but distinct from crowdsourcing and notable for their noncommercial nature (see Kleemann, Voss, and Rieder 2008).

15. Surowiecki (2005) discusses the "wisdom of the crowd." Granovetter's (1973) work anchors a vast literature on the importance of weak network ties in social life. See Desmond (2012) and Small (2017) for more examples of how people, often counterintuitively, rely on weak ties, including complete strangers, for comfort and support.

16. See McPherson et al. (2001) for an overview of the significance of homophily. Huber and Malhotra (2017) provide a demonstration of homophily's importance in the context of contemporary online dating.

17. This expression is from Granovetter (1973).

18. Multiple awards were established for the longitude problem, with larger awards going to solutions that could determine it with greater precision. Sobel (1995) chronicles this scientific prize and the story of the man who eventually solved it.

19. Howe (2006).

20. On Amazon Mechanical Turk and the "digital sweatshop," see Pittman and Sheehan (2016), Scholz (2012), and Semuels (2018). Hara et al. (2018) provide estimates of MTurk worker wages.

21. See Schor (2020) on the early promises of the "gig economy," critiques of its current implementation, and how the hypothetical benefits of the gig model might still be realized.

22. Williams and Wilson (2016) provide an overview of online funding methods used in the music industry and the "fan funding" model pioneered by ArtistShare. See Regner (2021) for an analysis of the viability of the patronage model for creative producers. Newport (2022) provides a brief history of the recent landscape of digital fundraising for creative work.

23. Platform fees for Indiegogo and Kickstarter are accurate as of Fall 2022. Leboeuf and Schwienbacher (2018) provide an overview of different models of crowdfunding and locate them in the broader context of entrepreneurial finance.

24. Howe (2009, 347). The quote by Danae Ringelman is from Clark (2012).

25. Strickler (2019, 11–12); Chapman (2016).

26. Findings on the role of campaign characteristics in crowdfunding success are from Hörisch (2015); Chan and Parhankangas (2017); Herzenstein et al (2011); Mitra and Gilbert (2014); Mollick (2014); and Parhankangas and Renko (2017).

27. Findings on the role of campaign organizers' location and networks on crowdfunding success are from Butticè et al. (2017); Mollick (2014); Zheng et al. (2014); Agrawal et al. (2015); Gallemore et al.(2019); Guenther et al. (2018); and Lin and Viswanathan (2016).

28. Findings on how campaign organizers' identity affects crowdfunding success are from Ahlers et al (2015); Pope and Sydnor (2011); Younkin and Kuppuswamy (2018); and Barasinka and Schäfer (2014). Ziegler et al. (2021) document gender differences in crowdfunding participation. See DiMaggio et al. (2016) and Hargittai (2011) on the digital divide.

29. Tosatto et al. (2019) make the point of crowdfunding having replaced "one master for another" in their recent evaluation of the large body of research on crowdfunding for creative and cultural projects. Attuel-Mendès (2017) discusses how banks and other traditional financial institutions participate in crowdfunding.

30. See the post by Kickstarter announcing its "Projects We Love" badges at https://www.kickstarter.com/blog/introducing-projects-we-love-badges.

31. Kickstarter, though a for-profit company, stands out among crowdfunding platforms for its actions to demonstrate a commitment to principles over profits. Notably, it became certified as a B Corporation in 2014 and a public benefit corporation in 2015, voluntarily committing itself to higher standards of transparency than are legally required. Its founders have repeatedly stated that they have no interest in selling the company or becoming publicly traded. Marquis (2020) recounts the rise of the B Corp movement and its potential impacts on contemporary corporate governance.

32. Bucher (2018) shows how algorithms shape our encounters with online platforms and argues for their close link to power and politics. See Burrell and Fourcade (2021) for examples of the ubiquity of algorithms in contemporary life and its implications.

33. See Benjamin (2019) and Noble (2018) on algorithms and racial injustice, Ferguson (2017) and Brayne (2020) on policing and criminal justice, Eubanks (2018) on government agencies, Christin (2020) and Petre (2021) on journalism, Rosenblat (2019) on work, and Feldstein (2021) and Tripodi (2022) on politics and misinformation.

34. C. O'Neil (2017).

35. See Galuszka and Brzozowska (2017) on crowdfunding for artistic endeavors, Schäfer et al. (2018) on scientific research, Hunter (2015) on journalism, (2018) on litigation, and Elmer and Ward-Kimola (2021) and Miller-Idriss (2020) on political campaigns, including for the far right. On depictions of crowdfunding as a digital safety net, see Harris (2017) and Lee and Lehdonvirta (2020). Wade (2022) analyzes the history of GoFundMe's positioning of itself as "the giving layer of the internet."

36. See Bobrow (2021) on Charles Best and the origins of DonorsChoose. The website funded its millionth project in 2018 (Paynter 2018). Meer et al. (2017) document a drastic decline in charitable giving and changing attitudes about the practice in the US following the Great Recession. Berliner and Kenworthy (2017) also link medical crowdfunding to austerity and the 2008 financial crisis.

37. Adams (2016) discusses the origins of GoFundMe. See Sisler (2012) and O'Neil on GiveForward, YouCaring, and other early services for medical crowdfunding.

38. See Lunden (2018) on tips and fees on GoFundMe. The quote by Dan Saper, CEO of YouCaring also appears in this article.

39. See Smith et al. (2016) for survey-based estimates of Americans' crowdfunding use in 2016. Chan (2017) features the quote by Jennifer Elwood of the Red Cross and discusses both Salvation Army and Red Cross forays into crowdfunding.

40. Adams (2016) reports on tips and fees on YouCaring. The press release by Indiegogo announcing the creation of a new platform, Generosity, can be found at https://go.indiegogo.com/blog/2015/10/generosity-by-indiegogo .html.

41. See Graham (2017) and Woolley (2017) on the acquisitions of GiveForward and CrowdRise, respectively, and Perez (2017) on Facebook's launch of its own GoFundMe competitor. The quote is from Lunden (2018), discussing GoFundMe's 2018 acquisition of YouCaring. The GoFundMe revenue estimate is from the company's 2020 annual report (GoFundMe 2020a).

42. The thinking behind welfare states is closely related to Marshall's (1950) concept of social citizenship, the idea that full membership in society requires a baseline level of equality among its members in terms of economic welfare, security, and opportunity. Governments achieve these conditions by providing public education, health care, and other services to ensure that a basic level of need is met for nearly everyone. Esping-Andersen (1990) provides an influential account of the varieties of welfare states around the world.

43. See Keller (1998) and Lubove (1986) for more on the social and political climate leading to the enactment of the Social Security Act of 1935. Amenta (2000), Piven and Cloward (1993), and Skocpol (1995) provide in-depth historical analyses of the origins of US social policy and its later development. See Katz (1996) and Trattner (1998) for more general histories of nineteenth- and twentieth-century charity and the rise of the welfare state in the US.

44. See Finkel (2006) and Tillotson (2008) for histories of nineteenth- and twentieth-century charity and the rise of the welfare state in Canada. See Esping-Andersen (1990) for characterizations of the major differences in welfare state arrangements around the world. Boychuk (2008) and Tuohy (1999) compare the US, Canada, and other countries in terms of the trajectories of their health-care policies.

45. See Esping-Andersen (1996) on the end of the "golden age" of the welfare state and Pierson (1996; 1994) on the politics of welfare state retrenchment.

46. See Harvey (2005) and Steger and Roy (2010) for introductions to neoliberalism, with special attention to Reagan and Thatcher. See Clark (2002) and Ilcan (2009) on neoliberalism in Canada, including under the Mulroney and Chrétien governments.

47. See Hacker (2019) on economic insecurity and the recent trajectory of health-care policy in the US. See Banting and Myles (2013) for a review of recent developments in the Canadian welfare state and health-care system.

48. Ganguli et al. (2020) discuss declining primary care use among insured Americans. Gilligan et al. (2018) provide statistics on the catastrophic

financial consequences of cancer diagnoses. Baird (2016) compares the financial burden of health care between the US and Canada, finding that the risk of incurring a large medical expense is 1.5–4 times higher in the US. See Law et al. (2018) and Holbrook et al. (2021) for recent research on cost-related prescription drug nonadherence in Canada.

49. See Piketty and Saez (2006) on the evolution of income inequality in the US and elsewhere over the course of the twentieth century. While income inequality roughly refers to how big the differences between rich and poor members of society are, poverty refers to how many people have insufficient income or other resources to meet their basic needs. Brady and Parolin (2020) find that deep and extreme poverty has increased in the US in recent decades and provide estimates of its prevalence. They also find that government benefits, like the Supplemental Nutrition Assistance Program (SNAP), have alleviated poverty over time.

50. Igra et al. (2021) examine medical crowdfunding uptake in response to the COVID-19 pandemic.

51. US Bureau of Labor Statistics (2021); Statistics Canada (2021); Alderman and Stevis-Gridneff (2020).

52. US Department of Labor (2020a, 2020b).

53. Parkinson and O'Kane (2020); Press (2020); Statistics Canada (2020).

54. Schwartz (2020); Cassella and Murphy (2020).

55. Finley (2020) and King (2020) discuss the technological challenges of implementing new benefit programs during the pandemic, including the shortage of programmers fluent in COBOL, a programming language from the 1960s. See Parrott et al. (2020) for early commentary and Haldeman et al. (2020) for a comprehensive analysis of the CARES Act.

56. Bivens and Shierholz (2020); Gale et al. (2020); and Narea (2020). See Cilke (2014) for estimates of the size of the US non-tax-filer population.

57. Nuñez and Ahmad (2020).

58. McGuinness and Zucker (2020); Graves (2003); Cohen et al. (2020). The CARES Act was succeeded by additional stimulus bills, namely the Consolidated Appropriations Act of 2021 and the American Rescue Plan (see Tankersley 2021).

59. Harris (2020). The US took steps to help with medical costs as well, but reports of surprise bills persisted (see J. S. King 2020).

60. Stewart (2020). See West and Hildebrand (1997) and Woodbury (2014) on the relationship between states and the federal government regarding unemployment support.

61. Cullen (2020); Robson (2020). Anecdotes about the surprising and frustrating obstacles to obtaining benefits are from Badger and Parlapiano (2020), McGeehan (2020), and Mazzei and Tavernise (2020). Later in the summer, amid rising concerns about fraudulent applications for government benefits, particularly by organized crime engaged in identity theft, Canadian authorities added additional validation measures to the application process. These

measures were still framed as seeking to balance security and efficiency for legitimate applicants. By the fall, nearly a million Canadians had also made use of a dedicated government portal for voluntarily paying back benefit money they had not been entitled to (Harris 2020).

62. Roman (2020).

63. Mulholland (2020). These physical features of cities and towns—churches, parks, and community centers—make up what Klinenberg (2019) calls social infrastructure. In addition to often providing in-kind services like meals and an internet connection, they provide less tangible benefits that help make social life possible and serve as a potent antidote to the modern ills of isolation and loneliness.

64. St-Denis (2020); Maroto et al. (2021). See Kalleberg (2011) on precarious work.

65. Arnold (2020).

66. McGeehan (2020). Nadine's Twitter post requesting help via Cash App can be found at https://twitter.com/NadineJosephs/status/126270680043399 9872.

67. GoFundMe (2020b).

68. GoFundMe's "COVID-19 Relief Fund" can be found at https://www .gofundme.com/f/covid19-relief-cause-fund. Statt (2020) reports on GoFund-Me's failed collaboration with Yelp. By Fall 2020, there was a good sense of the insecurity created by COVID-19, expressed in developments like upticks in food bank use and the risk of eviction and foreclosure (US Census Bureau 2020). Research on poverty during the pandemic (e.g., Parolin et al. 2021) has shown that government stimulus staved off the worst of the pandemic's economic effects.

Chapter 2

1. Of course it's more than demographics. The deeper sociological question animating our inquiry is what is the *habitus* of the crowdfunder? There's quite a bit of Pierre Bourdieu's work behind our thoughts in this section, and field theory has been helpful in thinking through the structure of the "field of crowdfunding" and its attendant positions and position-takings. For those interested in more, we suggest starting with Bourdieu (1990; 1996; 2000; 2019).

2. Although GoFundMe use is restricted to a handful of wealthy countries, note that crowdfunding as a whole is a global phenomenon, with various other platforms providing the service around the world (see Kenworthy 2019). On GoFundMe countries, see https://support.gofundme.com/hc/en-ca/ articles/360001972748-Countries-supported-on-GoFundMed.

3. On crowdfunding in France, see Boutigny and Leroux-Sostenes (2021).

4. Based on our data, Washington, DC is where campaigns dedicated to pets and animals make up the smallest share of all cases (less than 3 percent). By contrast, the share is largest in Vermont, making up almost 9 percent of all cases, followed closely by Rhode Island, New Hampshire, and Connecticut.

See Stoltz, Van Ness, and Bjerre (2020) for a discussion of the changing role of pets in financial decision-making, which also helps contextualize crowd-funding for pet-related costs.

5. For state data, see National Center for Education Statistics (2016).

6. For technological challenges facing Indigenous peoples living in remote Canada, especially Nunavut, see Tranter (2021).

7. Grabb and Curtis (2010) deal with regional-political variation in the US and Canada. They trace these changes to historical differences. A growing body of scholarship documents the creation of a distinct approach to social welfare in Quebec, especially since the 1990s, while the rest of Canada has been scaling it back (see Dinan and Noël 2020; Daigneault et al. 2021). Thanks to Jennifer Elrick for pointing this out.

8. We use "health care," rather than simply "medical," as an umbrella term to describe the wide variety of health and wellness campaigns we analyzed. Campaigns in this category correspond to those appearing in the "Medical, Illness, and Healing" GoFundMe fundraising category. Also note that these findings pertain to the person(s) *benefiting* from a crowdfunding campaign, who is often not the person who created and manages it (and certainly not in the case of campaigns benefiting infants and young children).

9. The small difference we observe in the proportion of men relative to women in our study sample isn't statistically significant and thus is indistin-guishable from the equal proportions we would expect to see. While we see parity in the representation of men and women in the overall pool of health-care appeals, this doesn't hold true when considering how campaigns actu-ally end up performing, something we discuss in Chapter 4. See Barcelos and Budge (2019) and Barcelos (2020) for more on the inequalities of transgender medical care and crowdfunding. Meerwijk and Sevelius (2017) estimate that about 1 in every 250 US adults are transgender, while the 2021 Canadian Census found that 1 in 300 Canadians aged 15 or older are transgender or non-binary (Statistics Canada 2022a).

10. Saleh et al. (2020), for example, find slightly larger percentages for chil-dren and smaller ones for adults, meaning that children in the US are roughly proportionally represented while children in Canada are slightly overrepre-sented. However, Saleh et al.'s estimates are based on cases seen on GoFund-Me's Discover page, where the most successful cases are chosen for display via algorithmic decision-making, and so should be taken as estimates of the frequency of different demographic groups in *successful* crowdfunding cases. A comparison of the estimates from these studies suggests that children's cases are more likely than adults' to do well.

11. See Cubanski et al. (2018) and Veall (2008) on poverty among seniors in the US and Canada, respectively. Curtis and Lightman (2017) discuss differ-ences between immigrants and the native-born in retirement.

12. See Statistics Canada (2022b) and Jones et al. (2021) for data from the 2021 Canadian and 2020 US censuses, respectively.

13. The front-stage and back-stage dramaturgical references are taken from Goffman (1978). As you might imagine, Goffman pointed out that there are things going on behind the social scenes that the audience doesn't see but are critical to the production.

14. See Powell and Kerr (2020) on US tuition and Varrella (2021) on Canadian tuition.

15. For general inequalities in medical crowdfunding, see Kenworthy (2020, 2021); Kenworthy et al. (2020). On Indigenous Canadians, see Lindsay (2021).

16. See Bray et al. (2018) for recent estimates of global cancer incidence.

Chapter 3

1. Two pieces by Vargas (2018b; 2018a) cover this story. In a related story, a man wanted to donate $15 to Jalloh but mistakenly gave $15,787. It took months to get it back, in large part because of the difficulty in getting substantive help from GoFundMe (think calling the cable company) and because Jalloh had no digital footprint. The inefficiencies resulting from digital-divide inequalities quickly became apparent.

2. On 2016 data, see Ryan (2018). On 2018 data, see Martin (2021).

3. Anderson and Kumar (2019) discuss poorer households' reliance on smartphones for accessing the internet; see also DiMaggio et al. (2016).

4. On disabilities and the internet, see Anderson and Perrin (2017) and Robinson et al. (2015). In thinking about digital inequalities by social group, it's worth considering sociologist Jen Schradie's (2019) *The Revolution That Wasn't: How Digital Activism Favors Conservatives*, about the grass-roots liberal organizers who don't have the capabilities to use social media effectively to organize and the well-funded conservative groups who do. This links to the discussion of union organizers helping Ista Jalloh.

5. For Social Security, see https://www.ssa.gov/ssnumber/ss5doc.htm; For Social Insurance, see https://www.canada.ca/en/employment-social-develop ment/services/sin/eligibility.html; on Canadian undocumented immigrants, see Goldring et al. (2009); on US undocumented immigrants, see Kamarck and Stenglein (2019).

6. Any quotes from GoFundMe are from its "Getting started" section, ac curate as of 2021. On health-care crowdfunding percentages, see Martinez (2019). This number is consistent with what GoFundMe itself has publicly stated regarding the number of health-care campaigns it hosts.

7. These values are based on the Bank of Canada's June 2020 conversion rate of C$1 to US$0.738.

8. These and other differences in sample-based estimates reported in this section are statistically significant.

9. See Budge et al. (2016), Grant et al. (2010), and Rosh (2017) on trans health-care access. We observed no significant differences in goal amounts between age or ethnic groups in our sample data.

10. The values for Canada are roughly 4 percent and 2 percent of the US health-care and education totals, respectively.

11. Monroe (2019). The quote by Rob Solomon appears in Fortt and Salinas (2018). Snyder (2021) and Stevenson (2020) criticize GoFundMe and its business model along these lines.

12. This sneakiness around tips is an example of a "dark pattern" in digital design—something we will unpack in detail in Chapter 4.

13. For more on friendfunding and health-care crowdfunding, see Borst et al. (2018) and Lee and Lehdonvirta (2020).

14. See Igra (2021) for more on donor capacity and crowdfunding inequality.

15. Leavitt (2021).

16. William Julius Wilson's groundbreaking 1987 work *The Truly Disadvantaged*, on social capital, network ties, and race in the 1980s, showed that because of structural changes tied to "White flight" from certain city neighborhoods, Black Americans, for example, were cut off from the network ties necessary to find employment. It's not what you know; it's who you know, but if you can't meet certain people because they've moved away to avoid you, that's a problem. The deeper point is the significant variation in the breadth of social networks, and race, class, and gender that have to be considered. See Lee and Lehdonvirta (2020) on regions with weaker ties having less crowdfunding success. Also see Cai (2018) on crowdfunding and social capital.

Chapter 4

1. Douglas (1995, 33). Thanks to Letta Page for making this connection.

2. Bate (2021).

3. Bonfiglio (2019).

4. For de Tocqueville ([1835] 2000), who traveled across the US in the nineteenth century, these habits were an essential expression of the American national character. The robust literature that extends from de Tocqueville emphasizes the importance of social ties and norms of reciprocity for fostering democracy and the pursuit of the public good. And Clemens (2020) shows how this voluntarism and reciprocity helped to build the very fabric of American identity. For more, see Bellah et al. (2007) and Lichterman (1996).

5. Snyder (2020), in *Exploiting Hope*, discusses the vulnerability we open ourselves up to and the possibilities for exploitation associated with new medical solutions, including crowdfunding. This period covers the beginning of the COVID-19 pandemic, whose economic consequences created surging demand for welfare crowdfunding. Our data suggests that campaigns created after March 2020 saw somewhat lower rates of success than those created before.

6. The majority of one-dollar campaign goals likely serve as placeholders. GoFundMe requires you to put in a dollar amount. Some welfare crowdfunders may be adopting a strategy popularized in real estate: beginning with

a low-ball amount in order to stimulate donations. It isn't completely clear whether or not this strategy is effective. Our data seems to hint that it isn't.

7. Concretely, if we drop all campaigns that were live for less than three weeks at the time of observation when calculating success among typical campaigns (i.e., the middle two-thirds by goal amount), the proportion that meet their goal changes from 12.1 to 13.4 percent. If we do this for the full range of goal amounts, we actually see the success rate fall. It's also worth considering a reasonable time for completing a campaign. Many of the costs that people turn to crowdfunding for (e.g., funeral, medical, tuition) are by their nature urgent, so that taking many weeks or months to meet a goal hardly counts as success. Our data can't tell us exactly how long campaigns tend to last; even if it could, the time a campaign spends on the platform may not be meaningful because many cases, especially when they don't take off right away, are left open for months and years until the platform itself eventually removes them.

8. The true extent of inequality in funds raised may be more extreme than we find based on our data. As we discuss in the Appendix, we believe that highly successful campaigns are more likely to stay online and visible longer to demonstrate how well the fundraising effort did. On the other hand, poorly performing campaigns are likely to be removed sooner to avoid being perceived as having failed. It's therefore much more likely that our analysis is missing low-funded campaigns rather than high-funded ones that were short-lived and so overlooked by our data collection because they were created and removed between our visits to GoFundMe. In other words, our approach to data collection likely undercounted the true number of low-earning campaigns, making our assessment of inequality conservative. If additional low-earning campaigns were to be added to our calculation, high-earning ones would become even rarer, making inequality as a whole even more severe. Igra et al. (2021) find similar inequality levels in a study of COVID-19-related medical crowdfunding.

9. These values are based on income earned, including capital gains, before taxes and government transfer payments (e.g., unemployment benefits). The numbers reported here are from tables 0 and A3 in the dataset in "World Bank Open Data" (2021), which updates the Piketty and Saez (2003) top income share series through 2018. Saez (2018) also provides a description of recent income inequality trends. The overall trend of steady or gradually increasing inequality in the US and Canada in recent years appears to have been disrupted, at least briefly, by the pandemic and the broad-based government economic aid that came with it.

10. According to the Organization for Economic Cooperation and Development, the 2017 US Gini (household disposable income) was 39. Other sources, like the Luxembourg Income Survey (https://www.lisdatacenter.org), provide similar estimates.

11. The values are very similar when looking at each country separately, although there are some differences between fundraising categories. Funds are somewhat more equally distributed for categories like pet-related costs (65) and more unequally distributed for community projects (85) and faith-based campaigns (76). The Gini for campaigns only in core welfare-related categories (health care, emergencies, funerals, and education) is 70. The South African Gini is from World Bank (n.d.).

12. The highest Gini for disposable income in the Standardized World Income Inequality Database (Solt 2020)—by far the most comprehensive collection of cross-nationally comparable income inequality measures— is 67.2, estimated for Namibia in 1994. The highest Gini for market income (pretax and pretransfer) in the database is 72.5, for South Africa in 2008. It's debatable whether disposable or market income is the most apt for comparison with crowdfunding earnings. We chose to highlight disposable income inequality since it gives a sense of actual consumable resources that individuals in different countries end up with. In crowdfunding, market and disposable "income" are one and the same since platforms don't engage in redistribution meaning that they don't "tax" high-earning campaigns and use the proceeds to make support payments to low-earning ones (although one interview respondent believed that they do). However, they certainly intervene by promoting some campaigns over others. The countries in which platforms operate, for their part, usually don't tax crowdfunding earnings (in the US, these are considered "personal gifts" and not taxable income in most cases). There are, of course, many important ways in which a crowdfunding platform differs from a country. We compare them here to give readers a general intuition about inequality on GoFundMe.

13. GoFundMe (2018).

14. See Boodman (2017).

15. *Fox 2 Detroit* (2018); Boynton (2020); Jefferson (2020).

16. Fottrell (2021).

17. See Schneiderhan (2011; 2015) for more on charity organizations, friendly visiting, and the move to combat fraud.

18. Cooley (1902).

19. For the privacy policy, see: https://www.gofundme.com/en-gb/c/privacy.

20. For GoFundMe revenue amounts, see Harris (2017) and MacMillan and Tan (2015).

21. See May (2020) and Campbell-Dollaghan (2016) for a general discussion of dark pattern design and GoFundMe; on Brignull see https://www.dark patterns.org/; on *Consumer Reports*, see Germain (2021). On FTC concerns, see Federal Trade Commission (2022).

22. Luguri and Strahilevitz (2021); Smith ([1776] 2003).

23. Adams (2016); Heller (2019), along these lines, discusses how "just getting the story out there" is insufficient for crowdfunding success.

24. Merton (1938) extensively theorized the role that luck plays in explaining and justifying what happens in our lives, particularly in American society; see also Sauder (2020) for a review of how luck factors into sociological thinking.

25. See Igra (2021).

26. See Smith et al. (2016), but note that this is for all crowdfunding, not just social welfare. See also Berliner and Kenworthy (2017). On low-income donors, see NORC (2021).

27. Igra (2021).

28. See Schneiderhan (2013) on using Taylor Swift song lyrics to make sense of mean peer reviews.

29. Mills (1959). Douglas (1995).

30. See Quinn and Schneiderhan (2023) for a discussion of the moral underpinnings of sociological research and how we might find purpose in trying to solve social problems in our community.

Chapter 5

1. This estimate of is from a survey by the research organization NORC at the University of Chicago (NORC 2021).

2. This period covers the beginning of the COVID-19 pandemic, whose economic consequences created surging demand for welfare crowdfunding. Our data suggests that campaigns created after March 2020 saw somewhat lower rates of success than those created before. See Igra et al. (2021) for a detailed analysis of COVID-19–related crowdfunding in the first months of the pandemic.

3. This image is often called Rubin's vase after the Danish psychologist Edgar Rubin.

4. This is a point that scholars of inequality have noted since the early days of the internet. See Hargittai (2002).

5. The psychological concept of "learned helplessness" is typically attributed to Seligman (1974) and refers to a sense of powerlessness resulting from repeated exposure to traumatic and averse events outside of one's control.

6. On tipping on GoFundMe, see Monroe (2019).

7. Berliner and Kenworthy (2017) were among the first to call attention to this problematic aspect of crowdfunding, and their article created a strong foundation for the ensuing conversation in the literature.

8. See Prasad (2018) and (2021) for more on how sociological ideas can be used to solve social problems and how focusing on social problems can help advance sociological understandings of the world. This specific formulation of "reconstruction" comes from Jürgen Habermas (1979, 95).

9. In a move widely condemned by developers and academics, Twitter ended its policy of free API use and switched to a paid model in February 2023.

10. See Cadogan (2021) for an example of critical statements by GoFundMe representatives about the state of the US social support system and how Go-FundMe has become a source of help for funding basic needs.

11. On the Algorithmic Justice League (https://www.ajl.org/), one of the leading organizations calling for this kind of work across all artificial intelligence platforms, see Vanian (2018).

12. See Cadogan (2021) on GoFundMe and the "giving layer." Wade (2022) provides a critical account of this concept.

13. Kang (2021).

14. Cadogan (2021).

15. Lorde (2018); Kenworthy (2020); Lothian-McLean (2020).

16. See Spade (2020), who is one of the leading thinkers on the importance of mutual aid in the twenty-first century. For more on mutual aid, see Fernandez (2020), Solnit (2020), Baiocchi et al. (2018), and Baiocchi (2020).

17. See Addams (2002) for the quote; see Schneiderhan (2015) for how this quote links to helping others in the past and present day.

18. See Japsen (2020) on the enduring popularity of Obamacare.

19. See Hoynes and Rothstein (2019) for a discussion of the potential role of universal basic incomes (UBI) in industrialized countries.

Appendix

1. See Google's introduction to sitemaps for website administrators at https://developers.google.com/search/docs/advanced/sitemaps/overview.

2. Salganik (2018).

3. The language describing deactivated campaigns as maintaining summary versions appears in GoFundMe's support documents as of late 2020 and is captured in an archived version of the page from Dec. 2020: https://web.archive.org/web/20201206012823/https://support.gofundme.com/hc/en-us/articles/203604074-How-Do-I-Delete-My-Fundraiser-. The collection period for the data analyzed in this book ended in January 2021.

4. See Feliciano and Kizer (2021); Igra (2021); Lukk et al. (2018).

References

Adams, Susan. 2016. "Free Market Philanthropy: GoFundMe Is Changing the Way People Give to Causes Big and Small." *Forbes*, October 19, 2016. https://www.forbes.com/sites/susanadams/2016/10/19/free-market-philanthropy-gofundme-is-changing-the-way-people-give-to-causes-big-and-small/.

Addams, Jane. 2002. *Democracy and Social Ethics*. Urbana, IL: University of Illinois Press.

Agrawal, Ajay, Christian Catalini, and Avi Goldfarb. 2015. "Crowdfunding: Geography, Social Networks, and the Timing of Investment Decisions." *Journal of Economics & Management Strategy* 24 (2): 253–74. https://doi.org/10.1111/jems.12093.

Ahlers, Gerrit K. C., Douglas Cumming, Christina Günther, and Denis Schweizer. 2015. "Signaling in Equity Crowdfunding." *Entrepreneurship Theory and Practice* 39 (4): 955–80. https://doi.org/10.1111/etap.12157.

Alderman, Liz, and Matina Stevis-Gridneff. 2020. "The Pandemic's Economic Damage Is Growing." *The New York Times*, July 7, 2020. https://www.nytimes.com/2020/07/07/business/EU-OECD-coronavirus-economic-reports.html.

Allan, Stuart, and Einar Thorsen. 2009. *Citizen Journalism: Global Perspectives*. Vol. 1. New York: Peter Lang.

Alvarez, R. Michael, Thad E. Hall, and Alexander H. Trechsel. 2009. "Internet Voting in Comparative Perspective: The Case of Estonia." *PS: Political Science & Politics* 42 (3): 497–505. https://doi.org/10.1017/S1049096509090787.

Amenta, Edwin. 2000. *Bold Relief: Institutional Politics and the Origins of Modern American Social Policy*. Princeton, NJ: Princeton University Press.

Amnesty International. 2022. "The Social Atrocity: Meta and the Right to Remedy for the Rohingya," September 29, 2022. Index no. ASA 16/5933/2022.

Anderson, Monica, and Madhumitha Kumar. 2019. "Digital Divide Persists Even as Lower-Income Americans Make Gains in Tech Adoption." *Pew Research Center* (blog), May 7, 2019. https://www.pewresearch.org/fact-tank/2019/05/07/digital-divide-persists-even-as-lower-income-americans-make-gains-in-tech-adoption/.

Anderson, Monica, and Andrew Perrin. 2017. "Disabled Americans Less Likely to Use Technology." *Pew Research Center* (blog), April 7, 2017. https://www.pewresearch.org/fact-tank/2017/04/07/disabled-americans-are-less-likely-to-use-technology/.

Aniftos, Rania. 2021. "A Timeline of Taylor Swift's Generosity." *Billboard*, March 23, 2021. https://www.billboard.com/music/music-news/timeline-taylor-swift-generosity-8481430/.

Arnold, Chris. 2020. "Unemployment Money Not Reaching Millions of People Who Applied." *NPR*, April 15, 2020. https://www.npr.org/2020/04/15/835174390/unemployment-money-not-reaching-millions-of-people-who-applied.

Attuel-Mendès, Laurence. 2017. "The Different Ways of Collaboration between a Retail Bank and Crowdfunding." *Strategic Change* 26 (2): 213–25. https://doi.org/10.1002/jsc.2121.

Badger, Emily, and Alicia Parlapiano. 2020. "States Made It Harder to Get Jobless Benefits. Now That's Hard to Undo." *The New York Times*, April 30, 2020. https://www.nytimes.com/2020/04/30/upshot/unemployment-state-restrictions-pandemic.html.

Bail, Chris. 2021. *Breaking the Social Media Prism*. Princeton, NJ: Princeton University Press.

Baiocchi, Gianpaolo. 2020. "The Utopian Counterfactual." *Thesis Eleven* (blog), August 13, 2020. https://thesiseleven.com/2020/08/14/the-utopian-counterfactual/.

Baiocchi, Gianpaolo, Marnie Brady, and H. Jacob Carlson. 2018. "Beyond the Market: Housing Alternatives from the Grassroots." *Dissent* 65 (4): 51–58. https://doi.org/10.1353/dss.2018.0074.

Baird, Katherine E. 2016. "The Financial Burden of Out-of-Pocket Expenses in the United States and Canada: How Different Is the United States?" *SAGE Open Medicine* 4 (January): 2050312115623792. https://doi.org/10.1177/2050312115623792.

Banting, Keith, and John Myles. 2013. *Inequality and the Fading of Redistributive Politics*. Vancouver: UBC Press.

Barasinska, Nataliya, and Dorothea Schäfer. 2014. "Is Crowdfunding Different? Evidence on the Relation between Gender and Funding Success from a German Peer-to-Peer Lending Platform." *German Economic Review* 15 (4): 436–52. https://doi.org/10.1111/geer.12052.

Barbrook, Richard, and Andy Cameron. 1996. "The Californian Ideology." *Science as Culture* 6 (1): 44–72. https://doi.org/10.1080/09505439609526455.

Barcelos, Chris A. 2020. "Go Fund Inequality: The Politics of Crowdfunding Transgender Medical Care." *Critical Public Health* 30 (3): 330–39. https://doi.org/10.1080/09581596.2019.1575947.

Barcelos, Chris A., and Stephanie L. Budge. 2019. "Inequalities in Crowdfunding for Transgender Health Care." *Transgender Health* 4 (1): 81–88. https://doi.org/10.1089/trgh.2018.0044.

Barrett, William P. 2021. "America's Top 100 Charities 2021." *Forbes*, December 13, 2022. https://www.forbes.com/lists/top-charities/.

Bartlett, Jamie. 2018. *The People vs. Tech: How the Internet Is Killing Democracy (and How We Save It)*. New York: Random House.

Bate, Ellie. 2021. "Taylor Swift Donates $50,000 to Family Whose Father Died of COVID-19." *BuzzFeed News*, March 24, 2021. https://www.buzzfeednews.com/article/eleanorbate/taylor-swift-andrea-donated-gofundme-covid-family.

Beito, David T. 2000. *From Mutual Aid to the Welfare State: Fraternal Societies and Social Services, 1890–1967*. Chapel Hill, NC: University of North Carolina Press.

Bellah, Robert N., Richard Madsen, William M. Sullivan, Ann Swidler, and Steven M. Tipton. 2007. *Habits of the Heart, with a New Preface: Individualism and Commitment in American Life*. Oakland, CA: University of California Press.

Benjamin, Ruha. 2019. *Race after Technology: Abolitionist Tools for the New Jim Code*. Medford, MA: Polity.

Benkler, Yochai, Robert Faris, and Hal Roberts. 2018. *Network Propaganda: Manipulation, Disinformation, and Radicalization in American Politics*. New York: Oxford University Press. https://doi.org/10.1093/oso/9780190923624.001.0001.

Berliner, Lauren S., and Nora J. Kenworthy. 2017. "Producing a Worthy Illness: Personal Crowdfunding amidst Financial Crisis." *Social Science & Medicine* 187: 233–42. https://doi.org/10.1016/j.socscimed.2017.02.008.

Bivens, Josh, and Heidi Shierholz. 2020. "Despite Some Good Provisions, the CARES Act Has Glaring Flaws and Falls Short of Fully Protecting Workers during the Coronavirus Crisis." *Economic Policy Institute* (blog), March 25, 2020. https://www.epi.org/blog/despite-some-good-provisions-the-cares-act-has-glaring-flaws-and-falls-short-of-fully-protecting-workers-during-the-coronavirus-crisis/.

Bobrow, Emily. 2021. "Charles Best Knows What Teachers Need." *The Wall Street Journal*, August 27, 2021. https://www.wsj.com/articles/charles-best-knows-what-teachers-need-11630081473.

Bonfiglio, Briana. 2019. "Jamison Novello, South Side High School Sophomore, Dies at 15." *LIHerald*, April 4, 2019. https://www.liherald.com/stories/jamison-novello-south-side-high-school-sophomore-dies-at-15,113342.

Boodman, Eric. 2017. "She Said She Had Cancer, and Neighbors Opened Their Wallets. Then a Stranger's Email Raised Questions." *Statnews*, November 1, 2017. https://www.statnews.com/2017/11/01/cancer-fundraising-fraud/.

Borst, Irma, Christine Moser, and Julie Ferguson. 2018. "From Friendfunding to Crowdfunding: Relevance of Relationships, Social Media, and Platform Activities to Crowdfunding Performance." *New Media & Society* 20 (4): 1396–414. https://doi.org/10.1177/1461444817694599.

Bourdieu, Pierre. 1990. *The Logic of Practice*. Stanford, CA: Stanford University Press.

———. 1996. *The Rules of Art: Genesis and Structure of the Literary Field*. Stanford, CA: Stanford University Press.

———. 2000. *Pascalian Meditations*. Stanford, CA: Stanford University Press.

———. 2019. *Distinction: A Social Critique of the Judgement of Taste*. London: Routledge.

Boutigny, Erwan, and Marie-Josèphe Leroux-Sostenes. 2021. "Dynamique du financement participatif territorial: vers une nouvelle perspective de financement?" *Annales des Mines—Gérer et comprendre* 143 (1): 3–12. https://doi.org/10.3917/geco1.143.0003.

Boychuk, Gerard W. 2008. *National Health Insurance in the United States and Canada: Race, Territory, and the Roots of Difference*. Washington DC: Georgetown University Press.

Boynton, Sean. 2020. "Accused Killer of Black Lives Matter Activist Oluwatoyin Salau Confessed to Police: Docs." *Global News*, June 24, 2020. https://globalnews.ca/news/7100413/oluwatoyin-salau-killing-confession/.

Brady, David, and Zachary Parolin. 2020. "The Levels and Trends in Deep and Extreme Poverty in the United States, 1993–2016." *Demography* 57 (6): 2337–60. https://doi.org/10.1007/s13524-020-00924-1.

Bray, Freddie, Jacques Ferlay, Isabelle Soerjomataram, Rebecca L. Siegel, Lindsey A. Torre, and Ahmedin Jemal. 2018. "Global Cancer Statistics 2018: GLOBOCAN Estimates of Incidence and Mortality Worldwide for 36 Cancers in 185 Countries." *CA: A Cancer Journal for Clinicians* 68 (6): 394–424. https://doi.org/10.3322/caac.21492.

Brayne, Sarah. 2020. *Predict and Surveil: Data, Discretion, and the Future of Policing*. Princeton, NJ: Princeton University Press.

Bucher, Taina. 2018. *If . . . Then: Algorithmic Power and Politics*. New York: Oxford University Press.

Budge, Stephanie L., Sabra L. Katz-Wise, and Michael V. Garza. 2016. "Health Disparities in the Transgender Community: Exploring Differences in Insurance Coverage." *Psychology of Sexual Orientation and Gender Diversity* 3 (3): 275. https://psycnet.apa.org/doi/10.1037/sgd0000169.

Burrell, Jenna, and Marion Fourcade. 2021. "The Society of Algorithms." *Annual Review of Sociology* 47 (1): 213–37. https://doi.org/10.1146/annurev-soc-090820-020800.

Buttic, Vincenzo, Massimo G. Colombo, and Mike Wright. 2017. "Serial Crowdfunding, Social Capital, and Project Success." *Entrepreneurship Theory and Practice* 41 (2): 183–207. https://doi.org/10.1111/etap.12271.

Cadogan, Tim. 2021. "GoFundMe CEO: Hello Congress, Americans Need Help and We Can't Do Your Job for You." *USA TODAY*, February 11, 2021. https://ww.usatoday.com/story/opinion/voices/2021/02/11/gofundme-ceo -congress-pass-covid-relief-desperate-americans-column/444042 5001/.

Cai, Cynthia Weiyi. 2018. "Disruption of Financial Intermediation by Fin-Tech: A Review on Crowdfunding and Blockchain." *Accounting and Finance (Parkville)* 58 (4): 965–92. https://doi.org/10.1111/acfi.12405.

Campbell-Dollaghan, Kelsey. 2016. "The Year Dark Patterns Won." *Fast Company*, December 21, 2016. https://www.fastcompany.com/3066586/ the-year-dark-patterns-won.

Carnevale, Anthony P., Tamara Jayasundera, and Dmitri Repnikov. 2014. "Understanding Online Job Ads Data." Georgetown University, Center on Education and the Workforce. https://cew.georgetown.edu/wp-content/ uploads/2014/11/OCLM.Tech_.Web_.pdf.

Cassella, Megan, and Katy Murphy. 2020. "States Overwhelmed by Previously Unimaginable Layoff Numbers." *Politico*, April 1, 2020. https://www.polit ico.com/news/2020/04/01/unemployed-workers-benefits-coronavirus -159192.

Castells, Manuel. 2012. *Networks of Outrage and Hope: Social Movements in the Internet Age.* Malden, MA: Polity.

Chan, C. S. Richard, and Annaleena Parhankangas. 2017. "Crowdfunding Innovative Ideas: How Incremental and Radical Innovativeness Influence Funding Outcomes." *Entrepreneurship Theory and Practice* 41 (2): 237–63. https://doi.org/10.1111/etap.12268.

Chan, Melissa. 2017. "How the Kindness of Strangers Became a Multi-Billion-Dollar Industry." *Time*, August 25, 2017. https://time.com/4912910/ crowdfunding-gofundme-youcaring/.

Chapman, Matthew. 2016. "Funding Businesses by Avoiding the Gate-keepers." *The Guardian*, August 11, 2016. https://www.theguardian.com/ small-business-network/2016/aug/11/growing-businesses-crowdfunding -indiegogo.

Christin, Angele. 2020. *Metrics at Work: Journalism and the Contested Meaning of Algorithms.* Princeton, NJ: Princeton University Press.

Cilke, James. 2014. "The Case of the Missing Strangers: What We Know and Don't Know about Non-Filers." *Proceedings. Annual Conference on Taxation and Minutes of the Annual Meeting of the National Tax Association.* .

Clark, David. 2002. "Neoliberalism and Public Service Reform: Canada in Comparative Perspective." *Canadian Journal of Political Science* 35 (4): 771–93. https://doi.org/10.1017/S0008423902778438.

Clark, Liat. 2012. "How to Get Your Crowdfunding Campaign to Indiegogo to the Top." *Wired UK*, October 19, 2012. https://www.wired.co.uk/article/how-to-indiegogo.

Clemens, Elisabeth S. 2020. "Civic Gifts: Voluntarism and the Making of the American Nation-State." Chicago: University of Chicago Press. https://press.uchicago.edu/ucp/books/book/chicago/C/bo45713286.html.

Cohen, Patricia, Ben Casselman, and Gillian Friedman. 2020. "An Extra $600 a Week Kept Many Jobless Workers Afloat. Now What Will They Do?" *The New York Times*, July 29, 2020. https://www.nytimes.com/2020/07/29/business/economy/unemployment-benefits-coronavirus.html.

Coleman, James S. 1988. "Social Capital in the Creation of Human Capital." *American Journal of Sociology* 94: S95–120. https://doi.org/10.1086/228943.

Cooley, Charles Horton. 1902. *Human Nature and the Social Order.* New York: Charles Scribner's Sons.

Covert, Bryce. 2019. "The Myth of the Welfare Queen." *The New Republic*, July 2, 2019. https://newrepublic.com/article/154404/myth-welfare-queen.

Cubanski, Juliette, Wyatt Koma, Anthony Damico, and Tricia Neuman. 2018. "How Many Seniors Live in Poverty?" Kaiser Family Foundation, November 19, 2018. https://files.kff.org/attachment/Issue-Brief-How-Many-Seniors-Live-in-Poverty.

Cullen, Catherine. 2020. "Ottawa Will Distribute Pandemic Money Now, 'Clean Up' Fraudulent Claims Later, PM Says." *CBC News*, May 12, 2020. https://www.cbc.ca/news/politics/clean-up-cerb-fraud-1.5566440.

Curtis, Josh, and Naomi Lightman. 2017. "Golden Years or Retirement Fears? Private Pension Inequality Among Canada's Immigrants." *Canadian Journal on Aging* 36 (2): 178–95. https://doi.org/10.1017/S0714980817000083.

Daigneault, Pierre-Marc, Lisa Birch, Daniel Béland, and Samuel-David Bélanger. 2021. "Taking Subnational and Regional Welfare States Seriously: Insights from the Quebec Case." *Journal of European Social Policy* 31 (2): 239–49. https://doi.org/10.1177/0958928721996651.

Desmond, Matthew. 2012. "Disposable Ties and the Urban Poor." *American Journal of Sociology* 117 (5): 1295–335. https://doi.org/10.1086/663574.

de Tocqueville, Alexis (1835) 2000. *Democracy in America*, translated by Harvey C. Mansfield and Delba Winthrop. Chicago: University of Chicago Press.

DiMaggio, Paul, Eszter Hargittai, Coral Celeste, and Steven Shafer. 2016. "Digital Inequality: From Unequal Access to Differentiated Use." In *Inequality in the United States: A Reader*, edited by John Brueggemann, 98–113. New York: Routledge.

Dinan, Shannon, and Alain Noël. 2020. "Quebec's Resilient Redistribution Model: Activation Policies in the 2010s." *Canadian Public Administration* 63 (3): 473–97. https://doi.org/10.1111/capa.12384.

Douglas, Susan Jeanne. 1995. *Where the Girls Are: Growing Up Female With the Mass Media.* New York: Times Books.

Ebersman, David A. 2012. "Form S-1 Registration Statement." Securities and Exchange Commission. https://www.sec.gov/Archives/edgar/data/1326801/000119312512034517/d287954ds1.htm.

Elliot, Michael. 2018. "Trial by Social-Media: The Rise of Litigation Crowdfunding." *University of Cincinnati Law Review.* 84: 529. https://scholarship.law.uc.edu/uclr/vol84/iss2/8.

Elmer, Greg, and Sabrina Ward-Kimola. 2021. "Political Crowdfunding and Campaigning on GoFundMe." *Canadian Journal of Communication.* 46 (4): 803–20. https://doi.org/10.22230/cjc.2021v46n4a3935.

Ember, Sydney. 2019. "Bernie Sanders Went to Canada, and a Dream of 'Medicare for All' Flourished." *The New York Times*, September 9, 2019. https://www.nytimes.com/2019/09/09/us/politics/bernie-sanders-health-care.html.

Esping-Andersen, Gøsta. 1990. *The Three Worlds of Welfare Capitalism*. Princeton, NJ: Princeton University Press.

———. 1996. "After the Golden Age? Welfare State Dilemmas in a Global Economy." In *Welfare States in Transition: National Adaptations in Global Economies*, edited by Gøsta Esping-Andersen, 1–31. London: SAGE Publications.

Espinoza, Javier. 2022. "How Big Tech Lost the Antitrust Battle with Europe." *Financial Times*, March 21, 2022. https://arstechnica.com/tech-policy/2022/03/how-big-tech-lost-the-antitrust-battle-with-europe/.

Etherington, Darrell. 2020. "Flexport, Arnold Schwarzenegger and Others Launch a Fund to Get Supplies to Front-Line Responders." *TechCrunch*, March 24, 2020. https://techcrunch.com/2020/03/24/flexport-arnold-schwarzenegger-and-others-launch-a-fund-to-get-supplies-to-frontline-responders/.

Eubanks, Virginia. 2018. *Automating Inequality: How High-Tech Tools Profile, Police, and Punish the Poor*. New York: Picador.

Faberman, Jason, and Marianna Kudlyak. 2016. "What Does Online Job Search Tell Us about the Labor Market?" *Economic Perspectives* 40 (1): 1–15. https://www.chicagofed.org/publications/economic-perspectives/2016/1-faberman-kudlyak.

Federal Trade Commission. 2022. "FTC Report Shows Rise in Sophisticated Dark Patterns Designed to Trick and Trap Consumers." September 15, 2022. https://www.ftc.gov/news-events/news/press-releases/2022/09/ftc-report-shows-rise-sophisticated-dark-patterns-designed-trick-trap-consumers.

Feldstein, Steven. 2021. *The Rise of Digital Repression: How Technology Is Reshaping Power, Politics, and Resistance*. New York: Oxford University Press.

Feliciano, Cynthia, and Jessica M. Kizer. 2021. "Reinforcing the Racial Structure: Observed Race and Multiracial Internet Daters' Racial Preferences." *Social Forces* 99 (4): 1457–86. https://doi.org/10.1093/sf/soaa065.

Ferguson, Andrew Guthrie. 2017. *The Rise of Big Data Policing: Surveillance, Race, and the Future of Law Enforcement*. New York: NYU Press.

Fernandez, Daniel. 2020. "Dean Spade on the Promise of Mutual Aid." *The Nation*, December 16, 2020. https://www.thenation.com/article/economy/interview-dean-spade/.

Ferrari, Elisabetta. 2020. "Technocracy Meets Populism: The Dominant Technological Imaginary of Silicon Valley." *Communication, Culture and Critique* 13 (1): 121–24. https://doi.org/10.1093/ccc/tcz051.

Finkel, Alvin. 2006. *Social Policy and Practice in Canada: A History*. Waterloo, ON: Wilfrid Laurier University Press.

Finley, Klint. 2020. "Can't File for Unemployment? Don't Blame Cobol." *Wired*, April 22, 2020. https://www.wired.com/story/cant-file-unemployment-dont-blame-cobol/.

Foroohar, Rana. 2018. "Year in a Word: Techlash." *Financial Times*, December 16, 2018. https://www.ft.com/content/76578fba-fca1-11e8-ac00-57a2a826423e.

Fortt, Jon, and Sara Salinas. 2018. "GoFundMe Used to Charge US Personal Campaigns, but Doesn't Anymore. Here's Why the CEO Thinks It's a Good Model to Follow." *CNBC*, April 14, 2018. https://www.cnbc.com/2018/04/14/gofundme-ceo-rob-solomon-our-insane-no-fee-business-model-works.html.

Fottrell, Quentin. 2021. "My Friends Raised $15,000 on GoFundMe While I Was Comatose after an Accident. But I Inherited $1 Million, and My Insurance Covered the Costs." *MarketWatch*, May 16, 2021. https://www.marketwatch.com/story/my-friends-raised-15000-on-gofundme-after-i-was-in-an-accident-but-i-inherited-1-million-and-my-insurance-covered-the-costs-2021-05-14.

Fox 2 Detroit. 2018. (text article), October 4, 2018. https://www.fox2detroit.com/news/woman-gets-28-5-months-to-15-years-for-faking-cancer-raising-over-30k.

Gallemore, Caleb, Kristian Roed Nielsen, and Kristjan Jespersen. 2019. "The Uneven Geography of Crowdfunding Success: Spatial Capital on Indiegogo." *Environment and Planning A: Economy and Space* 51 (6): 1389–406. https://doi.org/10.1177/0308518X19843925.

Galuszka, Patryk, and Blanka Brzozowska. 2017. "Crowdfunding and the Democratization of the Music Market." *Media, Culture & Society* 39 (6): 833–49. https://journals.sagepub.com/doi/10.1177/0163443716674364.

Ganguli, Ishani, Zhuo Shi, E. John Orav, Aarti Rao, Kristin N. Ray, and Ateev Mehrotra. 2020. "Declining Use of Primary Care among Commercially Insured Adults in the United States, 2008–2016." *Annals of Internal Medicine* 172 (4): 240–47. https://doi.org/10.7326/M19-1834.

Germain, Thomas. 2021. "New Dark Patterns Tip Line Lets You Report Manipulative Online Practices." *Consumer Reports*, May 19, 2021. https://www.consumerreports.org/digital-rights/dark-patterns-tip-line-report-manipulative-practices-a1196931056/.

Gilens, Martin. 1999. *Why Americans Hate Welfare: Race, Media, and the Politics of Antipoverty Policy*. Chicago: University of Chicago Press.

Gilligan, Adrienne M., David S. Alberts, Denise J. Roe, and Grant H. Skrepnek. 2018. "Death or Debt? National Estimates of Financial Toxicity in Persons with Newly-Diagnosed Cancer." *American Journal of Medicine* 131 (10): 1187–99. https://doi.org/10.1016/j.amjmed.2018.05.020.

Goffman, Erving. 1978. *The Presentation of Self in Everyday Life*. London: Harmondsworth.

GoFundMe. 2018. "Introducing 'True Stories of Good People,' GoFundMe's First Podcast." *Medium*, July 26, 2018. https://medium.com/gofundme-stories/introducing-true-stories-of-good-people-gofundmes-first-podcast-ab6d fbd6ffc6.

———. 2019. "GoFundMe 2019: A Year in Giving." https://www.gofundme .com/2019.

———. 2020a. "Inspire Hope: The GoFundMe 2020 Giving Report." https:// www.gofundme.com/2020.

———. 2020b. "Our New Fundraising Category—Rent, Food + Monthly Bills—Helps Address the Increase in Urgent Needs." *Medium*, October 22, 2020. https://medium.com/gofundme-stories/our-new-fundraising-cat egory-rent-food-monthly-bills-helps-address-the-increase-in-urgent -4dcd9d941178.

———. 2021. "GoFundMe's 2021 Giving Report." https://www.gofundme .com/c/gofundme-giving-report-2021.

Goldring, Luin, Carolina Berinstein, and Judith K. Bernhard. 2009. "Institutionalizing Precarious Migratory Status in Canada." *Citizenship Studies* 13 (3): 239–65. https://doi.org/10.1080/13621020902850643.

Grabb, Edward, and James Curtis. 2010. *Regions Apart: The Four Societies of Canada and the United States*. Oxford, UK: Oxford University Press.

Graham, Meg. 2017. "Competitor Acquires Chicago-Based Crowdfunding Site GiveForward." *Chicago Tribune*, March 29, 2017. https://www.chicagotri bune.com/business/blue-sky/ct-giveforward-youcaring-acquisition-bsi -20170329-story.html.

Granovetter, Mark S. 1973. "The Strength of Weak Ties." *American Journal of Sociology* 78 (6): 1360–80. https://www.journals.uchicago.edu/doi/ 10.1086/225469.

Grant, Jaime, Lisa Mottet, Justin Tanis, Jody L Herman, Jack Harrison, and Mara Keisling. 2010. "National Transgender Discrimination Survey Report on Health and Health Care." National Center for Transgender Equality/ National Gay and Lesbian Task Force. www.TheTaskForce.org/www .TransEquality.org.

Graves, Steven M. 2003. "Landscapes of Predation, Landscapes of Neglect: A Location Analysis of Payday Lenders and Banks." *The Professional Geographer* 55 (3): 303–17. https://doi.org/10.1111/0033-0124.5503017.

Grossman, Lev. 2006. "You—Yes, You—Are TIME's Person of the Year." *Time*, December 25, 2006. http://content.time.com/time/magazine/article/0,9171 ,1570810,00.html.

Guenther, Christina, Sofia Johan, and Denis Schweizer. 2018. "Is the Crowd Sensitive to Distance?—How Investment Decisions Differ by Investor Type." *Small Business Economics* 50 (2): 289–305. https://doi.org/10.1007/s11187 -016-9834-6.

Habermas, Jürgen. 1979. *Communication and the Evolution of Society*. Boston: Beacon Press.

Hacker, Jacob S. 2019. *The Great Risk Shift: The New Economic Insecurity and the Decline of the American Dream*. New York: Oxford University Press.

Haldeman, C., W. G. Gale, and G. Enda. 2020,). "Careful or Careless? Perspectives on the CARES Act." *Brookings*, March 27, 2020. 27https://www.brook ings.edu/blog/up-front/2020/03/27/careful-or-careless-perspectives-on -the-cares-act/.

Hao, Karen. 2021. "How Facebook Got Addicted to Spreading Misinformation." *MIT Technology Review*, March 11, 2021. https://www.technologyre view.com/2021/03/11/1020600/facebook-responsible-ai-misinformation/.

Hara, Kotaro, Abigail Adams, Kristy Milland, Saiph Savage, Chris Callison-Burch, and Jeffrey P. Bigham. 2018. "A Data-Driven Analysis of Workers' Earnings on Amazon Mechanical Turk." *Proceedings of the 2018 CHI Conference on Human Factors in Computing Systems*, Montreal, QC, April, 1–14.

Hargittai, Eszter. 2002. "Second-Level Digital Divide." *First Monday* 7 (4). https:// firstmonday.org/ojs/index.php/fm/article/download/942/864?inline=1.

———. 2019. "The Digital Reproduction of Inequality." In *The Inequality Reader*, 2nd ed., edited by David B. Grusky and Szonja Szelényi, 660–71. London: Routledge.

Harris, Ainsley. 2017. "How Crowdfunding Platform GoFundMe Has Created A $3 Billion Digital Safety Net." *Fast Company*, February 13, 2017. https:// www.fastcompany.com/3067472/how-crowdfunding-platform-gofund me-has-created-a-3-billion-digital.

———. 2018. "GoFundMe Keeps Gobbling Up Competitors, Says It's 'Very Good for the Market.'" *Fast Company*, April 4, 2018. https://www.fastcom pany.com/40554199/gofundme-keeps-gobbling-up-competitors-says-its -very-good-for-the-market.

Harris, Kathleen. 2020. "Trudeau Unveils $82B COVID-19 Emergency Response Package for Canadians, Businesses." *CBC News*, March 18, 2020. https:// www.cbc.ca/news/politics/economic-aid-package-coronavirus-1.5501037.

Harris, Robert L. 1979. "Early Black Benevolent Societies, 1780–1830." *The Massachusetts Review* 20 (3): 603–25. https://www.jstor.org/stable/25088988.

Harvey, David. 2005. *A Brief History of Neoliberalism*. Oxford, UK: Oxford University Press.

Heller, Nathan. 2019. "The Hidden Cost of GoFundMe Health Care." *The New Yorker*, June 24, 2019. https://www.newyorker.com/magazine/2019/07/01/the-perverse-logic-of-gofundme-health-care.

Herzenstein, Michal, Scott Sonenshein, and Utpal M. Dholakia. 2011. "Tell Me a Good Story and I May Lend You Money: The Role of Narratives in Peer-to-Peer Lending Decisions." *Journal of Marketing Research* 48 (SPL): S138–49. https://doi.org/10.1509/jmkr.48.SPL.S138.

Hindman, Matthew. 2008. *The Myth of Digital Democracy.* Princeton, NJ: Princeton University Press.

Holbrook, Anne M., Mei Wang, Munil Lee, Zhiyuan Chen, Michael Garcia, Laura Nguyen, Angela Ford, Selina Manji, and Michael R. Law. 2021. "Cost-Related Medication Nonadherence in Canada: A Systematic Review of Prevalence, Predictors, and Clinical Impact." *Systematic Reviews* 10 (1): 11. https://doi.org/10.1186/s13643-020-01558-5.

Hollis, Aidan, and Arthur Sweetman. 2001. "The Life-Cycle of a Microfinance Institution: The Irish Loan Funds." *Journal of Economic Behavior & Organization* 46 (3): 291–311. https://doi.org/10.1016/S0167-2681(01)00179-2.

Hrisch, Jacob. 2015. "Crowdfunding for Environmental Ventures: An Empirical Analysis of the Influence of Environmental Orientation on the Success of Crowdfunding Initiatives." *Journal of Cleaner Production* 107 (November): 636–45. https://doi.org/10.1016/j.jclepro.2015.05.046.

Howe, Jeff. 2006. "The Rise of Crowdsourcing." *Wired*, June 1, 2006. https://www.wired.com/2006/06/crowds/.

———. 2009. *Crowdsourcing: Why the Power of the Crowd Is Driving the Future of Business.* New York: Currency.

Hoynes, Hilary, and Jesse Rothstein. 2019. "Universal Basic Income in the United States and Advanced Countries." *Annual Review of Economics* 11 (1): 929–58. https://doi.org/10.1146/annurev-economics-080218-030237.

Huber, Gregory A., and Neil Malhotra. 2017. "Political Homophily in Social Relationships: Evidence from Online Dating Behavior." *The Journal of Politics* 79 (1): 269–83. https://doi.org/10.1086/687533.

Hunter, Andrea. 2015. "Crowdfunding Independent and Freelance Journalism: Negotiating Journalistic Norms of Autonomy and Objectivity." *New Media & Society* 17 (2): 272–88. https://journals.sagepub.com/doi/10.1177/1461444814558915.

Igra, Mark. 2021. "Donor Financial Capacity Drives Racial Inequality in Medical Crowdsourced Funding." *Social Forces*, July 2, 2021. https://doi.org/10.1093/sf/soab076.

Igra, Mark, Nora Kenworthy, Cadence Luchsinger, and Jin-Kyu Jung. 2021. "Crowdfunding as a Response to COVID-19: Increasing Inequities at a Time of Crisis." *Social Science & Medicine* 282 (August): 114105. https://doi.org/10.1016/j.socscimed.2021.114105.

Ilcan, Suzan. 2009. "Privatizing Responsibility: Public Sector Reform under Neoliberal Government." *Canadian Review of Sociology* 46 (3): 207–34. https://doi.org/10.1111/j.1755-618X.2009.01212.x.

Internal Revenue Service. 2021. "Exemption Requirements – 501(c)(3) Organizations." February 17, 2022. https://www.irs.gov/charities-non-profits/charitable-organizations/exemption-requirements-501c3-organizations.

Japsen, Bruce. 2020. "Poll: Obamacare More Popular Than Ever." *Forbes*, February 21, 2020. https://www.forbes.com/sites/brucejapsen/2020/02/21/poll-obamacare-more-popular-than-ever/.

Jefferson, J'na. 2020. "Death of Oluwatoyin Salau: What We Know So Far." *The Root*, June 15, 2020. https://www.theroot.com/death-of-oluwatoyin-salau-what-we-know-so-far-1844038831.

Jones, Nicholas, Rachel Marks, Robert Ramirez, and Merarys Ríos-Vargas. 2021. "2020 Census Illuminates Racial and Ethnic Composition of the Country." US Census Bureau, August 12, 2021. https://www.census.gov/library/stories/2021/08/improved-race-ethnicity-measures-reveal-united-states-population-much-more-multiracial.html

Kalleberg, Arne L. 2011. *Good Jobs, Bad Jobs: The Rise of Polarized and Precarious Employment Systems in the United States, 1970s–2000s*. New York: Russell Sage Foundation.

Kallio, Aki, and Lasse Vuola. 2020. "History of Crowdfunding in the Context of Ever-Changing Modern Financial Markets." In *Advances in Crowdfunding*, edited by R. Shneor,. L. Zhao, and B. T. Flåten, 209–39. Cham, Switzerland: Palgrave Macmillan.

Kamarck, Elaine, and Christine Stenglein. 2019. "How Many Undocumented Immigrants Are in the United States and Who Are They?" Brookings, November 12, 2019. https://www.brookings.edu/policy2020/votervital/how-many-undocumented-immigrants-are-in-the-united-states-and-who-are-they/.

Kang, Cecilia. 2021. "That Spotty Wi-Fi? There's $100 Billion to Fix It. *The New York Times*, April 1, 2021. https://www.nytimes.com/2021/04/01/technology/digital-divide-rural-wifi.html.

Katz, Michael B. 1996. *In the Shadow of the Poorhouse: A Social History of Welfare In America*, 2nd ed. New York: Basic Books.

Keller, Morton. 1998. *Regulating a New Society: Public Policy and Social Change in America, 1900–1933*. Cambridge, MA: Harvard University Press.

Kenworthy, Nora J. 2019. "Crowdfunding and Global Health Disparities: An Exploratory Conceptual and Empirical Analysis." *Globalization and Health* 15. https://doi.org/10.1186/s12992-019-0519-1.

———. 2020. "Opinion: Crowdfunding Is an Imperfect Weapon against the Pandemic." *Washington Post*, April 2, 2020. https://www.washingtonpost.com/opinions/2020/04/02/crowdfunding-is-an-imperfect-weapon-against-pandemic/.

———. 2021. "Like a Grinding Stone: How Crowdfunding Platforms Create, Perpetuate, and Value Health Inequities." *Medical Anthropology Quarterly*, March 12, 2021. https://doi.org/10.1111/maq.12639.

Kenworthy, Nora, Zhihang Dong, Anne Montgomery, Emily Fuller, and Lauren Berliner. 2020. "A Cross-Sectional Study of Social Inequities in Medical Crowdfunding Campaigns in the United States." *PLOS One* 15 (3): e0229760. https://doi.org/10.1371/journal.pone.0229760.

King, Ian. 2020. "An Ancient Computer Language Is Slowing America's Giant Stimulus." *Bloomberg*, April 13, 2020. https://www.bloomberg.com/news/articles/2020-04-13/an-ancient-computer-language-is-slowing-america-s-giant-stimulus.

King, Jaime S. 2020. "Covid-19 and the Need for Health Care Reform." *New England Journal of Medicine* 382 (26): e104. https://doi.org/10.1056/NEJM p2000821.

Kleemann, Frank, G. Günter Voss, and Kerstin Rieder. 2008. "Un(Der)Paid Innovators: The Commercial Utilization of Consumer Work through Crowdsourcing." *Science, Technology & Innovation Studies* 4 (1): 5–26. https://www.researchgate.net/publication/42632427_UnderPaid_Innovators_The_Commercial_Utilization_of_Consumer_Work_through_Crowdsourcing.

Klinenberg, Eric. 2019. *Palaces for the People: How Social Infrastructure Can Help Fight Inequality, Polarization, and the Decline of Civic Life*. New York: Broadway Books.

Klinkenberg, Marty. 2019. "How the Humboldt Broncos Tragedy Was Further Complicated by a $15.2-Million Outpouring of Support." *The Globe and Mail*, March 14, 2019. http://myaccess.library.utoronto.ca/login?qurl =https%3A%2F%2Fwww.proquest.com%2Fblogs-podcasts-websites%2F how-humboldt-broncos-tragedy-was-further%2Fdocview%2F23824 94513%2Fse-2%3Faccountid%3D14771.

Law, Michael R., Lucy Cheng, Ashra Kolhatkar, Laurie J. Goldsmith, Steven G. Morgan, Anne M. Holbrook, and Irfan A. Dhalla. 2018. "The Consequences of Patient Charges for Prescription Drugs in Canada: A Cross-Sectional Survey." *CMAJ Open* 6 (1): E63–70. https://doi.org/10.9778/cmajo .20180008.

Leavitt, Kieran. 2021. "'This Is Insane': Facebook Blocked This Family from Raising Money for a Wheelchair Van." *Toronto Star*, April 1, 2021. https:// www.thestar.com/politics/federal/2021/04/01/this-is-insane-facebookv-blocked-this-family-from-raising-money-for-a-wheelchair-van.htm l?utm_source=share-bar&utm_medium=user&utm_campaign=user -share.

Leboeuf, Gaël, and Armin Schwienbacher. 2018. "Crowdfunding as a New Financing Tool." In *The Economics of Crowdfunding: Startups, Portals and Investor Behavior*, edited by Douglas Cumming and Lars Hornuf, 11–28. Cham, Switzerland: Springer International Publishing.

Lee, Sumin, and Vili Lehdonvirta. 2020. "New Digital Safety Net or Just More 'Friendfunding'? Institutional Analysis of Medical Crowdfunding in the United States." *Information, Communication & Society* 25 (8): 1151–75. https://doi.org/10.1080/1369118X.2020.1850838.

Lichterman, Paul. 1996. *The Search for Political Community: American Activists Reinventing Commitment.* New York: Cambridge University Press.

Lin, Mingfeng, and Siva Viswanathan. 2016. "Home Bias in Online Investments: An Empirical Study of an Online Crowdfunding Market." *Management Science* 62 (5): 1393–414. https://doi.org/10.1287/mnsc.2015.2206.

Lindsay, Bethany. 2021. "Indigenous People in B.C. 75% More Likely to End Up in ER, Report Says." *CBC News*, February 4, 2021. https://www.cbc.ca/news/canada/british-columbia/bc-health-care-racism-report-update-1.5900527.

Lorde, Audre. 2018. *The Master's Tools Will Never Dismantle the Master's House.* London: Penguin Books.

Lothian-McLean, Moya. 2020. "Why Crowdfunding Is No Replacement for the Welfare State." *The Guardian*, September 2, 2020. https://www.theguardian.com/commentisfree/2020/sep/02/crowdfunding-welfare-state-pandemic.

Lubove, Roy. 1986. *The Struggle for Social Security, 1900–1935.* Pittsburgh, PA: University of Pittsburgh Press.

Luguri, Jamie, and Lior Jacob Strahilevitz. 2021. "Shining a Light on Dark Patterns." *Journal of Legal Analysis* 13 (1): 43–109. https://doi.org/10.1093/jla/laaa006.

Lukk, Martin, Erik Schneiderhan, and Joanne Soares. 2018. "Worthy? Crowdfunding the Canadian Health Care and Education Sectors." *Canadian Review of Sociology* 55 (3): 404–24. https://doi.org/10.1111/cars.12210.

Lunden, Ingrid. 2017. "GoFundMe Drops 5% Platform Fee for U.S. Personal Campaigns, Adds Tips." *TechCrunch*, November 30, 2017. https://techcrunch.com/2017/11/30/gofundme-drops-5-platform-fee-for-u-s-personal-campaigns-adds-tips/.

———. 2018. "GoFundMe Acquires YouCaring as Charitable Crowdfunding Continues to Consolidate." *TechCrunch*, April 3, 2018. https://techcrunch.com/2018/04/03/gofundme-acquires-youcaring-as-charitable-crowdfunding-continues-to-consolidate/.

Mac, Ryan, and Brianna Sacks. 2020. "'The Black Lives Matter Foundation' Raised Millions. It's Not Affiliated With the Black Lives Matter Movement." *BuzzFeed News*, June 15, 2020. https://www.buzzfeednews.com/article/ryanmac/black-lives-matter-foundation-unrelated-blm-donations.

MacMillan, Douglas, and Gillian Tan. 2015. "GoFundMe Founders to Reap a Fortune in Buyout." *The Wall Street Journal*, June 24, 2015. https://www.wsj.com/articles/BL-DGB-42425.

Maroto, Michelle Lee, David Pettinicchio, and Martin Lukk. 2021. "Working Differently or Not at All: COVID-19's Effects on Employment among People with Disabilities and Chronic Health Conditions." *Sociological Perspectives* 64 (5): 876–97. https://doi.org/10.1177/07311214211012018.

Marquis, Christopher. 2020. *Better Business: How the B Corp Movement Is Remaking Capitalism*. New Haven, CT: Yale University Press.

Marshall, T. H. 1950. *Citizenship and Social Class and Other Essays*. New York: Cambridge University Press.

Martin, Michael. 2021. "Computer and Internet Use in the United States: 2018." US Census Bureau, April, 21, 2021. https://www.census.gov/library/publications/2021/acs/acs-49.html.

Martinez, Gina. 2019. "GoFundMe CEO: One-Third of Fundraisers Are for Medical Costs." *Time*, January 29, 2019. https://time.com/5516037/gofundme-medical-bills-one-third-ceo/.

Matchan, Linda. 2015. "From Homeless to Harvard, with the Help of Crowdfunding." *Boston Globe*, April 24, 2015. https://www.bostonglobe.com/metro/2015/04/23/toronto-woman-goes-from-homeless-harvard-with-help-crowdfunding-site/28Q3rfjitQtfIYjmnEsWqM/story.html

Mattern, Ashleigh. 2018. "By the Numbers: The Humboldt Broncos GoFundMe." *CBC News*, August 15, 2018. https://www.cbc.ca/news/canada/saskatchewan/humboldt-broncos-gofundme-numbers-1.4786381.

May, Chris. 2020. "People Donate Billions through GoFundMe. Where It Goes Is Not Guaranteed." *Street Roots*, November 18, 2020. https://www.streetroots.org/news/2020/11/18/people-donated-billions-through-gofundme-where-it-goes-not-guaranteed.

Mazzei, Patricia, and Sabrina Tavernise. 2020. "Florida Is a Terrible State to Be an Unemployed Person." *The New York Times*, April 23, 2020. https://www.nytimes.com/2020/04/23/us/florida-coronavirus-unemployment.html.

McCullough, Brian. 2018. *How the Internet Happened: From Netscape to the IPhone*. New York: Liveright Publishing.

McGeehan, Patrick. 2020. "'I Cry Night and Day': How It Took One Woman 8 Weeks to Get Unemployment." *The New York Times*, May 8, 2020. https://www.nytimes.com/2020/05/08/nyregion/unemployment-benefits-ny-coronavirus.html.

McGuinness, Tara Dawson, and Gabriel Zucker. 2020. "Congress Appropriated $300 Billion in Relief Payments to Individuals and Families—but Poor Delivery May Prevent Tens of Millions of Americans from Ever Accessing Them." *New America*, April 8, 2020. http://newamerica.org/pit/reports/relief-payments-poor-delivery-may-prevent-tens-of-millions-of-americans-from-accessing/.

McPherson, Miller, Lynn Smith-Lovin, and James M Cook. 2001. "Birds of a Feather: Homophily in Social Networks." *Annual Review of Sociology* 27 (1): 415–44. https://doi.org/10.1146/annurev.soc.27.1.415.

Meer, Jonathan, David Miller, and Elisa Wulfsberg. 2017. "The Great Recession and Charitable Giving." *Applied Economics Letters* 24 (21): 1542–49. https://doi .org/10.1080/13504851.2017.1319556.

Meerwijk, Esther L., and Jae M. Sevelius. 2017. "Transgender Population Size in the United States: a Meta-Regression of Population-Based Probability Samples." *American Journal of Public Health* 107 (2). https://doi.org/10.2105/ AJPH.2016.303578.

Merton, Robert K. 1938. "Social Structure and Anomie." *American Sociological Review* 3 (5): 672–82. https://doi.org/10.2307/2084686.

Mezrich, Ben. 2010. *The Accidental Billionaires: The Founding of Facebook.* New York: Anchor Books.

Miller, Claire Cain. 2008. "How Obama's Internet Campaign Changed Politics." *Bits Blog* (blog), November 7, 2008. https://bits.blogs.nytimes.com/ 2008/11/07/how-obamas-internet-campaign-changed-politics/.

Miller-Idriss, Cynthia. 2020. *Hate in the Homeland: The New Global Far Right.* Princeton: Princeton University Press.

Mills, C. Wright. 1959. *The Sociological Imagination.* New York: Oxford University Press.

Mitra, Tanushree, and Eric Gilbert. 2014. "The Language That Gets People to Give: Phrases That Predict Success on Kickstarter." In *CSCW '14: Proceedings of the 17th ACM Conference on Computer Supported Cooperative Work & Social Computing,* 49–61. New York: Association for Computing Machinery. https://doi .org/10.1145/2531602.2531656.

Mollick, Ethan. 2014. "The Dynamics of Crowdfunding: An Exploratory Study." *Journal of Business Venturing* 29 (1): 1–16. https://doi.org/10.1016/j .jbusvent.2013.06.005.

Monroe, Rachel. 2019. "When GoFundMe Gets Ugly." *The Atlantic,* November 2019. https://www.theatlantic.com/magazine/archive/2019/11/gofund me-nation/598369/.

Mosendz, Polly, and Suzanne Woolley. 2017. "Collecting Money after a Mass Shooting Is Easy. Giving It Away Is Tricky." *Bloomberg,* November 21, 2017. https://www.bloomberg.com/news/articles/2017-11-21/collecting-money -after-a-mass-shooting-is-easy-giving-it-away-is-tricky.

Mulholland, Elizabeth. 2020. "Canada's Most Vulnerable Need Extra Help in Getting COVID-19 Help." *Policy Options,* June 4, 2020. https://policyoptions .irpp.org/magazines/june-2020/canadas-most-vulnerable-need-extra -help-in-getting-covid-19-help/.

Nachtwey, Oliver, and Timo Seidl. 2020. "The Solutionist Ethic and the Spirit of Digital Capitalism." *SocArXiv,* October 29, 2020. https://doi.org/10.31235/ osf.io/sgjzq.

Narea, Nicole. 2020. "Immigrants Have Helped Keep Essential Services Running. But Those without Legal Status Have No Financial Safety Net." *Vox,*

May 5, 2020. https://www.vox.com/2020/5/5/21244630/undocumented
-immigrants-coronavirus-relief-cares-act.

National Center for Education Statistics. 2016. "Number and Percentage of Households with Computer and Internet Access, by State: 2016" (table). *Digest of Education Statistics*. https://nces.ed.gov/programs/digest/d17/tables/dt17_702.60.asp.

Newport, Cal. 2022. "The Rise of the Internet's Creative Middle Class." *The New Yorker*, June 15, 2022. https://www.newyorker.com/culture/culture-desk/the-rise-of-the-internets-creative-middle-class.

Noble, Safiya Umoja. 2018. *Algorithms of Oppression: How Search Engines Reinforce Racism*. New York: NYU Press.

NORC at the University of Chicago. 2021. "Millions of Americans Continue to Donate to Crowdfunding Sites to Help Others Pay Medical Bills Despite Economic Hardships of the Pandemic." *NORC* (blog), April 1, 2021. https://www.norc.org/NewsEventsPublications/PressReleases/Pages/millions-of-americans-continue-to-donate-to-crowdfunding-sites-to-help-others-pay-medical-bills-despite-economic-hardships.aspx.

Norris, Pippa. 2001. *Digital Divide: Civic Engagement, Information Poverty, and the Internet Worldwide*. New York: Cambridge University Press.

Nuez, Stephen, and Hallah Ahmad. 2020. "Where the CARES Act Went Wrong." *The Hill*, April 18, 2020. https://thehill.com/opinion/white-house/493458-where-the-cares-act-went-wrong.

Nyabola, Nanjala. 2018. *Digital Democracy, Analogue Politics: How the Internet Era Is Transforming Politics in Kenya*. London: Zed Books.

Nylen, Leah. 2022. "Tech Antitrust Bill Threatens to Break Titans' Grip on Internet." *Bloomberg*, July 26, 2022. https://www.bloomberg.com/graphics/2022-tech-antitrust-bill/.

O'Mara, Margaret. 2019. *The Code: Silicon Valley and the Remaking of America*. New York: Penguin Press.

O'Neil, Cathy. 2017. *Weapons of Math Destruction: How Big Data Increases Inequality and Threatens Democracy*. New York: Crown.

O'Neil, Luke. 2017. "For People Crowdfunding Health Care, Going Viral Is a Matter of Life or Death." *Esquire*, March 28, 2017. https://www.esquire.com/news-politics/a54132/go-viral-or-die-trying/.

Parhankangas, Annaleena, and Maija Renko. 2017. "Linguistic Style and Crowdfunding Success among Social and Commercial Entrepreneurs." *Journal of Business Venturing* 32 (2): 215–36. https://doi.org/10.1016/j.jbusvent.2016.11.001.

Parkinson, David, and Josh O'Kane. 2020. "Unemployment Claims Reach Nearly One Million as Businesses Battered by Coronavirus Pandemic." *The Globe and Mail*, March 25, 2020. https://www.theglobeandmail.com/business/article-unemployment-claims-reach-nearly-one-million-as-businesses-battered-by/.

Parolin, Zachary, Sophie Collyer, Megan Curran, and Christoper Wimer. 2021. "Monthly Poverty Rates among Children after the Expansion of the Child Tax Credit." *Poverty and Social Policy Brief 20412*. New York: Center on Poverty and Social Policy, Columbia University. https://ideas.repec.org/p/aji/briefs/20412.html.

Parrott, Sharon, Chad Stone, Chye-Ching Huang, Michael Leachman, Peggy Bailey, Aviva Aron-Dine, Stacy Dean, and LaDonna Pavetti. 2020. "CARES Act Includes Essential Measures to Respond to Public Health, Economic Crises, but More Will Be Needed." Center on Budget and Policy Priorities, March 27, 2020. https://www.cbpp.org/research/economy/cares-act-includes-essential-measures-to-respond-to-public-health-econo mic-crises.

Paynter, Ben. 2018. "DonorsChoose Just Funded Its 1 Millionth Project." *Fast Company*, January 31, 2018. https://www.fastcompany.com/40524322/donorschoose-just-funded-its-1-millionth-project.

Perez, Sarah. 2017. "Facebook Introduces Personal Fundraising Tools, Donate Buttons in Facebook Live for Pages." *TechCrunch* (blog), March 30, 2017. https://techcrunch.com/2017/03/30/facebook-introduces-personal-fund raising-tools-donate-buttons-in-facebook-live/.

Petre, Caitlin. 2021. *All the News That's Fit to Click: How Metrics Are Transforming the Work of Journalists*. Princeton, NJ: Princeton University Press.

Pickett, Kate E., and Richard G. Wilkinson. 2009. *The Spirit Level: Why Greater Equality Makes Societies Stronger*. New York: Bloomsbury.

Pierson, Paul. 1994. *Dismantling the Welfare State? Reagan, Thatcher and the Politics of Retrenchment*. New York: Cambridge University Press.

———. 1996. "The New Politics of the Welfare State." *World Politics* 48 (2): 143–79. https://doi.org/10.1353/wp.1996.0004.

Piketty, Thomas. 2014. *Capital in the Twenty-First Century*, translated by Arthur Goldhammer. Cambridge, MA: Belknap Press.

Piketty, Thomas, and Emmanuel Saez. 2003. "Income Inequality in the United States, 1913–1998." *Quarterly Journal of Economics* 118 (1): 1–41. https://academic.oup.com/qje/article-abstract/118/1/1/1917000?redirectedFrom=fulltext

———. 2006. "The Evolution of Top Incomes: A Historical and International Perspective." *American Economic Review* 96 (2): 200–05. https://doi.org/10.12 57/000282806777212116.

Pittman, Matthew, and Kim Sheehan. 2016. "Amazon's Mechanical Turk a Digital Sweatshop? Transparency and Accountability in Crowdsourced Online Research." *Journal of Media Ethics* 31 (4): 260–62. https://doi.org/10.1080/23736992.2016.1228811.

Piven, Frances Fox, and Richard Cloward. 1993. *Regulating the Poor: The Functions of Public Welfare*. New York: Vintage.

Plucinska, Joanna. 2015. "GoFundMe Raised Its Donation Cap Thanks to Taylor Swift." *Time*, July 13, 2015. https://time.com/3955074/gofundme-tay lor-swift-donation/.

Pope, Devin G., and Justin R. Sydnor. 2011. "What's in a Picture? Evidence of Discrimination from Prosper.Com." *Journal of Human Resources* 46 (1): 53–92. https://doi.org/10.3368/jhr.46.1.53.

Powell, Farran, and Emma Kerr. 2020. "See the Average College Tuition in 2020–2021." *US News & World Report*, September 14, 2020. https://www.usnews.com/education/best-colleges/paying-for-college/articles/paying-for-college-infographic.

Prasad, Monica. 2018. "Problem-Solving Sociology." *Contemporary Sociology* 47 (4): 393–98. https://journals.sagepub.com/doi/10.1177/0094306118779810.

———. 2021. *Problem-Solving Sociology: A Guide for Students*. New York: Oxford University Press.

Press, Jordan. 2020. "Nearly 5.4 Million Receiving Emergency Federal Aid as Requests Climb." *The Globe and Mail*, April 13, 2020. https://www.theglobeandmail.com/canada/article-nearly-54-million-receiving-emergency-federal-aid-as-requests-climb/.

Puckett, Cassidy. 2022. *Redefining Geek: Bias and the Five Hidden Habits of Tech-Savvy Teens*. Chicago: University of Chicago Press. https://press.uchicago.edu/ucp/books/book/chicago/R/bo137270726.html.

Putnam, Robert D. 2000. *Bowling Alone: The Collapse and Revival of American Community*. New York: Simon and Schuster.

Quadagno, Jill S. 1994. *The Color of Welfare: How Racism Undermined the War on Poverty*. New York: Oxford University Press.

Quinn, Kaitlyn, and Erik Schneiderhan. Forthcoming. "Leaving the Sequestered Byway: A Forward Look at Sociology's Morals and Practical Problem-Solving." In *Handbook of the Sociology of Morality*. Vol. 2. New York: Springer.

Rafalow, Matthew H. 2020. *Digital Divisions: How Schools Create Inequality in the Tech Era*. Chicago: University of Chicago Press.

Ravenscraft, Eric. 2022. "What Is the Metaverse, Exactly?" *Wired*, April 25, 2022. https://www.wired.com/story/what-is-the-metaverse/.

Regalado, Antonio. 2018. "Two Sick Children and a $1.5 Million Bill: One Family's Race for a Gene Therapy Cure." *MIT Technology Review*, October 23, 2018. https://www.technologyreview.com/2018/10/23/139429/two-sick-children-and-a-15-million-bill-one-familys-race-for-a-gene-therapy-cure/.

Regner, Tobias. 2021. "Crowdfunding a Monthly Income: An Analysis of the Membership Platform Patreon." *Journal of Cultural Economics* 45 (1): 133–42. https://doi.org/10.1007/s10824-020-09381-5.

Robinson, Laura, Shelia R. Cotten, Hiroshi Ono, Anabel Quan-Haase, Gustavo Mesch, Wenhong Chen, Jeremy Schulz, Timothy M. Hale, and Michael J. Stern. 2015. "Digital Inequalities and Why They Matter." *Information, Communication & Society* 18 (5): 569–82. https://doi.org/10.1080/1369118X.2015.1012532.

Robson, Jennifer. 2020. "Radical Incrementalism and Trust in the Citizen: Income Security in Canada in the Time of COVID-19." *Canadian Public Policy* 46 (S1): S1–18. https://doi.org/10.3138/cpp.2020-080.

Roman, Karina. 2020. "EI Claimants Are Going Weeks without Income as Federal Call System Slows to a Crawl." *CBC News*, May 1, 2020. https://www.cbc.ca/news/politics/employment-insurance-ei-cerb-covid-coronavirus-pandemic-1.5549617.

Rosenblat, Alex. 2019. *Uberland: How Algorithms Are Rewriting the Rules of Work*. Oakland, CA: University of California Press.

Rosh, Samuel. 2017. "Beyond Categorical Exclusions: Access to Transgender Healthcare in State Medicaid Programs." *Columbia Journal of Law and Social Problems* 51 (1): 1–38. http://jlsp.law.columbia.edu/wp-content/uploads/sites/8/2017/11/51-Rosh.pdf.

Ryan, Camille. 2018. "Computer and Internet Use in the United States: 2016," ACS Report no. 39. US Census Bureau. https://www.census.gov/library/publications/2018/acs/acs-39.html.

Saez, Emmanuel. 2018. "Striking It Richer: The Evolution of Top Incomes in the United States." In *Inequality in the 21st Century*, edited by David B. Grusky and Jasmine Hill, 39–42. New York: Routledge.

Saleh, Sameh N., Ezimamaka Ajufo, Christoph U. Lehmann, and Richard J. Medford. 2020. "A Comparison of Online Medical Crowdfunding in Canada, the UK, and the US." *JAMA Network Open* 3 (10): e2021684. https://doi.org/10.1001/jamanetworkopen.2020.21684.

Salganik, Matthew J. 2018. *Bit by Bit: Social Research in the Digital Age*. Princeton: Princeton University Press.

Sauder, Michael. 2020. "A Sociology of Luck." *Sociological Theory* 38 (3): 193–216. https://doi.org/10.1177/0735275120941178.

Schfer, Mike S., Julia Metag, Jessica Feustle, and Livia Herzog. 2018. "Selling Science 2.0: What Scientific Projects Receive Crowdfunding Online?" *Public Understanding of Science* 27 (5): 496–514. https://journals.sagepub.com/doi/10.1177/0963662516668771.

Schneiderhan, Erik. 2013. "Peer Reviewers: Why You Gotta Be So Mean." *The Chronicle of Higher Education*, July 22, 2013. https://www.chronicle.com/article/peer-reviewers-why-you-gotta-be-so-mean/.

Schneiderhan, Erik. 2007. "Jane Addams and Charity Organization in Chicago." *Journal of the Illinois State Historical Society* 100 (4): 299–327. https://www.academia.edu/en/612243/Jane_Addams_and_Charity_Organization_in_Chicago.

———. 2011. "Pragmatism and Empirical Sociology: The Case of Jane Addams and Hull-House, 1889–1895." *Theory and Society* 40 (6): 589. https://doi.org/10.1007/s11186-011-9156-2.

———. 2015. *The Size of Others' Burdens: Barack Obama, Jane Addams, and the Politics of Helping Others*. Stanford, CA: Stanford University Press.

———. 2016. "Jane Addams on Creativity and Power in Social Service." In *Service Sociology and Academic Engagement in Social Problems*, edited by A. Javier Treviño and Karen M. McCormack, 45–60. London: Routledge.

Scholz, Trebor. 2012. *Digital Labor: The Internet as Playground and Factory*. London: Routledge.

Schor, Juliet. 2020. *After the Gig: How the Sharing Economy Got Hijacked and How to Win It Back*. Oakland, CA: University of California Press.

Schradie, Jen. 2019. *The Revolution That Wasn't: How Digital Activism Favors Conservatives*. Cambridge, MA: Harvard University Press.

Schwartz, Nelson D. 2020. "'Nowhere to Hide' as Unemployment Permeates the Economy." *The New York Times*, April 16, 2020. https://www.nytimes .com/2020/04/16/business/economy/unemployment-numbers-coronavi rus.html.

Securities and Exchange Commission. 2004. "Form S-1 Registration Statement under the Securities Act of 1933: Google Inc.," April 29, 2004. https:// www.sec.gov/Archives/edgar/data/1288776/000119312504073639/ds1.htm.

Seligman, Martin E. 1974. "Depression and Learned Helplessness." In *The Psychology of Depression: Contemporary Theory and Research*, xvii, 318. Oxford, UK: John Wiley & Sons.

Semuels, Alana. 2018. "The Internet Is Enabling a New Kind of Poorly Paid Hell." *The Atlantic*. January 23, 2018. https://www.theatlantic.com/business/ archive/2018/01/amazon-mechanical-turk/551192/.

Seth, Angie. 2015. "Once-Homeless Toronto Woman Crowdfunds More than $60K for Harvard Tuition." *Global News*, April 17, 2015. https://globalnews .ca/news/1945257/once-homeless-toronto-woman-crowdfunds-more -than-60k-for-harvard-tuition/.

Sisler, Julia. 2012. "Crowdfunding for Medical Expenses." *Canadian Medical Association Journal* 184 (2): E123–24. https://doi.org/10.1503/cmaj.109-4084.

Skocpol, Theda. 1995. *Protecting Soldiers and Mothers: The Political Origins of Social Policy in the United States*. Cambridge, MA: Belknap Press.

Small, Mario Luis. 2017. *Someone to Talk To*. Oxford, UK: Oxford University Press.

Smith, Aaron 2009. "The Internet's Role in Campaign 2008." *Pew Research Center: Internet, Science & Tech* (blog), April 15, 2009. https://www.pewre search.org/internet/2009/04/15/the-internets-role-in-campaign-2008/.

———. 2015. "Searching for Work in the Digital Era." *Pew Research Center: Internet, Science & Tech* (blog), November 19, 2015. https://www.pewresearch.org/ internet/2015/11/19/searching-for-work-in-the-digital-era/.

———. 2016. "Which Americans Donate to Crowdfunding Platforms." *Pew Research Center: Internet, Science & Tech* (blog), May 19, 2016. https://www.pewre search.org/internet/2016/05/19/collaborative-crowdfunding-platforms/.

Smith, Adam. (1776) 2003. *The Wealth of Nations*. Edited by Edwin Cannan. New York: Bantam Classic.

Snyder, Jeremy. 2021. "GoFundMe Is Becoming a Social Safety Net—An Inequitable One." *Undark*, April 8, 2021. https://undark.org/2021/04/08/gofund me-inequitable-social-safety-net/.

———. 2020. *Exploiting Hope: How the Promise of New Medical Interventions Sustains Us—And Makes Us Vulnerable*. Oxford, UK: Oxford University Press.

Snyder, Jeremy, Peter Chow-White, Valorie A. Crooks, and Annalise Mathers. 2017. "Widening the Gap: Additional Concerns with Crowdfunding in Health Care." *The Lancet Oncology* 18 (5): e240. https://doi.org/10.1016/S1470-2045(17)30259-0.

Snyder, Jeremy, Annalise Mathers, and Valorie A. Crooks. 2016. "Fund My Treatment! A Call for Ethics-Focused Social Science Research into the Use of Crowdfunding for Medical Care." *Social Science & Medicine* 169 (November): 27–30. https://doi.org/10.1016/j.socscimed.2016.09.024.

Snyder, Jeremy, Marco Zenone, Valorie Crooks, and Nadine Schuurman. 2020. "What Medical Crowdfunding Campaigns Can Tell Us about Local Health System Gaps and Deficiencies: Exploratory Analysis of British Columbia, Canada." *Journal of Medical Internet Research* 22 (5): e16982. https://doi.org/10.2196/16982.

Sobel, Dava. 1995. *Longitude: The True Story of a Lone Genius Who Solved the Greatest Scientific Problem of His Time*. New York: Walker and Company.

Solnit, Rebecca. 2020. "'The Way We Get through This Is Together': Mutual Aid under Coronavirus." *The Guardian*, May 14, 2020. http://www.theguardian.com/world/2020/may/14/mutual-aid-coronavirus-pandemic-rebecca-solnit.

Solt, Frederick. 2020. "Measuring Income Inequality across Countries and over Time: The Standardized World Income Inequality Database." *Social Science Quarterly* 101 (3): 1183–99. https://doi.org/10.1111/ssqu.12795.

Soril, Lesley J. J., Ted Adams, Madeleine Phipps-Taylor, Ulrika Winblad, and Fiona M. Clement. 2017. "Is Canadian Healthcare Affordable? A Comparative Analysis of the Canadian Healthcare System from 2004 to 2014." *Healthcare Policy* 13 (1): 43–58. https://doi.org/10.12927/hcpol.2017.25192.

Spade, Dean. 2020. *Mutual Aid: Building Solidarity during This Crisis (and the Next)*. London: Verso Books.

Srnicek, Nick. 2017. *Platform Capitalism*. Malden, MA: Polity.

Statistics Canada. 2020. "Labour Force Survey, June 2020," July 10, 2020. https://www150.statcan.gc.ca/n1/daily-quotidien/200710/dq200710a-eng.htm.

———. 2021. "Labour Force Characteristics by Province, Monthly, Seasonally Adjusted," June 4, 2021. https://www150.statcan.gc.ca/t1/tbl1/en/tv.action?pid=1410028703.

———. 2022a. "Canada Is the First Country to Provide Census Data on Transgender and Non-Binary People," April 27, 2022. https://www150.statcan.gc.ca/n1/daily-quotidien/220427/dq220427b-eng.htm.

———. 2022b. "The Canadian census: A rich portrait of the country's religious and ethnocultural diversity," October 26, 2022. https://www150.statcan.gc.ca/n1/daily-quotidien/221026/dq221026b-eng.htm.

Statt, Nick. 2020. "Yelp to Stop Auto-Creating Fundraisers after Outrage from Business Owners." *The Verge*, March 26, 2020. https://www.theverge.com/2020/3/26/21196446/yelp-gofundme-coronavirus-automatic-opt-in-fundraiser-pause.

St-Denis, Xavier. 2020. "Sociodemographic Determinants of Occupational Risks of Exposure to COVID-19 in Canada." *Canadian Review of Sociology/Revue Canadienne de Sociologie* 57 (3): 399–452. https://doi.org/10.1111/cars.12288.

Steger, Manfred B., and Ravi K. Roy. 2010. *Neoliberalism: A Very Short Introduction*. New York: Oxford University Press.

Stevenson, Seth. 2020. "The Dark Side of GoFundMe." *Slate*, December 9, 2020. https://slate.com/business/2020/12/gofundme-dark-side-fraud-social-media-health-care.html.

Stewart, Emily. 2020. "We Can End America's Unemployment Nightmare." *Vox*, September 16, 2020. https://www.vox.com/the-highlight/21430930/covid-unemployment-600-cares-act-the-great-rebuild.

Stiglitz, Joseph E. 2012. *The Price of Inequality: How Today's Divided Society Endangers Our Future*. New York: W. W. Norton.

Stoltz, Dustin S., Justin Van Ness, and Mette Evelyn Bjerre. 2020. "The Changing Valuation of Dogs." *Sociological Forum (Randolph, NJ)* 35 (4): 1183–205. https://doi.org/10.1111/socf.12643.

Strickler, Yancey. 2019. *This Could Be Our Future: A Manifesto for a More Generous World*. New York: Penguin.

Surowiecki, James. 2005. *The Wisdom of Crowds*. New York: Anchor Books.

Swedberg, Richard. 2014. *Theorizing in Social Science: The Context of Discovery*. Stanford, CA: Stanford University Press.

Tankersley, Jim. 2021. "To Juice the Economy, Biden Bets on the Poor." *The New York Times*, March 6, 2021. https://www.nytimes.com/2021/03/06/business/economy/biden-economy.html.

The Salvation Army. 2021. "2021 Annual Report." https://s3.amazonaws.com/usn-cache.salvationarmy.org/e1941a3f-50f7-490e-b6ad-d06b71094lab_2021-SAL-Entire-Annual-Report.pdf.

Tilly, Charles. 2002. *Stories, Identities, and Political Change*. New York: Rowman & Littlefield.

———. 2006. *Why?* Princeton, NJ: Princeton University Press.

Tosatto, Jann, Joe Cox, and Thang Nguyen. 2019. "An Overview of Crowdfunding in the Creative and Cultural Industries." In *Handbook of Research on Crowdfunding*, edited by Hans Landström, Annaleena Parhankangas, and Colin Mason, 269–302. Northampton, MA: Edward Elgar.

Tranter, Emma. 2021. "'Deeply Disturbing': Nunavut Internet Still Slower, More Costly Than Rest of Country." *Toronto Star*, January 24, 2021. https://www.thestar.com/news/canada/2021/01/24/deeply-disturbing-nunavut-internet-still-slower-more-costly-than-rest-of-country.html.

Trattner, Walter I. 1998. *From Poor Law to Welfare State: A History of Social Welfare in America*. 6th ed. New York: Free Press.

Tripodi, Francesca Bolla. 2022. *The Propagandists' Playbook: How Conservative Elites Manipulate Search and Threaten Democracy*. New Haven: Yale University Press.

Tufekci, Zeynep. 2018. *Twitter and Tear Gas: The Power and Fragility of Networked Protest*. New Haven, CT: Yale University Press.

Tuohy, Carolyn Hughes. 1999. *Accidental Logics: The Dynamics of Change in the Health Care Arena in the United States, Britain, and Canada*. New York: Oxford University Press.

United Way Worldwide. 2020. "2020 Annual Report." https://s3.amazonaws .com/uww.assets/site/annual_report/2020/2020_Annual_Report_FINAL .pdf.

US Bureau of Labor Statistics. 2021. "Civilian Unemployment Rate." https:// www.bls.gov/charts/employment-situation/civilian-unemployment-rate .htm.

US Census Bureau. 2020. "Week 17 Household Pulse Survey: October 14–October 26." November 4, 2020. https://www.census.gov/data/tables/2020/ demo/hhp/hhp17.html.

U.S. Department of Labor. 2020a. "Unemployment Insurance Weekly Claims." April 16, 2020. https://oui.doleta.gov/press/2020/072320.pdf.

———. 2020b. "Unemployment Insurance Weekly Claims." July 23, 2020. https://oui.doleta.gov/press/2020/072320.pdf.

Vallas, Steven, and Juliet B. Schor. 2020. "What Do Platforms Do? Understanding the Gig Economy." *Annual Review of Sociology* 46 (1): 273–94. https:// doi.org/10.1146/annurev-soc-121919-054857.

Vanian, Jonathan. 2018. "Unmasking A.I.'s Bias Problem. *Fortune*, June 25, 2018. https://fortune.com/longform/ai-bias-problem/.

Vargas, Theresa. 2018a. "'I Know How It Feels': More than 100 Reach out to Help Immigrant Woman Who Lost Her Dulles Job." *Washington Post*, August 3, 2018. https://www.washingtonpost.com/local/i-know-how-it-feels-more -than-100-reach-out-to-help-immigrant-woman-who-lost-her-dulles -job/2018/08/03/ccf5cbb2-96ac-11e8-80e1-00e80e1fdf43_story.html.

———. 2018b. "Perspective: A Stranger Meant to Donate $15 to a GoFundMe Page. He Accidentally Gave More than $15,000." *Washington Post*, September 9, 2018. https://www.washingtonpost.com/local/a-stranger-meant-to -donate-15-to-a-gofundme-page-he-accidentally-gave-more-than-15000/ 2018/09/08/6a3de272-b2bb-11e8-aed9-001309990777_story.html.

Varrella, Simona. 2021. "Canada: Undergraduate Tuition Fee by Province 2020/21." *Statista*, March 9, 2021. https://www.statista.com/statistics/733512/ tuition-fee-for-full-time-canadian-undergraduates-by-province/.

Veall, Michael R. 2008. "Canadian Seniors and the Low Income Measure." *Canadian Public Policy* 34: S47–58. https://doi.org/10.3138/cpp.34.Supplement. S47.

Wade, Matt. 2022. "'The Giving Layer of the Internet': A Critical History of GoFundMe's Reputation Management, Platform Governance, and Communication Strategies in Capturing Peer-to-Peer and Charitable Giving Markets." *Journal of Philanthropy and Marketing*, October 20, 2022. https://doi.org/10.1002/nvsm.1777.

West, Thomas E., and Gerard Hildebrand. 1997. "Federal-State Relations." In *Unemployment Insurance in the United States: Analysis of Policy Issues*, edited by Christopher J. O'Leary and Stephen A. Wandner, 545–98. Kalamazoo, MI: W. E. Upjohn Institute for Employment Research.

Williams, Justin A., and Ross Wilson. 2016. "Music and Crowdfunded Websites: Digital Patronage and Artist-Fan Interactivity." In *The Oxford Handbook of Music and Virtuality*, edited by Sheila Whiteley and Shara Rambarran, 593–612. New York: Oxford University Press. https://doi.org/10.1093/oxfordhb/9780199321285.013.33.

Wilson, William J. (1987) 2012. *The Truly Disadvantaged: The Inner City, the Underclass, and Public Policy*, 2nd ed. Chicago: University of Chicago Press.

Woodbury, Stephen A. 2014. "Unemployment Insurance." In *The Oxford Handbook of U.S. Social Policy*, edited by Daniel Béland, Kimberly J. Morgan, and Christopher Howard. New York: Oxford University Press. https://doi.org/10.1093/oxfordhb/9780199838509.013.022.

Woodcock, Jamie, and Mark Graham. 2020. *The Gig Economy: A Critical Introduction*. Medford, MA: Polity.

Woolley, Suzanne. 2017. "American Health Care Tragedies Are Taking Over Crowdfunding." *Bloomberg*, June 12, 2017. https://www.bloomberg.com/news/articles/2017-06-12/america-s-health-care-crisis-is-a-gold-mine-for-crowdfunding.

World Bank. n.d. "World Bank Open Data." Accessed June 23, 2021. https://data.worldbank.org/.

Wylie, Christopher. 2019. *Mindf*ck: Cambridge Analytica and the Plot to Break America*. New York: Random House.

Younkin, Peter, and Venkat Kuppuswamy. 2018. "The Colorblind Crowd? Founder Race and Performance in Crowdfunding." *Management Science* 64 (7): 3269–87. https://doi.org/10.1287/mnsc.2017.2774.

Zheng, Haichao, Dahui Li, Jing Wu, and Yun Xu. 2014. "The Role of Multidimensional Social Capital in Crowdfunding: A Comparative Study in China and US." *Information & Management* 51 (4): 488–96. https://doi.org/10.1016/j.im.2014.03.003.

Ziegler, Tania, Rotem Shneor, Karsten Wenzlaff, Krishnamurthy Suresh, Felipe Ferri de Camargo Paes, Leyla Mammadova, Charles Wanga, et al. 2021. "The 2nd Global Alternative Finance Market Benchmarking Report." *SSRN*, November 9, 2021. https://doi.org/10.2139/ssrn.3957488.

Zuboff, Shoshana. 2019. *Age of Surveillance Capitalism: The Fight for a Human Future at the New Frontier of Power*. London: Profile Books.

Index

CPSIA information can be obtained
at www.ICGtesting.com
Printed in the USA
JSHW020048270723
45479JS00002B/2